THE CHINESE AT THE NEGOTIATING TABLE

THE CHINESE AT THE NEGOTIATING TABLE

Style and Characteristics

Alfred D. Wilhelm, Jr.

National Defense University Press
Washington, DC

National Defense University Press Publications

To increase general knowledge and inform discussion. NDU Press publishes monographs, proceedings of University-sponsored symposia, and books relating to U.S. national security, especially to issues of joint, combined, or coalition warfare, peacekeeping operations, and national strategy. The Press occasionally publishes out-of-print defense classics, historical works, and other especially timely or distinguished writing on national security, and it is the home of *JFQ: Joint Force Quarterly*, a forum for examining joint and combined warfare and exchanging ideas of importance to all services.

NDU Press publications are sold by the US Government Printing Office. For ordering information, call (202) 783-3238, or write to Superintendent of Documents, US Government Printing Office, Washington, DC 20402.

Library of Congress Cataloging-in-Publication Data

Wilhelm, Alfred D.
The Chinese at the negotiating table: style and characteristics/
Alfred D. Wilhelm, Jr.
p. cm.
Includes bibliographical references and index.
1. United States—Foreign relations—China. 2. China—Foreign relations—United States. 3. United States—Foreign relations—1945-1989. 4. China—Foreign relations—1949- 5. Negotiation. 6. Diplomatic negotiations in international disputes. I. Title
E183.8.C5W55 1991
327.73051—dc20 92-11931
CIP

First printing, February 1994

TO THE MEMORY OF
ANNABELLE SCHAS MILLER
March 14, 1921 – September 15, 1984

Her love was a constant source of strength;
her faith, a boundless source of encouragement.

CONTENTS

LIST OF ILLUSTRATIONS

FOREWORD

WHEN, IN 1972,the United States opened trade negotiations with the People's Republic of China—after 23 years of little contact owing to the absence of diplomatic recognition—most representatives were uncertain how to negotiate with the Chinese. What little they knew had come through foreign reports and from transcripts of the Panmunjon negotiations in Korea. But once China opened its doors, a great deal was at stake for both nations.

In this volume Alfred Wilhelm examines the process of negotiating with the Chinese, using historical examples and analyses of cases from 1953 to the present. He debunks the myth of legendary Chinese patience, assesses American reaction to negotiating with the Chinese, and analyzes the Chinese approach to negotiations. He reveals elements of continuity in Chinese behavior that surfaced during talks with the United States since as early as 1949.

The United States will likely continue to increase its contacts with China as that nation modernizes and opens up to the world. Because the Chinese have approached negotiation in a consistent pattern, even to such details as what clothes they wear and which way they want the chairs to face, American negotiators can prepare themselves to work more advantageously with their PRC counterparts. This book shows the way.

Paul G. Cerjan
Lieutenant General, US Army
President, National Defense University

PREFACE

THE PRC'S RELATIONS WITH THE UNITED STATES have been characterized by highly visible and politically charged negotiations. This has been true whether the PRC's policies were based on opposition to the United States, as in the 1950s, or on managing opposition to a common Soviet threat in the 1970s and early 1980s. The international attention given these negotiations reflected their importance as symbols of international and domestic changes being pursued by both sides. As the 20th century closes, it appears that the next decade is likely to bring major changes in the global distribution of power, including a larger role of the PRC. China's growing capabilities will extend its influence as a major player far beyond the Asia-Pacific region to that of an international power. Sino-American relations will grow in importance and complexity, and bilateral and multilateral negotiations will become even more frequent as the opportunities for cooperation and conflict increase.

In a recent policy paper titled "United States and China Relations at a Crossroads," published by the Atlantic Council of the United States and the National Committee on United States-China Relations, 77 prominent Americans highlighted the changes that have been taking place in China and the implications for the future. They concluded that at present, "China is the Asia-Pacific region's major source of economic growth," but that it is "increasingly an important force in the world economy, and that it will be a major force in the next century if current trends continue." The question of how to accommodate to change in China has been one of the few constraints in US policy and promises to be one of its biggest challenges in the next century.

Negotiations presage change. For four decades, the environment for Sino-American bilateral negotiations has been conditioned by the preoccupation of both sides with changes and the fear of challenges to their respective national security. In the future, national security decision makers will be challenged by an even broader array of threats. The prevention or resolution of military issues will remain important to global peace and security but will be less likely to dominate the agenda in deference to such issues as the promotion of investment and trade, job creation, world environmental degradation, preventing drug traffic, improving public health, human rights and the economic and political development of Hong Kong and Taiwan (over long-standing concerns about their physical security). Greater emphasis, inevitably requiring a strong negotiator, will be placed on resolving differences over weapons sales and the reduction or destruction of nuclear, chemical, and biological weapons.

From the very beginning, the negotiating strategies and tactics of the PRC's leaders challenged the United States. In the future, as Chinese and American interests brush up against each other over an even widening array of critical issues, negotiations will play a even greater role in managing the relationship. The Chinese approach the table with a style that benefits from and is encumbered by thousands of years of experience filtered through 40 years of international experience in which the Chinese had to conceal their weaknesses and make maximum use of their limited strengths. When I sat across from Ambassador Wang Bingnan at Geneva and later at Warsaw in the late 1950s, both sides had much to learn about the other. As Dr. Wilhelm suggests, however, we may have been the more disadvantaged. Both sides made many mistakes and probably lost many opportunities to advance their interests because of their limited understanding of the strategies and tactics plus the strengths and weaknesses of the other. Washington was slow to recognize either Zhou Enlai's brilliance or his game plan. If we had, we might have been able to avoid some of the difficulties of the next three decades. From this book's peek behind the Chinese cloak of secrecy, it appears that the same can be said of the insights of Beijing about America.

Negotiations are the product of the efforts of a team, not of the brilliance of one man. How China accomplishes this task is different from that of the United States, but they do negotiate and they do compromise. For the Chinese, diplomacy is a continuous bargaining process that periodically peaks in formal negotiations where progress is codified. Concessions and compromises tend to be tactical and generally over techniques. Compromises over strategic objectives are much more difficult to accommodate and generally tend to be conditional and temporary. And there is a human dimension that Dr. Wilhelm introduces into our understanding of how the Chinese negotiate. Despite the criticism of some observers, I knew Ambassador Wang Bingnan to be a first-class diplomat and a superb negotiator. The author's approach to understanding the Chinese negotiating style takes us behind the mask of formal diplomacy and gives us an important glimpse at the Chinese negotiator and the importance of his place on the Chinese team. He also gives us a practical methodology for attempting to set aside the emotions of nationalism and judgements of right and wrong, and for objectively evaluating any given set of negotiations so as to understand how the Chinese view the process. Only through such understanding can any negotiator hope to find a practical and enduring compromise.

The environment of the future will change much about how the Chinese negotiate. As the private sector grows and the PRC government is further decentralized to accommodate modernization, a greater number of people will be involved in negotiations with the United States. Nevertheless, our negotiator would be well advised to consider the Chinese experience in negotiating with Americans when conducting negotiations with the Chinese. They can be assured that the next generation of Chinese negotiators will have benefitted from the experiences of their mentors.

Ambassador U. Alexis Johnson

ACKNOWLEDGMENTS

I MADE A PLEDGE of confidentiality to the active and retired Chinese, Japanese, and Korean officials, and to the Chinese now living outside the PRC, who generously gave of their time to be interviewed for this study. They included participants in or observers of Sino-American negotiations from 1945 to 1983 or, in the case of the Japanese, people who had participated in Sino-Japanese negotiations from the mid-1970s to 1983. I am deeply indebted to these more than forty individuals whom I am not free to acknowledge by name.

Richard H. Solomon, Michael Oksenberg, and Charles W. Freeman were particularly helpful in the formative stages of this study. Ambassador U. Alexis Johnson generously gave of his time for many interviews and to read and make suggestions on portions of the manuscript. Dr. Huan Guocong reviewed the study and made suggestions for improvement, as did several Chinese officials and students residing in the United States. I received strong moral support and much helpful criticism from Professors Clifford P. Ketzel, Daniel Bays, Chae-Jin Lee, and Ronald A. Francisco at the University of Kansas. Joseph W. Harned and the Atlantic Council of the United States made it possible for me to travel twice to the People's Republic of China, as well as to visit Japan, Korea, Hong Kong, and Singapore, where many of the interviews were conducted.

My wife, Candace Wilhelm, typed and edited many drafts and offered numerous helpful suggestions. She and my three children, Alfred, Kimberly, and Michael, sacrificed many evenings, weekends, and holidays so that this study might be completed. Without their love and support I could not have finished.

ALFRED D. WILHELM JR.

INTRODUCTION

A CAREFUL REVIEW of the record of Sino-American negotiations at Panmunjom in the 1950s, at Geneva and Warsaw in the 1950s and 1960s, Beijing and Washington in the 1970s, and of the related experiences of American businessmen in more recent years, suggests that there is a discernible Chinese diplomatic negotiating style, at least in negotiations with Americans. Identifying this Chinese style would assist American negotiators in the future to be more effective. Also, according to several scholars and diplomats of the People's Republic of China (PRC), it would encourage the Chinese to systematically examine their style, something they have never done before. Such knowledge on both sides would reduce misunderstandings and tensions in future negotiations, enhance the prospects for mutually satisfactory conclusions, and broaden understanding of international negotiations in general.

From the founding of the People's Republic of China in 1949 until the normalization of relations with the United States in 1979, there were no official relations between the two countries. Yet for most of this period more substantive diplomatic interaction took place between these two major powers than between China and the Western nations that normalized relations with the PRC earlier. Furthermore, most of this interaction culminated at the negotiating table.

The results of these negotiations have frustrated most informed American observers over the years in one of two general ways. Although the United States has been the greater political, economic, and military power, to some observers the Chinese somehow seemed to extract concessions from the United States disproportionate to their apparent power. Particularly during the 1950s and 1960s, the success of the Chinese was credited to their adherence to the "unscrupulous tenets of Marxism-Leninism-

Maoism." Although today ideology is less frequently credited for the successes of Chinese negotiators, some American observers believe that the Chinese approach to negotiations continues to enable China to benefit most from the Sino-American relationship.

Other Americans would not agree that the Chinese are more successful, but are frustrated over the lost opportunities for both the United States and the PRC. They point out that cultural differences have generated misunderstandings that have hindered both sides from achieving their goals via negotiated solutions. In general, these differences have been or could have been overcome with patience and more complete knowledge of each other. For these observers, the problems in government-to-government negotiations have resulted from each side's misinterpretation of the other's interests in the negotiations.

From both viewpoints, neither the negotiating process nor the results have been satisfactory. Inherent in this dissatisfaction is an awareness that the Chinese approach negotiations differently than Americans do.

Importance for US Policy

Sino-American negotiations since 1949 have taken place during five distinct periods as defined by Beijing's perceptions of the degree to which US and PRC interests were complementary or in conflict. In the first period, 1949-1953, the PRC entered into the Korean armistice negotiations with the United States, both sides seeking to end their battlefield competition. These negotiations ended Mao's self-imposed political isolation from the West, begun in 1950.

During the second period, 1954-1970, Beijing sought to break through the diplomatic fence the United States had erected to contain China. Talks between ambassadors from the PRC and the United States were pursued first at Geneva and then later at Warsaw. The atmosphere was strained and distrustful because of the distinct conflict both sides saw between their interests.

Following several years of another, even more severe period of self-imposed diplomatic isolation during the Cultural Revolution, the concomitant collapse of Sino-Soviet relations, and the development of a Soviet military threat to against China, Beijing encouraged to US overtures for a rapprochement. As a result, China and the United States normalized relations in 1979. By the mid-1970s, such scholars as Michael Pillsbury and A. Doak Barnett were speculating about the possibility of US arms sales to the PRC.[1] Within a decade, Beijing's leaders had purchased US military equipment and technology and were asking for even more sophisticated technology.

In the fourth period, 1979–1989, despite differences over some major interests, negotiations were frequent and focused on the expansion of bilateral relations based on common economic and security interests. Bilateral trade climbed from about $750 million in 1973 to over $18.7 billion in 1989; US investment in China rose from $116 million total in projects from 1979 through 1981 to $645 million in 1989 in 276 projects; and China purchased approximately $500 million dollars in equipment under the US Foreign Military Sales program. Substantive, high-level exchanges and negotiations were frequent over a broad spectrum of government activities. This heady period of expanding relations was suddenly and severely setback following the US condemnation of the Chinese government's brutal suppression of the demonstrators in Tiananmen Square on 4 June 1989, and the resultant imposition of sanctions by the United States and others.

The fifth period opened in the months following Tiananmen with both sides angry and uncertain as to how complementary the relationship would be in the wake of major adjustments in the international environment. The familiar constraints of the bipolar world disappeared with the collapse of the East European Communist regimes, the demise of the Warsaw Pact, the eruption of the Persian Gulf War, the implosion of the USSR, the reemergence of ethnic conflict and nationalism as threats to global security, and the collapse of Somalia highlighting Third World distress.

Even as the old order was crumbling, a new one was emerging. The United Nations achieved new levels of cooperation in dealing with Cambodia, Iraq, and Somalia. The European Community continued moving toward integrated markets and unified political and monetary institutions, the North American Free Trade Area concept offered prospects for new regional cooperation and wealth, and the East Asian nations experienced economic growth and varying degrees of political liberalization.

These changes and the possibility of a reduced American presence in the Pacific area have resulted in calls for regional security cooperation being advanced by many in the region. At the same time, China is experiencing an enhanced self-image as a function of its rapid economic growth (an estimated 12 percent in 1992); an increase in the PRC's international role especially evident in the UN Security Council; and by the end of 1992 a resumption of pre-Tiananmen relations with all nations less the United States and the opening of new relations with nations previously denied, such as South Korea.

In this environment the United States is seen Beijing as the center of a unipolar world that has the potential of being more hostile for China than the bipolar world of the past two decades. At a time when China's confidence as a major power is maturing and increasingly others respect China accordingly, the United States appears to some Chinese to be less willing to cooperate with China. And most Chinese believe that cooperation is necessary if China's reforms are to continue. Despite the intense criticism in the United States of China's human rights practices, there clearly are areas ranging from security to economic where the United States and China have common interests. For example, in the first 9 months of 1992, Americans invested $1.64 billion in 1,892 projects, over twice the total invested in 1989. It is in this new "sweet and sour" environment that formal cross-table negotiations between the PRC and the United States will deal with the issues of human rights conditions in China, arms control and counter-proliferation of weapons of mass destruction, destruction of nuclear weapons, trade and investment, the environment, energy, technology transfers, population, and global health (e.g., AIDS).

Just as the international and domestic policy environments in which Sino-American negotiations take place have varied considerably, so have the subsequent interpretations by social scientists, politicians, and policymakers of the Chinese negotiating style in each of these cases. Most of these interpretations have been negative, reflecting varying degrees of dissatisfaction with both Chinese methods and the results of the negotiations. Some of the more recent characterizations, like Dr. Henry Kissinger's, have shown respect, even admiration for selected Chinese techniques and results. The differences between the policy environments of each period and between the Western characterizations of the Chinese negotiating style of each period suggest a lack of continuity in the Chinese approach to negotiations, particularly in terms of strategies and tactics. Consequently, for the average Washington policymaker, unable under daily pressures to personally assess records of the past, the histories of these negotiations seem to offer little insight into current Chinese negotiating behavior. But the frustration that accompanies extensive experience in dealing with China usually fosters an awareness of culturally based differences in negotiating behavior and an intuitive sense of the importance of previous Chinese negotiating behavior to interpreting these differences.

From a policy perspective it is important to determine whether there is a Chinese diplomatic negotiating style. Although no study of how the Chinese government negotiates with the US government can provide a comprehensive blueprint of future Chinese negotiating behavior, this study does assess the early Sino-American negotiation experience in an attempt to provide some insight into the pressures that shape Chinese negotiating strategy. It also discusses Chinese motivation for using various maneuvers and techniques when dealing with Americans.

Importance for Negotiation Theory

Western literature concerning negotiation theory, strategies, and techniques draws primarily on the European experience. From the earliest descriptive expositions by such observers as Bacon (1597) and Decallieres (1716) to the most recent innovations in quantitative analysis, the stated and implied assumptions behind these analyses are essentially derived from Western logic and experiences. The logic and experiences of Asian negotiators have not been represented among the cases and data from which negotiation theories have been developed. This lack of worldwide representation argues against J. Harsanyi's suggestion that negotiation theories are universally applicable.[2] If, as Gordon Rule argues, negotiation is an art, not a science—suggesting that negotiating styles may be as culture dependent as other art forms—

then even wider variations in negotiation styles than previously recognized are likely.[3]

The scope of negotiation studies is also a limiting factor. Most studies to date have focused on either the negotiating process or the outcome. The least developed approach for studying negotiations is the identification of the pressures that shape the strategy, maneuvers, and techniques employed. Game theorists, economists, and sociologists generally have made assumptions about the environment in order to isolate the negotiation process, to mitigate concern about the sources of pressures, and to portray the negotiators as unitary, rational opponents. These approaches have produced useful insights, but their predictive power for even simple negotiations is weak.

Considering the complexity of the interaction between the environment, process, and outcome of international negotiations, some observers have concluded that a theory of negotiations is impossible. For example, Otomar Bartos argues that the human element in negotiations is too complex for a deterministic model or theory of negotiations to be possible.[4] Generalizations about negotiations have been constructed inferentially, using assumptions that tend to oversimplify the complexities of the environment— particularly variations between cultures—and encourage many to think that what may be an indeterminate process is determinant.

Also constraining is the tendency in the West to accept the idea that the negotiation styles of communist countries are similar.[5] This judgment tends to underplay cultural distinctions by focusing narrowly on ideology as the principal determinant of a communist nation's negotiating style. Even Fred Ikle's study of negotiations inadequately stresses culturally derived differences in style.[6]

Of the limited empirical research and analysis that have been focused on the Asian negotiator and his environment using Asian sources, the most successful is by Michael Blaker.[7] Using the Japanese Foreign Ministry's equivalent to the *Foreign Relations of the United States* series, Blaker analyzed 18 Japanese international negotiations to ascertain whether there is a distinctive Japanese bargaining style. His analysis suggests some negotiation precepts are common to East and West, but that some are unique to the Japanese experience, or possibly by extension to Sinic culture-oriented societies.

Research on how the PRC negotiates is even more limited than that on negotiations of other Asian countries. Scholarly access, whether by Chinese or foreign scholars, to data involving Chinese foreign policy decisions and processes continues to be severely restricted, although some improvements have been made in recent years. Most of the available records on Chinese actions and attitudes are based on the observations of American or other foreign participants in negotiations with the Chinese.

William Vatcher's account of the Korean armistice negotiations, supplemented by Admiral C. Turner Joy's diary of his 10 months as chief US delegate, is a fairly complete account from an American perspective.[8] Arthur Dean has written a brief account of his experiences in negotiating with Huang Hua during the Korean peace talks.[9] Kenneth Young has analyzed the Geneva-Warsaw Ambassadorial Talks through 1967, and each of the American ambassadors who participated has provided a brief account in his memoirs of his own role in the talks.[10] Arthur Lall similarly analyzed "Peking's attitudes toward negotiations in Asia," based on his experiences at Geneva in 1961-62.[11] So far, Chinese accounts are limited to the memoirs of Ambassador Wang Bingnan, in which he describes his experiences in Geneva and Warsaw.[12]

Information concerning Sino-American negotiations of the 1970s is episodic and incomplete, existing largely in the memoirs of American participants in those negotiations and in the public records. Declassified US government records were not yet available for most of this study, as they are for some of the earlier periods, making interviews with participants and close observers from both sides even more important.

Efforts to define the Chinese style appear in the works of Kenneth Young and in an insightful study of the Chinese commercial negotiating style by Lucien Pye.[13] Pye also made recommendations for US diplomatic negotiations based on the conclusions he drew from a series of interviews with businessmen experienced in negotiating with the Chinese. Nearly all of these memoirs and studies, however, evaluate Chinese actions in terms of American negotiating practices rather than from the Chinese perspective.

The Chinese style of negotiating, according to the Chinese scholars and diplomats I interviewed, has never been analyzed in China. It is a subject about which relatively little is known. In terms of theory, such a study would facilitate modification and extension of existing negotiation theory and open the door to a more historic approach.

A leading student of international negotiations, I. W. Zartman, argues the need to bring narrow approaches to the study of negotiations together in order to develop a concept better able to deal with all the major forces affecting the negotiator.[14] I believe that such a new analysis is necessary if Americans are to work successfully with Chinese negotiators now and in the future. Americans must comprehend the logic and experiences of Chinese negotiators in order to broaden their own base of understanding and build better approaches to negotiations in general.

Organization

To accomplish this task, I have organized this undertaking into topical chapters and two case studies, the topical chapters treating the subject theoretically, the case studies treating it practically and concretely. The first chapter contrasts the definition and connotations of the word *negotiation* as used in the United States with the Chinese words most commonly used in translating the word *negotiation.* I emphasize the difference between the connotations of *negotiations* for US diplomats and the connotations for PRC diplomats of the approximately equivalent Chinese words.

The second chapter suggests a framework for analyzing Sino-American negotiations. It is derived from a review of the theoretical literature on negotiations, available documents concerning specific negotiations, and extensive interviews with American and Chinese diplomats, both active and retired, who have participated in or closely observed Sino-American negotiations since 1945.

The third chapter characterizes the principal Chinese negotiators that US negotiators faced from 1951 to 1979. Despite assertions to the contrary by some Chinese I interviewed, China's negotiators generally share some characteristics useful to them in the negotiating process. I highlight characteristics that are reinforced by China's process for selecting its negotiators and preparing them for their job—particularly those characteristics that parallel the ideals of Marxism-Leninism and those heavily influenced by Chinese culture.

Two case studies then use the framework of chapter 2 to analyze the Military Armistice and Political Talks at Panmunjom, Korea (1951-1953), and the Ambassadorial Talks in Geneva and Warsaw (1955-1970). I do not believe there is yet adequate documentation of, or access to officials involved in, the talks leading to normalization of Sino-American relations (1971-1979) to warrant a separate case study. Episodic information from 1971 to 1979 was useful, though, in supporting the framework I develop in chapter 2.

A concluding chapter evaluates the utility of my framework for analyzing the negotiations, makes comparisons, draws conclusions about the Chinese style of negotiation, and offers predictions about how this style is likely to change in the future.

This study does not attempt to develop a definitive model of Chinese negotiations. Instead it tries to move beyond mere description of negotiations and identify critical Chinese perceptions of negotiations—ways of thinking about or reacting to the process. At the close, I suggest questions that American negotiators should address before, during, and after diplomatic negotiations with the Chinese.

Methodology

Analyzed together, negotiations theory and actual US negotiating practice in Sino-American relations are mutually reinforcing, each illuminating the other. To similarly illuminate the Chinese perspective of these bilateral negotiations, I have supplemented the historical record of the negotiations with interviews of Chinese officials and scholars who participated in the negotiation process. These interviews are especially important because of the difficulty of researching the Chinese perspective of past negotiations with Americans. We have seen some improvements in terms of foreign access to Chinese academics, newsmen, and officials, but official Chinese policy does not encourage such research. The Chinese environment is therefore resistant to these types of inquiry. Unlike the United States, the PRC is not yet willing to make the early records from its diplomatic archives available to foreign researchers; they are only available, selectively, to a very small number of Chinese scholars.[15]

Also valuable, in addition to the interviews, are the memoirs of former officials, especially when official archive materials are not yet available. Former senior US officials rush comparatively unrestrained to publish their memoirs before the American public forgets them. By contrast, senior Chinese officials have only recently been permitted—and selectively encouraged—to write about their experiences.[16] For the immediate future, these Chinese memoirs probably will be limited in number, broad, and factual, adding a personal tone to the official histories but contributing relatively little in the way of specific detail or insights into the rationale or process of foreign policy decisions.[17] A few other less senior Chinese officials have been permitted to write of their experiences, but only if they do so collectively.[18]

Chinese officials, both active and retired, appeared less worried after 1983 about granting in-depth interviews concerning past foreign and defense policy decisions and the efforts to implement these decisions. Substantive dialogue is no longer restricted to a relatively small number of conversations with top officials or to diplomatic conversations designed to convey messages informally between governments. On the other hand, I was unable to use effectively a systematic interview process involving such tools as standarized questionnaires. One person would selectively complete a questionnaire or answer certain kinds of questions orally, while others wouldn't even consider them. Some people would accept only general questions to which they responded with lengthy monologues, thereby limiting the number of questions. Others would only deal with specific questions to which they gave short and general answers or the reactions of party leaders.

Memories of the "anti-rightist" campaign of the late 1950s and of the Cultural Revolution hung like a cloud over many of these interviews, exaggerating the Communist Party's remaining requirements for secrecy. This self-imposed restriction made many people interviewed reluctant to be specific, particularly when they couldn't foresee how the conversation might be interpreted by or affect others. To compensate, I promised those interviewed that I would not associate them by name with specifics in the study. Although helpful, this condition was not a panacea, for it neither created trust nor completely eliminated concerns about party regulations or the reactions of party leaders.

Another limiting factor was the possibility that Chinese I interviewed had acquired some of their information about the negotiation process from reading Western descriptions rather than from personal experiences. Many of those interviewed had indeed read extensively in Western accounts of Sino-American relations. Several had done research in the United States. They often asked if I had read a particular account, as a reference point for our conversation and to learn more about me—and possibly so that they wouldn't rely too heavily in their discussion on materials with which I was familiar. I tried to minimize such bias by interviewing the same person more than once and by interviewing more than one person with similar experiences. Nevertheless, I might have failed to detect some answers constructed to support the party's current policy objectives vis-a-vis the United States.

Despite the limitations of the historical record and of the interviewing environment, with the assistance of those interviewed, this study does go beyond mere description to identify critical Chinese perceptions of diplomatic negotiations, particularly as directed toward the United States.

Chapter 6 of this book reviews style and types of negotiators, offers historical insights, discusses the strategy of conflict, and highlights the five Chinese characteristics that influence the way the Chinese approach and act in negotiations. Awareness of these characteristics and some understanding of their implications in past Sino-American negotiations offer rewards for Americans who negotiate with the Chinese in the future.

THE CHINESE AT THE NEGOTIATING TABLE

1.
CROSS-CULTURAL DEFINITIONS

We should not refuse to enter into negotiations because we are afraid of trouble and want to avoid complications, nor should we enter into negotiations with our minds in a haze. We should be firm in principle, we should also have all the flexibility permissible and necessary for carrying out our principles.

—Mao Tse-tung
5 March 1949

RESPONDING TO THE PROBLEM of the moment in early 1949, Mao counseled the Communist Party's Central Committee to negotiate, but with special guidelines. Although the end of the civil war was in sight, the Nationalists, with more than a million troops, were still dangerous. The Nationalists' January 1949 peace initiative had evoked hopes of an early peace among many of the communist leaders. But the communists also feared that solutions involving accommodation and assimilation would leave "vestiges of counterrevolution and its political influence" that "disposing of the enemy by fighting" would not. Mao's proposal to negotiate meant accepting these problems temporarily while organizing to "dispose" of them, primarily through re-education, even though such solutions would take much time and would "not be quite as effective as the solution by fighting."[1] This practical, obvious accommodation was a tactical expedient, a conciliatory gesture, not the enduring strategic compromise that the Nationalists and their Western supporters wanted.

Albeit a response for the moment, it was shaped by Mao's years of experience in negotiations with his opponents, his study of Marxism-Leninism, and his intimate knowledge of the Chinese classics.[2] Mao's offer to the Chinese Nationalists was conciliatory and temporizing rather than compromising; it was essentially a moral, not a legal judgment on the issue. It was not a compromise in the idealized Western sense of an enduring concession—even over principle—for the purpose of mutual gain "based on some fair standard independent of the will of either side."[3] For the practical, legal-minded Westerner, such a temporary concession establishes long-term precedent. But for Mao, his concessions were indeed temporary and were not the baseline from which to begin any future negotiations, as interpreted by Westerners.

Because the practical difference between these two ways of perceiving concessions made during a negotiation is small, some Western analysts conclude that the Chinese do compromise their principles—despite their claims to the contrary. But although the near-term difference between Communist Chinese conciliations and Western concessions is minimal, the long-term difference is potentially great. This difference over the meaning of concessions spawned much of the frustration and reciprocal distrust of the 1950s and 1960s, and it continues today to cause misunderstanding and frustration in Sino-American relations.

During interviews in 1983 and 1984 with American and Chinese diplomats, I gradually realized that each group's expectations of negotiations as a process were somewhat different. Neither side, though, was fully cognizant of these differences or able to articulate them. These differences are reflected even in the various meanings of the word *negotiations.*

Of course the connotations of the term *negotiations* differed somewhat for each diplomat interviewed, depending on his personal experiences and cultural background—even among the theoretically more intellectually disciplined Chinese diplomats, who were all successful party members. In general, however, for Americans the term implied emphasis on compromise or a quid pro quo to resolve conflict, along with an emphasis on law and judicial systems as bases for determining what is just and for ensuring compliance. The Chinese tended to emphasize the permanence and self-evident truth of their principles, the use of conditional and non-permanent agreements to constrain conflict until these truths or principles prevail, and moral suasion as a basis for achieving conformity and thus harmony.

Each of the American negotiators charged with representing the interests of the United States in bilateral negotiations with the Chinese from 1949 to 1979 has noted that the Chinese approach negotiations somehow differently than the Americans do. The Chinese seemed to expect something slightly different from the *process*, as separate from the issues. To study the Chinese approach to negotiations, we can begin by searching for cross-culturalequivalence between the concepts inherent in the English word *negotiations* and its Chinese equivalents.

The word *negotiate* appears in English in at least a half dozen different sematic contexts, including financial dealings, overcoming of obstacles, and settlement of problems. Each usage carries different meaning, yet all are related and influence the connotations of the others. When translated into Chinese, *negotiate* becomes a different word in each context. The explicit meanings conveyed by the Chinese terms do not cover the same range of usage as in English, and each Chinese term is related to a set of Chinese words that add connotations to the term different from those in English. The connotations or implicit meanings a word acquires beyond its denoted or explicit meaning greatly complicate the translator's task of conveying ideas between two dissimilar cultures through their dissimilar languages. The subtle differences in the definitions of *negotiate* in two commonly used English language dictionaries suggest some of the difficulty of the translator's task even before the connotations derived from personal experiences and circumstances of the users are considered.

The word *negotiate* as it might be used in a diplomatic affairs context was defined in the *Random House College Dictionary* as "to deal or bargain with another"[4] and in *The New Merriam- Webster Pocket Dictionary* as "to confer with another so as to arrive at the settlement of some matter."[5] The first implies a degree of compromise by the use of the words *bargain* and *deal.* These two words denote an agreement that settles what each party shall give or take. The second definition does not necessarily convey the idea of compromise, merely discussing and resolving a problem or, as from the Latin origin, *neg* (not) + *otium* (leisure), carrying on business.

Robert Ekvall, a Chinese-English translator of considerable ability and experience, described the problem as follows:

> If we draw a circle to present the sematic content of a word and take the centering of the word, its placement, to show its nuance and slant, we discover two things. First, it is impossible in the same or any other language to find another word whose circle of meaning is exactly the same size. Second, even the circles which are approximate in size are not centered or placed alike, but are above or below, to one side or the other. They are never exactly superimposed and matching, and as a consequence many circles cut into that of the

> given word. If any one of those circles cut into and comprehends more than 50 percent of the area of meaning, it becomes a candidate for equivalency and is one of the many from which the interpreter, taking into account nuance, circumstance, history and course of the argument, and many other considerations, must select the right word, or one as right as possible. Always, there is that 49 percent or less of meaning which is lacking in the new circle.[6]

Among observers and practitioners of American foreign policy, there is a general consensus that the term *negotiations* carries an even stronger connotation of compromise than that suggested by the previously mentioned dictionary definitions. Dr. Fred Iklé cautions against this tendency among American negotiators because it often leads them to assume unilaterally the role of a mediator.[7] So commonly accepted is this perception that in the *International Relations Dictionary*, *negotiation* is defined as "a diplomatic technique for the peaceful settlement of differences and the advancement of national interests. The objectives of negotiation are accomplished by compromise and accommodation reached through direct personal contact. . . . negotiated agreements imply both sides are willing to make mutually acceptable concessions (quid pro quo)."[8] Note that this US definition assumes both compromise and concessions.

"Negotiations" between two countries is normally translated in Chinese as *tanpan* (谈判) . The first syllable or character, *tan* (谈) , means to talk, chat, discuss, or that which is talked about or discussed. [9] The second syllable or character, *pan* (判) , means (a) to distinguish, discriminate; (b) to sentence, condemn. The combined word, *tanpan*, means to negotiate or to resolve matters involving two parties through mutual consultations.[10]

Comparing the "circle of meaning" of *tanpan* and *negotiations*, according to the definitions I have cited, reveals an overlap that meets Ekvall's criteria for equivalency. But the sematic content of *tanpan* does not appear to contain the implication of compromise. *Tanpan* involves a more deliberative and decisive process of problem solving. It does not preclude compromise, but neither does it suggest it.

Most of the Chinese officials I interviewed had considerable experience as interpreters and were thus familiar with the problem of matching the semantic content of words between Chinese and English. To develop a comparative perspective, I interviewed people in Beijing, Hong Kong, Tokyo, and Washington who are not PRC citizens but who routinely translate between Chinese and English. During these interviews, the range of connotations for *tanpan* as a noun varied widely depending on the background of each individual. For no one did the circle of meaning of *tanpan* and *negotiation* exactly superimpose. To some, the meaning was straightforward, obvious, doctrinal; to others, the meaning was complicated by memories and hostile emotions. Yet, common to most of these understandings were a number of ideas that suggest reinforcement and modernization of some traditional approaches to negotiations, with Marxist-Leninist values.

Most of those interviewed agreed that *tanpan* suggests a specific problem sufficiently serious that both sides are interested in seeing it does not get any worse. They saw little if any harmony and trust between the parties negotiating, the environment itself supporting latent if not open hostility—a sense of struggle. Principles are at stake for both parties, and neither is expected or likely to compromise its principles. Because of the seriousness of the problem, however, some way will be found to work together, such as an accommodation on a lesser issue. *Tanpan* has been used to describe the negotiations conducted between the People's Republic of China and the United States at Panmunjom, the Ambassadorial Talks held in Geneva and Warsaw, the Taiwan arms sales talks, and the trade talks of 1983. It is also used to describe Sino-Soviet talks. It was not generally used, however, to describe the negotiations that led to the normalization of Sino-American relations.

Huitan (会谈) was used to refer to the normalization talks. This compound word is composed of the character *hui* (会),which means (as a verb) (a) to get together, assemble; (b) to meet, see; (or as a noun) (c) meeting, gathering, conference, party. Coupled with *tan*(谈), the compound denotes *talks*. Those interviewed felt that it also connotes some trust between the participants and no hostility. No significant conflict of opinion would be expected between participants of such talks, although no agreement is necessarily expected to result either. It is a fairly neutral term as it pertains to the relationship between the participants.

When two countries have a friendly relationship, *huishang* (会商) is the appropriate term. *Shang* means, as a verb, to discuss, consult; or, as a noun, business, commerce, trade. The combination means to hold a conference or consultation. *Shang* seems to add a degree of trust and similarity in point of view to the meeting of the two sides.

Xieshang (协商) is an even friendlier term, meaning to consult or to talk. It connotes an even greater level of trust and similarity of viewpoint on principles than *huishang* does. A *xieshang* discussion would be some level of family matter, a matter between Chinese.

This semantic typology of words related to talks and negotiations is not intended to be either definitive or rigid. The use of these terms depends upon each individual's experiences, the circumstances of speech or writing, and a host of other considerations including how the government chooses to use them. The meaning of a term, particularly the connotative meaning of a combination of symbols (characters), tends to change over time according to common usage. Although each of the individual characters comprising the various terms can be found in Chinese sources from as early as 1100 B.C., none of the combinations discussed above is found in such early sources. In fact, only one combination, *tanpan*, appears in the 1937 edition of the *Ci Yuan* dictionary published in Shanghai.[11] The relatively recent acceptance into common usage of these word combinations is typical of the changes that gradually occur in a complex language to meet new circumstances.[12]

Despite differences in denotations and connotations of these words, though, for all the Chinese interviewed, use of any one of the words, particularly *tanpan*, as a noun or adjective in the title for a particular meeting suggested certain expectations for that meeting. Particularly important for this study was the consistency with which Chinese officials believed that intergovernmental discussions described by the word *tanpan* were likely to be concerned with struggle over a serious problem that the participants wanted to keep from getting out of hand. The participants in such discussions would have principles that they would be unable or unwilling to compromise, but in order to contain the issue—as Mao argued for in 1949—they would be prepared to be flexible enough to find some common ground for an agreement that would not compromise their ability ultimately to achieve their principles.

2.
A CONSTRUCT FOR NEGOTIATIONS

Negotiation is one form of struggle against imperialism. Necessary compromises can be made in negotiations, so long as the principle of upholding the fundamental interests of the people is observed. But if one regards negotiations as the main means, or even the sole means, of striving for peaceful coexistence and does not scruple to sell out the fundamental interests of the people in order to seek compromises with imperialism, that is not peaceful coexistence but capitulationist coexistence. And it will only result in endangering world peace.[1]

—Spokesman of the Chinese
Government
September 1, 1963

THIS QUOTATION IS FROM one of a series of open letters to the leaders of the Soviet Union strongly criticizing major Soviet foreign policy decisions and actions regarding the future of relations between the Communist countries and the West, particularly the United States. From the Chinese perspective, the Soviets made unilateral compromises with the United States that violated Marxist-Leninist principles and threatened China's fundamental interests. Soviet actions were hegemonistic. Their compromises injured the nationalistic pride of the Chinese who had "stood up" in 1949 and recovered their independence from the West, only to have the Soviets make decisions in 1963 that, if allowed to stand unchallenged, would unilaterally usurp the prerogatives of the Chinese as well as other Communist countries. Particularly significant to this study, Khrushchev had violated Chinese negotiating principles by converting peaceful coexistence with the imperialists (the United States) from a tactic or temporary negotiation concession into a strategic objective or permanent compromise. To the Chinese, bilateral relations with the United States should be dealt with as a dynamic bargaining process in which peaceful coexistence was but one of several instruments available to Moscow's negotiators. Once again Moscow failed.

Previously, the Soviets had needed the cooperation of the other Communist nations in defending against the inevitable nuclear war that would be launched by the United States. Now the Soviets rather chauvinistically argued that the imperialists' fear of Soviet missiles would defend the Soviet world. Yet the Chinese had witnessed the Soviets' shortcomings as negotiators, experienced the self-interest of Soviet foreign policy, and now increasingly feared the reemergence of Russian imperialism in the form of Soviet hegemonism. As surrogates for Moscow during the Korean War, the Chinese found the Korean War costly. Later, Soviet support for China during the Sino-American Taiwan Straight crisis of 1958 was weak and during the 1962 Sino-Indian crisis, it was nonexistent. Soviet hegemonistic tendencies were confirmed when, eschewing Marxist-Leninist principles, they placed missiles in Cuba. Then China was excluded from the mid-1963 test-ban agreement, reinforcing Soviet efforts to block China's achievement of a self-defense capability and full independence.[2]

From the objectives, strategy, and tactics of the Soviets to the results of their formal negotiations, the Soviet approach to dealing with the United States aggravated the Chinese. With more than a decade of experience in dealing with the Americans, first in Korea and later in Geneva and Warsaw, the Chinese had developed strong opinions about how to manage bilateral relations with the United States. The Soviets violated every precept the Chinese knew to be essential to effective bargaining. By selectively compromising these basic principles in their analysis of reality, the Soviets compromised the ability of the socialist nations (particularly the PRC) to achieve long-term objectives for the sake of short-term Soviet benefits.

This chapter presents a framework for describing and analyzing the Chinese approach to negotiations with the United States. First is a description of how the Chinese have used negotiations, both as a tactic and as a strategy, in their efforts to manage the overall US-PRC bilateral relationship as a bargaining process. Next follows a description of the primary interests or objectives of China's Communist leaders that the bargaining process must support, and of the derivative principles of foreign relations that establish the boundaries of the bargaining process within which China's diplomatic representatives must operate. Following a discussion of how traditional social values and Marxist values appear to influence contemporary Chinese thinking about negotiations, a construct is proposed depicting the evolving contemporary negotiations process, as a framework within which to collect and analyze information concerning Sino-American negotiations. The chapter concludes with a discussion of selected maneuvers and techniques that make up the core of Chinese negotiating tactics.

Managing the Relationship

Despite the implicit assertion by the Chinese in 1963 that their approach to negotiations with the United States differed from that of the Soviets, Americans didn't notice. The vocabulary and tone of the open letters were distracting. The Chinese affinity in the 1960s for strong rhetoric and hyperbole in their public statements reinforced the belief of most Americans in the 1950s that the Chinese had copied the Soviet diplomatic negotiating style. Thus Chinese negotiators, like the Soviets, were viewed as being radically different from their American counterparts: They were "deceptive and duplicitous, secretive and suspicious, inflexible and implacable, contentious and contemptuous."[3] (Several of the Chinese interviewed made similar evaluations of the American negotiators.)

Some Western diplomats, scholars, journalists, and analysts interviewed believed that a lack of understanding of the Chinese negotiating style and its cultural roots was primarily responsible for Americans' negative evaluations of Chinese negotiators. These Westerners believe the change in Sino-American relations since the 1960s has allowed a friendlier tone to replace the hostile nature of earlier negotiations, but they believe the lack of understanding still exists. Their opinion is that Americans lack the long-term perspective of the Chinese and are vulnerable to psychological manipulation by the Chinese masters of interpersonal relations. Conversely, the American fascination with agreements of excruciating detail and execution to the letter of the law overwhelms the Chinese negotiator. Concerned with reaching an agreement in principle (achieving a spirit of agreement), the Chinese often feel the details must carry a hidden, tricky meaning contravening the spirit of the agreement sought.

Others, including a few of the Chinese interviewed, contended that any cultural differences were superficial. They believed friendly relations had brought a change in the Chinese style, indicated by the concessions the Chinese have frequently made, particularly since beginning to pursue the Four Modernizations strategy in the late 1970s. Several Americans further argued that the apparent intransigent style of the 1950s and 1960s is not predictive of the Chinese diplomatic negotiating style of the 1980s, 1990s, and beyond.[4] Despite these differences of opinion, largely over the degree to which the Chinese will compromise, these observers generally agreed that the two sides often seemed to employ negotiations for different tactical and strategic purposes.

Negotiations as a tactic. By their nature, formal diplomatic negotiations involve mutual dependence and effort to avoid conflict as well as, paradoxically, a degree of competition, conflict, and tension. Threats, whether they involve withholding rewards or inflicting punishment, are as integral to such negotiations as are compromise and cooperation. Formal negotiations probably precede or follow war as often as they prevent it. Yet Western writers tend to deemphasize the agressive, competitive use of formal diplomatic negotiations. Rather, they focus on the mutual benefits of international negotiations as a cooperative exercise in resolving conflicts.[5] Conversely, the Chinese tend to emphasize the value of formal, face-to-face negotiation as another tactical "form of struggle" against the United States.

Tactical compromises are acceptable to the Chinese when the situation dictates, but concessions must not sacrifice *principles* essential to the accomplishment of long-term or strategic objectives. Formal negotiations are a problem-solving process involving the selective use of a variety of tactics and techniques, including bargaining concessions, as circumstances dictate.

The description "negotiation as one form of struggle" suggests that the Chinese are not motivated to meet the United States halfway or to match concessions on the basis of impartiality. Rather, the Chinese consider a face-to-face negotiation as a means to reduce opposition to their point of view. Negotiation is one of the tools available to the nation's leaders for persuading their opponents of the moral correctness of the Chinese position. When and how formal negotiations are used depend on "objective reality," the nature of the change to be effected, the level of hostility between China and the United States, the amount of time available, and the cost. These are the same considerations that enter into planning for the use of such other tools of persuasion as peaceful coexistence, deterrence, revolution, and war.

Negotiations as a strategy. Also explicit in the open letters of 1963 is the Chinese view that China's long-term relationship with the United States in one of *continual struggle or conflict.* Whether viewed in the socialist's terms of a struggle against the oppression of imperialism or in terms of the nationalist's concern for equality and independence, the struggle since 1949 has been to change, step by step, the attitudes, patterns of interaction, and the accepted norms of the United States with respect to the PRC. This concept of having to struggle continually to preserve its identity persisted in China into the post-1979 era in which relations were "normalized" and defined as "friendly, but non-aligned." The Chinese continue to see the relationship as a continual struggle for self-reliance (or power) and equality, which Americans and others who are more powerful would deny to the PRC.

Even in the mid-1940s, despite their naivete about the United States, the central leadership of the Chinese Communist Party (CCP) was sensitive to the importance of influencing the nature and pace of the development of Sino-American relations. For the party's leaders, the virulence of America's political and economic policies toward China had been a two-edged sword: On the one hand, the Americans had been supportive of China's "self-strengthening" efforts; on the other, they hindered the revolution.

Toward gaining for the PRC a position of self-determination in the relationship, according to several old cadre participants of the time, the new Communist government spurned US efforts in 1949 and 1950 to establish diplomatic relations and "cleansed the society of the vestiges of (US) imperialism."[6]

According to those interviewed, by 1954 the PRC was ready to resume relations with the Western World. Ambassador Wang Bingnan has described the situation as one in which the "party had greatly eliminated the social foundations of imperialism in China—the counterrevolutionary forces and the ideas of worshiping, dreading, and fawning on the United States." Chairman Mao said that it was necessary "to clean house before inviting guests in."[7] Ready to resume receiving guests, Beijing approached the suggestion of Ambassadorial Talks in Geneva with the idea that if China could improve relations with the United States, relations with other Western nations would soon follow.[8] The Chinese initiative at Geneva was rejected by the United States, and not until after the Cultural Revolution—the second cleansing of Chinese society—did a consensus begin to emerge in Beijing that favored Deng Xiaoping's desire to encourage US support for China's development through the Four Modernizations policy.[9] As in 1954, the United States held, and continues today to hold, the key to the easing or elimination of Western restrictions on strategic trade and cooperation with the PRC.[10]

Zhou Enlai was the principal architect of the strategy for managing Sino-American relations. It has been a strategy in continual evolution, a strategy of persuasion, a strategy for building on previous experiences; the strategy's development proceeded much like Zhou's own development as a negotiator. As a student, Zhou early rejected the idea that orders from strong leaders were sufficient to ensure the Chinese people's acceptance of new ideas, values, and norms. The people must be persuaded of the correctness of changes through example, study, and experience, moving them gradually, but more resolutely, from their old ideas to the new.

For the three decades before 1949, persuasion was a way of life for Zhou, whether as a crowd-pleasing orator, as a newspaper editor and writer, or in one-on-one conversations. He perfected the skills of conciliation and political compromise while learning to exploit fully the very limited leverage of the struggling infant party.[11]

During those long years of conflict, most of it with the stronger Kuomintang (KMT) party, Zhou mastered what Thomas Schelling calls the "strategy of conflict"—the awareness that most if not all "conflict situations are essentially bargaining situations." The ability of one conflicting party to gain its ends depends greatly on the choices or decisions of the other party, which can be influenced by persuasion, conciliation, and compromise.[12]

From Zhou's vantage point, the 30 years of relations between the CCP and the KMT were a continuous bargaining situation. During long interludes between rounds of formal negotiations, each side attempted to influence the choices and decisions of its opponent. For Zhou, negotiations assumed a strategic dimension, as a means of managing the relationship.

Relations with the United States would also involve a conflict over ideas and values between parties of disparate levels of power. Relations with the United States, if conducted by Western rules, would have been as one-sided as David's fight with Goliath would have been had David fought by the conventional rules of the day—with heavy body armor and spear—instead of using that which he knew best, his sling. So it was natural for Zhou also to manage Sino-American relations as a continual bargaining process, in which military power is but one of the tools to be exploited.

A highly respected People's Liberation Army (PLA) general and military strategist, Zhou, like Mao, understood the influence of military actions on an opponent's decisions. Winning was important to Zhou, but he knew that victory is seldom absolute and is not always necessary to strengthen one's bargaining position—one even can lose the battle and still win the war. Gains in war are relative because war is destructive, not creative. From experience, Zhou also knew that the persuasive influence of military capability is often strongest when that capability is left unused.

Military capability was an important element in Zhou's repertoire, but only one element. Persuasion by force, he knew, is seldom enduring. In managing the bargaining process, Zhou focused on developing a conceptual framework and supporting organizational structure that emphasized persuasion and conciliation without rejecting the option of force. Zhou preferred to affect the choices and decisions of other countries' leaders through third parties. His Foreign Ministry, therefore, was organized to set the stage for and complement the efforts of the PRC's formal diplomatic negotiators through such third parties as the domestic and international media, third country representatives, and non-governmental delegations.

Usually, these third parties are participants in what the Chinese call people-to-people relations. Managed by extensions of the Chinese Foreign Ministry known as Friendship Associations, people-to-people activities develop "friends" for the Chinese people among such diverse American interest groups as sports associations (the most famous having to do with ping-pong), schools and churches, journalists, scientists, and businessmen. Long before the normalization of relations, the Chinese applied pressure on US decisionmakers via such interest groups.

Once Sino-American relations were normalized, government-to-government interactions offered another medium for affecting US choices. Congressional delegations carried messages, Chinese ministers and American secretaries exchanged visits, and delegations at international conferences exchanged views. Again, considerable energy was expended in an effort to manage these exchanges so as to influence the bargaining environment positively.

The third medium involves party-to-party relations, normally with other Communist parties. While such relations have not been established between the CCP and US political parties, the CCP has established relations with some major non-Communist parties in Western Europe in recent years. During interviews with leading Communist Chinese for this study, questions about the Chinese Communist Party and its role in Sino-American relations generally were politely but firmly turned aside because party-to-party relations have not been established. Although a convenient way to protect the Party's privacy, this Chinese refusal to talk serves the equally useful function of minimizing the opportunities for bilateral discussions that might lead to the corruption or "peaceful evolution" of the theories and logic behind the political, social, and economic structure of the PRC.

China chooses to act through formal negotiations with the United States when people-to-people and government-to-government exchanges have generated an opportunity to advance Chinese interests that is best exploited by face-to-face talks. Beijing might see the potential results of a bilateral agreement as important to China's fundamental interests; or should the United States desire an agreement of only nominal value to China, the PRC might see the negotiations as an opportunity influencing US and world opinion in support of some other Chinese goal.

The adjournment of a formal negotiation session with a signed document does not conclude the negotiation over that particular subject. Implementing an agreement will require continuous reinterpretation of the intentions of the agreement according to the realities of the moment. The agreement establishes a baseline or plateau from which future negotiations can begin, a springboard to further discussions on issues the United States might have thought settled.

No matter how seemingly novel or unprecedented the subject of a specific formal negotiation, for the Chinese, longstanding political antecedents give the negotiations purpose and meaning beyond the issue at hand. The formal negotiations' long-term implications for "the fundamental interest of the people" are, in general, more important to the central leadership than the immediate implications of the issue in dispute. The immediate result, of course, might be crucial to a specific, sometimes visible interest group, but the broader strategy still takes priority. In this broader strategic context, negotiations involve more than just the act of sitting down to the conference table to discuss a bilateral issue and concluding with a joint communique or a signed document. Formal negotiations are another one of the tools used to support the negotiating strategy by which China's leaders attempt to influence the evolution of Sino-American relations toward achieving the fundamental interest of the Chinese people.

Fundamental Interests of the People

Since 1949 the Communist Party of China has faced a problem that China's leaders of the previous century repeatedly tried but failed to solve: How to modernize China without becoming dependent on, and thus exploited by, the West. Since 1949 each Chinese administration has staked its survival on having the correct program to fulfill "The nation's long-cherished ideal . . . to turn this poor backward country into an independent, prosperous, and powerful state."[13] Each administration has, in large part, failed. According to several Chinese interviewed, the Four Modernizations—a comprehensive policy for the long-term agricultural, industrial, scientific and technological, and military development of China—is the current administration's equivalent to a national security policy for achieving the fundamental objectives of the people: independence, development, and security.

Independence. After "100 years of suffering and humiliation due to Western imperialism," the objective or principle of independence cannot be compromised. China's leaders are determined to avoid any relationship that might appear to subordinate China's interests—political, ideological, economic, cultural, or military—to "any big power or bloc of powers." The economic "self-sufficiency" policy of the 1960s was the result of this xenophobia carried to the extreme by ideological fervor, an over-reaction that has since been moderated. To assuage foreign concerns, former Premier Zhao Ziyang continually emphasized "China's current policy of opening to the outside world is not a mere subjective wish but a reflection of the objective necessity. China has opened its door and will never close it again."[14] His conservative successor, Premier Li Peng, has even more fervently affirmed in public his administration's commitment to the "open door policy."

The qualifiers of this very positive assertion are the principles of "self-reliance" and "equality and mutual benefit." Americans often overlook or downplay these qualifiers in their excitement to take advantage of the opening of the door to China's potentially vast market. These qualifiers mean that the price for entering that open door is unqualified assistance to the Chinese in developing their own talents and resources—development that is, at least in most cases, the prerequisite to achieving "equality and mutual benefit." Consequently, the process will often appear to favor the Chinese: the door swings inward more often than outward. In implementing their open door policy, China's leaders are determined that China will not become dependent upon or be exploited by anyone, particularly the United States, "dependence and exploitation" being defined by the Chinese according to the situation at any particular time.

Development. When the Party adopted the Four Modernizations policy, development—not capitalist development but socialist socioeconomic development—became the keystone objective. The Party is determined that the modernization process will succeed. In accordance with the "scientific method," in which experimentation with various principles is followed by application of those principles that work, China's leaders have made major economic changes in the direction of a market economy, including real estate, commodity, and stock markets, but they have determined that the process will be separate and distinct from capitalist modernization. Although the blueprint is not yet fully and clearly drawn, "China is building socialism with its own distinctive features."[15] The CCP will continue to "lead the Chinese people ultimately to the creation of a Communist social system."[16]

Security. For China's leaders, the pursuit of the first two objectives, independence and development, has depended on their evaluation of China's security. Fears of world war or large-scale conflict with a major power have resulted in a deferrence to security concerns. For decades, China considered its security threatened by the large number of Soviet troops along the Sino-Soviet and Sino-Mongolian borders, Soviet presence in Afghanistan, Soviet support for Vietnam, and Soviet-American nuclear confrontation. Despite the demise of the Soviet Union, China's greatest physical threat continues to be from the north, where an unstable Russia has Pacific-oriented conventional and nuclear land, air, and sea forces, and the neighboring newly independent states have volatile ethnic minorities with interests in China's border regions. Japan is a major potential threat, and Vietnamese activity in the South China Sea, along with instability in South Asia and on the Korean peninsula, has the greatest potential for near-term crises. The PRC also has felt threatened for decades by a "US policy of discrimination against China in economic and trade affairs, US policies toward Taiwan, technology transfers, the Law of the Sea, and arms control," all of which have been exacerbated by the US export of its social values, e.g., human rights. Although China continues to be concerned about the "hostile nature" of the international order and the threat of "things foreign,"[17] the prospect of world war has been sufficiently low since the early 1980s, for China to devote greater resources to development.

The relative importance of security to the objectives of independence and development depends on more than a net assessment of opposing military forces. Security exists when there is a net positive correlation of all forces that support China over those inimical to China's interest. Thus, security can be most effectively increased by coordinating China's domestic, foreign, military, and economic policies.

The United States has been and will continue through the foreseeable future to be a crucial positive and negative influence on China's ability to achieve each of its national objectives. Beijing has perceived the United States at different times as either an asset or a liability, and those perceptions have determined the degree to which the Chinese deal with the United States in a hostile or friendly manner. The fact that in 1984, 5 years after the normalization of relations, the PRC still could not classify the United States as a friend[18] highlights the difficulty the Chinese have had in assessing the relative value of the United States as a positive influence. Even the positive US influence on China's economic development and security from Soviet aggression (anti-hegemonism) did not outweigh the perceived negative influence of the United States on China's independence, socio-economic development, and security. In fact, since the events in Tiananmen Square in 1989 and the collapse of the Soviet Union, Chinese concerns about the negative influence of the United States in these areas has increased about as dramatically as has China's need for US investment, science, and technology, in light of the 1991 Gulf War and the worldwide recession.

Principles of Foreign Relations

To manage relations with the United States as a continual bargaining situation is to encourage change continually. But how much change and by whom? Traditionally, other nations and peoples were expected to conform with China's norms and values. Even in the declining years of the Qing Dynasty (1644-1912), pressures from the West to conform to international practice resulted in little more than minimal institutional changes.[19] Further, the basic attitude that the rest of the world should conform has changed little with the transferal of power to the CCP. However, the CCP also knows that fundamental change by others comes slowly and only with "patient persuasion and guidance."

Knowing who should change, the next questions are what should the non-Chinese world learn and how should the principles be transmitted? As a society, the Chinese learned long before the Communists came to power that the only enduring way to change the norms and values of a society is through education. With memorization as their core teaching method, the Chinese are accustomed to transmitting or teaching norms and values—their objectives or principles—with the aid of numbered catchwords as mnemonic devices. Behind such easily memorized principles as those found in the "five relationships" of Confucius or Mao's "five antis" are complex political constructs. Consequently, it was natural for China's new leaders gradually to translate their emerging foreign policy principles into such expressions, first for internal consumption and second as a pedagogical device for educating the West concerning the foreign policy of the PRC. The central construct or derivative set of foreign policy principles for this purpose is the "Five Principles of Peaceful Coexistence."

Origin of the five principles of peaceful coexistence. In early 1949, as the Communist Party assumed its national responsibilities, foreign policy increasingly became the subject of public statements. One such statement by Zhou Enlai in April 1949 to a group of university professors gathered in Beijing focused on eliminating the vestiges of imperialism. In discussing the foreign policy themes and principles required for this task, he emphasized independence, equality, self-reliance, mutual benefit, and the handling of problems peacefully "on just grounds, to our advantage and with restraint."[20] By the end of June 1949, a more sharply defined set of principles emerged in Mao's remarks concerning the establishment of relations "with all foreign countries on the basis of equality, mutual benefit, and mutual respect for territorial integrity and sovereignty."[21]

Later, the PRC experienced the "aggression" of the United States in Korea and American "interference" in China's internal affairs concerning Taiwan. These experiences resulted in further emphasis on respect for sovereignty with the addition of the 1949 formulation of principles concerning nonaggression and noninterference. Then Lenin's concept of "Peaceful Coexistence" was added to neutralize concerns generated by earlier efforts at exporting revolution. The utility of the "Five Principles of Peaceful Coexistence" was tested during the negotiation of the PRC's first treaty with India (April 1954) and included therein:[22]

- Mutual respect for each other's territorial integrity and sovereignty
- Mutual nonaggression
- Mutual noninterference in each other's internal affairs
- Equality and mutual benefit
- Peaceful coexistence.[23]

A year later, in April 1955, the "Five Principles of Peaceful Coexistence" gained international attention when Zhou Enlai opened a diplomatic offensive at the Asian-African Solidarity Conference in Bandung to gain a more respected and responsible role for the PRC in the international community. Zhou asserted that by following the five principles listed below, countries with "different social systems" can achieve peaceful coexistence and settle disputes through negotiations.[24] Except for a hiatus during the Cultural Revolution, these principles have continued as the standard against which China's leaders measure the PRC's bilateral relations with the US and other non-socialist nations.[25]

International law versus the five principles. Along with the establishment of Imperial China's first centralized foreign office in 1861, there was an effort in the 1860s by a small number of Chinese reformists to introduce international law systematically to China. They reasoned that to deal effectively with the West, China must master both international law and the secrets of Western military technology.[26] Chinese frustrations with this effort at transplanting Western ideas, as well as with Western laws, were succinctly described in 1891 by a Chinese diplomat who observed that "International law is just like Chinese statutory law—reasonable but unreliable. If there is right without might, the right will not prevail."[27]

The theoretical discussions of international law in China during the mid to late 1950s reflect an effort similar to that of the 1860s, only more critical of "western hypocrisy." For example, one Chinese author argued that the principle of peaceful coexistence is not only consistent with the principles of international law but is the premise thereof and should be practiced by all nations. Furthermore, the other four principles have also been important international concerns, but they too are frequently violated by the West. Since these principles are only selectively practiced by the West, the application of international law by the West is obviously self-serving.[28] Thus, by urging universal adoption of the Five Principles—as a standard by which to measure the justness of Western laws—Zhou attempted to seize the moral high ground within the international community. There appeared to be little about the Five Principles with which the West could disagree. On the other hand, the possibility of a hidden agenda concerned US Secretary of State Dulles and others. These principles were based on Chinese experiences, moral obligations, and principles and not on Western experiences and legal precedents. Different historical experiences and cultural values result in laws that are meaningful in one system and irrelevant in the other—a maxim reaffirmed in the mid-1980s.

Initially, in 1955, the Five Principles were ignored by US policymakers because of their uncertainty as to what the Chinese intended by them.[29] Nearly two decades later in the "Shanghai Communique" of 28 February 1972, the United States endorsed these principles and then reaffirmed that endorsement in the Joint Communique of 15 December 1978, concerning the establishment of relations, and again in the Joint Communique of 17 August 1982.[30] These US actions, however, have not satisfied the Chinese. Prior to 1972, the United States was criticized by the Chinese for not adopting the Five Principles; since 1972 the United States has been criticized for not living up to the Five Principles the United States had thrice affirmed. In 1984, Premier Zhao Ziyang stated in the "Report on the Work of the Government" to the National People's Congress that

> China maintains good relations with many developed countries . . . on the basis of the Five Principles of Peaceful Coexistence. . . . There remains an obstacle to the development of Sino-US relations, namely, the Taiwan question. It will be possible to make steady and sustained progress in Sino-US relations so long as the United States strictly abides by the principles established in the Sino-US joint communiques."[31]

In effect, the Five Principles of Peaceful Coexistence are a moral code for judging the correctness of the China policy of the United States, a code to which the Chinese have the interpretive keys. In a political context, Chinese principles are a substitute for international law. This does not mean that the Chinese ignore international law, or US domestic law, but they do criticize these laws whenever they run counter to the Five Principles or other principles derived therefrom.

As broad general foreign policy axioms, the Five Principles are applicable to any issue involving Chinese and American interests. Principles associated with specific international, regional, and bilateral issues are logical derivatives of these axioms; exceptions are rare. These specific principles are simply asserted as if their validity is self-evident, requiring no explanation. Such principles can be used as fences to protect subjects the Chinese do not wish to negotiate, either with the United States or domestically. For example, the principle of mutual noninterference in each other's internal affairs has been used to defect international criticism of the Chinese government's reactions to domestic political and religious opposition, such as in Tibet and Tiananmen Square. However, predicting the degree to which China's leaders may insist or temporize on the immediate attainment of these specific principles depends on an admixture of factors not well understood by Americans or many Chinese. The level of immediate commitment to attaining a principle may be a function of external factors over which there is no immediate control or it may simply be a function of priority. But how does the organizational process decide what can be achieved and determine the priority for implementation? How is competition between bureaucracies and factions manifest? Or at the aggregate level, how does Beijing evaluate the "objective reality" of the moment and determine its negotiating strategy? More than an anecdotal understanding of these processes must await the opening of the PRC's historical records to the public.

In 1951 China made clear to the United States and the United Nations that its terms for discussing the cessation of hostilities in Korea included the withdrawal of UN forces, the return of Taiwan, and the representation of China in the United Nations by the PRC.[32] Yet none of these specific objectives was achieved prior to the Armistice Talks. For whatever military, political, or economic reasons, Beijing laid these principles aside for the moment. But they were not eliminated. Those principles resurfaced during the Armistice Talks and, where they have not been fulfilled, more than 30 years later they remain principles to be fulfilled.

The Five Principles are important to China's leaders in terms of Sino-American relations because they provide both a frame of reference within which principles concerning specific issues can be logically presented and argued, and because they provide a moralistic foreign policy yardstick based on Chinese norms and values against which Beijing can publicly evaluate and struggle against the policies, norms, and values of the United States. These principles provide the necessary tactical flexibility to accommodate "objective reality" without losing direction. Agreements that are to some extent ideologically undesirable can be reached for the interim without Chinese domestic opposition becoming excessively concerned that the agreement will evolve into a permanent one. Agreements that don't adhere to the Five Principles and derivative principles are, by definition, incomplete and subject to reconsideration as objective conditions evolve in favor of the Chinese solution. Conversely, retrogression from these principles would be unacceptable. This moralistic "we are a principled people" approach has often aggravated US negotiators and policymakers. Nevertheless, China's consistency and perseverance with this approach over the long term have resulted in the gradual acceptance by world public opinion of many of China's formerly "obdurate and uncompromising" positions.

The Chinese Negotiation Style

In summarizing American experiences in negotiations with the PRC from 1953 to 1967, Kenneth Young described the Chinese negotiating style as "adversary negotiations." Mirroring the conclusions of the Chinese diplomat of 1891, Young concluded that unless the United States exercises "both diplomacy and power, negotiation with Peking is unlikely or impossible."[33] Conversely, in 1971 Henry Kissinger found the Chinese style of getting to a defensible position in one concessionary jump satisfying. He felt it was somewhat ironic when he was castigated later for using the tactic of "preemptive concession," a tactic he adopted from the Chinese for use in other negotiations as well.[34]

Normalization of relations in 1979 brought an even greater change in American perceptions of the Chinese style of negotiation, as a seemingly endless stream of US officials and private citizens traveled to Beijing to negotiate their respective parts of an expanding array of agreements. With the hostility of the 1950s and 1960s replaced by the charm of Chinese hospitality and the rapidly increasing number of agreements, the experiences of earlier decades seemed irrelevant to an understanding of how the Chinese negotiate today.[35] Yet, when these periods are compared and examined as elements of a dynamic strategic continuum of negotiations by which Sino-American relations are managed by the Chinese, rather than as individual episodes, some consistencies appear. The Chinese show patterns of traditional and Marxist logic along with cultural habits and norms that result in a preference for principles versus laws and the implementation of agreements per the spirit of the agreement versus the detailed letter of the law. Domestic politics and bureaucratic standards also combine to generate a degree of consistency and continuity in the evolving rationale, process, and tactics of the Chinese style of negotiation.

The influence of tradition. Traditionally, the Chinese have preferred to resolve conflicts through mediation. Philosophically, agreement or harmony ranked high on the scale of virtues, motivated in part by the awareness that conflict carried the potential for the violence that could break down the social order essential to China's agrarian society.[36] Parties negotiated with each other directly; mediation conducted at the lowest possible level was the rule; the court system was to be avoided.[37] Mediation was informal and began with one of the parties calling on a third person or peer, such as a friend, to persuade the other party to fulfill his obligations. If this low-level parley was unsuccessful, the next meeting was usually either group mediation, involving a number of peers offering advice, or mediation by a respected person, often a retired official. Successive steps involved local clan or village leaders with the county (*xian*) court as the first formal alternative. Public pressure for the participants to accept a mediator's recommendation increased significantly with each step in the process. First, the mediator stood to "lose face" if his recommendation was not adopted. Second, the greater the mediator's respectability ("face," or *mianzi*) and rank, the greater the likelihood of public support for his recommendations. Failure could mean loss of face for the mediator and public disapproval of the participants. Public disapproval was a powerful force, for it placed the prestige of each participant's face in jeopardy. Prestige or public reputation, critical to the achievement of wealth and power, would be lowered by such criticism. Public disapproval also threatened the other aspect of a face—*lian*—by casting doubt on one's good character and personal integrity and jeopardizing the comfort and convenience that comes with respectability.[38] In essence, life was an endless series of negotiations over face. Interdependence, not individualism, was rewarded. Social isolation was and remains a terrible punishment. Only those outside the system, such as the outlaw, were exempt from this endless series of negotiations over face.

This mediation process minimized contact between opponents to avoid exacerbating the dispute. It was a process of continual struggle to exert or resist pressure or moral persuasion by each of the opponents on the other, by the mediator on the participants, or by participants on the public. Righteousness or principle was an important element of the pressure applied, though subject to the overriding need for harmony.

The use of violence to resolve disputes was discouraged by this system, but not eliminated. When quarrels erupted into violence, they did so with considerable force, occasionally escalating into clan wars aand resulting in lost lives and resources. While land was the basis of a clan's power, it was only as productive as the amount of labor added. The loss of lives in a clan war could seriously affect a clan's future. War created pressures to return to negotiations and a settlement in light of the new circumstances.

The imperial government of the Qing dynasty (1644-1912) seldom had sufficient local military capability to resolve forcibly each clan dispute and it thus preferred to stand aside until the government's legitimacy was seriously threatened. Nevertheless, the threat of government involvement, with its accompanying costs to the participants in the dispute, was a constraining influence, and conflict was often limited by tacit agreement to avoid government intervention. Futhermore, the fear of escalation that government involvement would bring provided a face-saving excuse for returning to mediation. The resumption of negotiations was arranged by third parties, but the final settlement was handled directly by the principals.[39]

This system for resolving disputes plus a court system focused primarily on criminal law were the essence of China's relatively effective imperial legal system. But there was also a negative side to this traditional system—might too often made right. In the name of harmony, public opinion was vulnerable to the pressures of wealth, politics, and force. Passiveness before injustice too often passed for harmony. Furthermore, the traditional approach didn't stand up well in disputes with the West during China's "100 years of humiliation" where the mediators were working between cultures rather than within one. Deprived of a shared cultural milieu, the mediators often found their role reduced from mediator to messenger.

China's legal system was essentially a system of duties and obligations rather than rights. Rights as a concept did not develop in Chinese law in the same manner as in the West; in China, rights were both determined and sustained by moral obligations. For the Chinese, the West's emphasis on rights and guaranteeing rights more through laws than ethics often led to decisions in the West that shocked the moral sense of the Chinese.[40] An example from Western international law was the ceding of former German concessions in Shandong, a coastal province south of Beijing, to Japan at the May 1919 Paris Peace Conference, rather than returning them to China.

Believing themselves a victim of the West's "unjust" legal systems, Chinese intellectuals for over a century have not trusted the West's legal system to be a suitable replacement for China's traditional approach. Despite its many foibles, exceptions, and variations, informal mediation remains the societal norm. Even with the advent of the CCP the Chinese have continued to favor third-party "go-betweens" to mediate a dispute or in some way facilitate the mediation process. The Chinese still try to avoid direct confrontation between opponents until after both have shown their commitment to finding a mutually acceptable solution through mediation. At this point, the opponents are needed only to resolve final details and seal the agreement. The Chinese also are influenced still by public opinion, but more than ever recognize the public's vulnerability to pressures. This preference for the traditional approach both reinforces and is reinforced by the Chinese tendency to distrust Western approaches.

The influence of Marxist rationale. In the Marxist view, all knowledge is acquired directly through personal experience or indirectly through the experiences of others. Thus, experience becomes the material of a materialist theory of knowledge. On the premise that continued experience over time will change reality, knowledge can advance next to the rational stage of conception, judgment, and inference. This is the dialectic's thought process for a theory of knowledge. At this point in the development of knowledge, according to Mao, "logical knowledge is capable of grasping the development of the surrounding world in its totality, in the international relations of all its aspects."[41] Having been scientifically reconstructed, this knowledge reflects "objective reality." The next step is to apply this new understanding of the laws of the "objective world" to changing the world. These laws or theories may be wrong—according to Mao many are—but through the test of practice they can be corrected.[42] On the basis of the Marxist theory of knowledge, the experiences of the CCP have validated the wisdom of traditional Chinese rationale that judged the logic of Western law as unacceptable for China.

CCP attitudes since 1949 toward law and conflict resolution have continued to be essentially anti-legal. A brief experiment with the Soviet legal model during the mid-1950s ended with the "Anti-Rightist" campaign. The Chinese Communist Party and its preference for moral principles (as defined by Marxist-Leninist ideology) became supreme in legal matters. Traditional informal mediation practices have been adapted, with most civil disputes resolved through people's mediation committees, other non-legal specialists, and public pressure.[43] Even today, as China opens to the West, Chinese courts remain oriented toward criminal cases versus arbitration cases. Mediation of cases involving Westerners is handled by specialized agencies, not courts of law.[44]

Communist thought has not totally supplanted the "three religions and nine schools of thought" of traditional China, but its influence is pervasive and particularly strong where the Party has focused its attention on the weaknesses of the traditional system.[45] If righteousness fails to prevail in the resolution of conflict (contradicting Marx), the principles or laws of Marxism-Leninism-Maoism (the new righteousness) will correct the weakness.[46] Although the violence of the Cultural Revolution and other campaigns leaps to mind to suggest that harmony is unimportant to Communists, in theory it is essential.[47] It is a condition within which lesser contradictions are laid aside, as in a united front, to permit a unified effort to resolve a principal contradiction. And it is the first of "two stages of motion for all things" within the "law of the unity of opposites." Although Mao argued that contradiction exists in all things, he also said that contradictions "will not become intensified into antagonism in all things"—a concept similar to traditional thought.[48]

The violent cyclical swings since 1949 between seeing antagonism in all contradictions (the radical ideologue) and seeing antagonism only in some (the pragmatist) can also be viewed as a swing between resolving conflict by force or by mediation. China's foreign policy toward the United States from 1949 to 1979 shifted with these domestic changes. The contradictions in Sino-American relations did not always intensify into antagonism or active hostility, although antagonism dominated much of the period.

Interviews in six major cities of the PRC in 1983 and 1984 with party members and non-party members alike suggest that maybe the Party has found a workable combination of mediation and force such that the violent extremes of the past will not be repeated. The Party's approach through a united front is responsible to the traditional society's call for harmony. On the other hand no Party member interviewed would argue that all contradictions between China and the United States could be resolved by non-antagonistic methods; they only "hoped so."

The importance of Marxism-Leninism-Maoism to the rationale for the Chinese approach to negotiations has been strongly argued. Kenneth Young, for instance, stressed the importance of party discipline, the Communist's distrust of imperialism, and the moral imperative of Marxism-Leninism-Maoism in determining the Chinese Communist's adversarial approach to negotiations. Arthur Lall stressed the Communist's "hard to understand emphasis on contradictions" and China's traditional, "though unjustified," superiority complex. Others have stressed the commonality between Soviet and Chinese Communist approaches. These conclusions, however, are too narrow. Veteran party cadres made it clear during interviews that ideology has not been and is not now the sole significant determinant of the Chinese style of negotiation. Although the CCP shares a common ideological heritage with the Communist Party of the USSR, it is clear by the CCP's own claims that communism as practiced in China is unique to China. As indicated earlier, there are patterns of logic remaining from traditional China that the Party has altered little if any. Furthermore, as virulent as feelings in the early 20th century were against Western imperialism, there is reason to believe that even without the discipline and doctrine of the Communist Party, the Chinese today would be tough negotiators. One has only to examine the Nationalist government's negotiating record with the United States to realize how tough.

The evolving contemporary process. The contemporary Chinese negotiating style with respect to negotiations with the United States is both constant and ever changing. It is rooted in time-honored patterns of interaction that have been reinforced and only slightly modified by China's "100 years of humiliation" in dealing with the West and by the Communist Party's own Marxist values to produce what China's current leaders might call a "socialist negotiating style with Chinese characteristics." The Chinese negotiator's current style is further defined by an enduring set of foreign relations principles designed primarily by Zhou Enlai to achieve the nation's primary interests of independence, economic development, and security. These principles were designed as China's alternative to the West's "unreliable system of international relations and law." But the Chinese system is also continually changing and reforming on the margins to accommodate the government's most recent national security policy—the latest of which is the "Four Modernizations" policy—and experiences in dealing with the United States. It is a negotiating style that both defines the PRC's "grand strategy" for relations with the United States and the tactics to be used in formal negotiations. The contemporary process as described in the sections that follow is illustrated in the case studies in chapters 4 and 5.

As Marxists, China's leaders have managed Sino-American relations since 1949 as a contradiction between two competing social systems. Within the Marxist paradigm, resolution of the principal contradiction is paramount; all other contradictions are secondary and subordinate and thus not necessarily antagonistic. Throughout most of this period the US-PRC contradiction was the principal one. The nationalistic views of China's leadership reinforced their Marxist views of the United States. The United States was the epitome of the economic and technological strength of the West that was responsible for China's exploitation and its resultant backwardness. However, as international and domestic circumstances changed, competition or antagonism between the PRC and the Soviet Union became the principal contradiction, forcing the PRC-US contradiction into a secondary and supporting role that resulted in cooperation between the PRC and the United States to deal with the Soviets as a mutual problem.[49] As the United States lowered its military profile in Asia and the conflict with the Soviet Union became the primary contradiction, concerns about the United States were lowered enough to permit efforts "to learn from the West in order to oppose foreign aggression."

Throughout the period covered by this study, China's leaders used something comparable to Schelling's "strategy of conflict." They instinctively handled the bilateral relationship as a continuing bargaining process. Though influenced by both Marxist and Western conventions, the implementation of the strategy was basically along traditional Chinese lines in which China's negotiators first worked their way up through a hierarchy of third parties before turning to more formal instruments of power. They sought to influence international public opinion; to deal through such third persons as respected private citizens, the press, and people's organizations; to work with such "respected persons" as third country diplomats, leaders, and members of international organizations; to use direct negotiations; and finally, in most cases, to use military force to demonstrate resolve rather than destroy or conqueror.

The process at the aforementioned strategic level is much the same as that used tactically during direct, formal negotiations. Both the strategic and tactical process can be analyzed in five fairly distinct phases:

- Prenegotiation phase or indirect engagement
- Convening the conference or direct engagement
- Evaluating possible outcomes or sizing the opponent
- Hard bargaining and closure
- Postconference phase.

Prenegotiation phase. For the Chinese, as emphasized by those interviewed, this is the most critical phase. In theory, everything that has occurred in the past has the potential for influencing the outcome of direct negotiations and may, under some circumstances, predetermine the outcome. While the cosmological nature of this view may appear to some to be unmanagable, the Chinese have a different perception. History is important in China. It has always been a means to explain the present. The relationship of the present situation to the past is like that of an individual to his lineage. He is simultaneously unimportant and all important, undifferentiated and unique; a person is the product of his lineage and is but one of many in an endless history. On the other hand, he has the potential for breaking the line or redirecting the future. So it is with any particular conference. The future of the PRC does not rest on any single conference, yet what is done at any one conference is part of a long chain of events that determines what can or can not be accomplished in the future.

Before negotiations at any level begin, the central leadership will have assessed the "objective reality" and determined its objectives vis-a-vis the principal "contradiction" as well as the strategy for achieving those objectives. In 1949-1950 the CCP sought to deter the United States from achieving preponderant power and influence in China and East Asia. The strategy was to "lean to one side" toward the USSR in joint opposition to the US. By 1954 the leadership perceived a need to correct the tilt and open the door to cooperation with the United States. However, the preconditions were too great for the United States, and the Chinese domestic window of opportunity closed a few years later. By the early 1970s, the Soviet Union was perceived as the principal threat, and China saw the need to shift its strategy from the somewhat ambivalent one of the late 1960s toward a strategy that favored the United States over the USSR in a ratio of about 70 to 30.[50]

Changes in strategy require changes in subordinate objectives. Even with the best of information, however, it is not always clear how to pursue new objectives. The problem has been more difficult for China's leaders because their knowledge of the US has always been limited. In 1949 it was limited to the experiences of a few returned students and contact by a small group of party leaders with Americans during World War II and during the postwar negotiations. The result was the gradual evolution of a trial and error approach in the development of Sino-American policy. One US diplomat, experienced in negotiating with the Chinese, described the Chinese approach as being "similar to that of an engagement between two military forces with limited or no knowledge of the other. Both sides reconnoiter by fire searching for targets, attempting to ascertain the intentions of the other." Chinese probing techniques included making statements of general principles on subjects of special concern and making assertions that the United States should take certain actions because of the debt it owed China as a victim of US imperialism. Official and unofficial reactions in the United States, and to some extent elsewhere in the world, helped the Chinese identify where US and PRC interests were in conflict, as well as determine the level of US resistance to China's objectives.

As "heads begin to pop up and targets are identified," more detailed information is sought and possible solutions explored. Third parties are used to test ideas and probe resistance in the United States to Chinese positions. Efforts are made to influence the perceptions of various elements of the US body politic and the international community.

When the Chinese believe they have identified tentative solutions, they begin preparations for direct, formal negotiations. Ideally these are not meetings to find solutions but meetings where solutions explored through third parties are ratified and stated for the record. However, miscalculations are made and plans can fail. It's always a gamble to go to the negotiation table, for third-party solutions are seldom based on complete information about any of the participants. The Chinese are certainly aware of the possibility of failure and come prepared to use the conference to achieve what Dr. Iklé calls "side-effects," at least maneuvering the United States into the position of appearing at fault for the failure to reach an agreement.

Preparations for the conference are extensive and thorough. The best possible combination of negotiators and staff is assembled. The historical record is reviewed exhaustively (the Chinese are meticulous record keepers). Accounts by US diplomats of previous negotiations are translated and studied. Illustrating the effort expended in preparation, one interviewee reported that Premier Zhao Ziyang read Ambassador Cabot's little-known account of his experiences at the Warsaw Talks as part of the Premier's preparation for dealing with the United States.

Although each negotiator and each conference are different, full consideration is given to taking advantage of the peculiarities of each, particularly from a psychological perspective. Nothing is consciously left to fate.

Convening the conference. In the Chinese game of strategy known as *weiqi* (*Go* in Japan), the beginner is often confused by what appears to be the studied randomness with which the experienced player positions his pieces. It's not until much later that the beginner perceives the logic of the placement of each piece. An important principle to *weiqi* players is the concept of maintaining the initiative (*xianshou*) on both the defensive as well as the offensive. Similar to the *weiqi* beginners, Western negotiators can become temporarily confused by the unexpected opening moves of China's negotiators. The nature of the problem, US perceptions of who has the advantage, and what the next move of the Chinese would logically be, don't seem to correlate well with the apparent self-assurance and purposefulness, even arrogance, of the Chinese negotiator, who, from an American viewpoint, is usually at a disadvantage. US uncertainty is cultivated. Each step leading to the conference is calculated to give the Chinese negotiator the initiative. The Chinese want each succeeding move by the United States to be dependent on their moves. Should the initiative be lost, considerable effort is expended to recover it.[51]

The location of the conference sets the stage. The preference for a location is Beijing, where access to historical records, staff, and the collective decision structure is best. One Chinese official noted that he feels very uncomfortable when in Europe, because of the long lines of communication that limit direct access to the Foreign Ministry's archives and staff as well as "policy" developments (I read this as developments in factional politics) in Beijing. He also felt threatened by the big advantage the United States derives from its efficient record retrieval,

Courtesy National Archives

Kaesong, site of the first negotiations between the United States and representatives of the new government of China.

assisted in recent decades by its preeminence in the development and use of computers. He assumed that the US Government stores its historical records and other data needed for negotiations so that they are available instantaneously almost anywhere in the world.

The city of Beijing is not always acceptable to the United States nor is it necessarily the best location for the Chinese. When it is not, the Chinese make every effort to utilize the advantages of the chosen location while minimizing its disadvantages; psychological aspects of the location are often more important than the physical. Americans have tended to assess the importance placed by the North Koreans and the Chinese on Kaesong as the initial conference site for the Korean Armistice Talks as an effort to place the UN team on the defense psychologically.[52] What tends to be overlooked is the positive psychological advantage that accrued to the Chinese team by being located in a culturally compatible environment as compared to the alien environment aboard the West European hospital ship originally proposed by the United Nations as a neutral environment.

The tone of the conference is determined to a great extent by the tenor of Sino-American relations and the nature of the issue. The hostile tone of the armistice conference in Korea reflected the enmity of the battlefield as well as the revolutionary's struggle against a century of Western imperialism. The negotiations in 1984 pertaining to military technology transfers were predicated more on interests held in common; thus, the tone was more cooperative and less focused on areas of disagreement.

Because of the highly personalized nature of Chinese politics, the Chinese insist that conference procedures and interpersonal relations during the conference reflect the nature of the relationship between the two countries. Accustomed to intensely managing interpersonal relations, the Chinese often reflect a stylized response to the conference's tone in their personal mannerisms. This could appear as the invective of a hostile personal relationship or the amenities associated with personal friendships.

The single most significant action during this phase is the development of an agenda. The agenda proposed by the Chinese tends to be constructed around proposals that each side has suggested or implied, often through third parties are acceptable. The proposed agenda is a reasonably accurate statement of Chinese objectives and what they believe to be the basis for a principled settlement. The agendas proposed at Kaesong in July 1951 and at Geneva for the Ambassadorial Talks were both constructed around principles the Chinese felt the Americans had accepted and that were acceptable to the Chinese once they had reformatted them. The Chinese expected in both cases to reach a quick settlement and move on to a more important set of issues at a higher level of negotiation.[53]

When US negotiators reject the Chinese agenda, the Chinese feel the United States misrepresented its intentions to the third parties during the pre-negotiation phase, and are not prepared to reach a settlement. If the Chinese decide to discontinue the negotiations, they will in essence return to the prenegotiation phase's objectives of pressuring those interested in the issue (international and US public, mediators, and the US government) to accept the validity of China's principles.

If the initial agenda proposal is rejected, the Chinese refocus their efforts on revising the agenda to support their efforts to influence attitudes and opinions. The agenda becomes a strategy and to some extent a media schedule for persuading interested parties. Through the agenda, the rules of engagement are established and subjects to be discussed are limited or expanded and then ranked, according to Chinese perceptions, from the easiest to the more difficult. The agenda is the framework that permits control of the pace of the conference; it helps determine who has the initiative, facilitates success (e.g., by placing the more easily solved issue first), and influences the rules and assumptions for resolving conference issues.

Evaluating possible outcomes. This phase can easily become the most demanding and exasperating phase, if in the pre-negotiation phase the probable settlement wasn't accurately identified. During the negotiations leading up to the Shanghai communique, this phase was relatively brief, while during the armistice negotiations and the Ambassadorial Talks it extended into years.

The purpose of this phase is to size the opposition, to draw out the US position with minimum exposure of China's. Efforts to pressure the US into revealing its negotiating position range from the threat and use of force to the most subtle psychological efforts. The extreme form of the first pressure is reflected in the well known "Fight, Fight, Talk, Talk" tactic employed during the Korean Armistice Talks.

At the subtle end, Chinese maneuvers to dominate the agenda and set the pace help exploit American vulnerabilities to being trapped between the "minute hand" and some self-imposed deadline. Creating the impression through comments and physical mannerisms that the Chinese have infinite patience reinforces this initiative. The patient countenance of a stoic and remarks like "If it cannot be reunited in 100 years, then it will be reunited in 1000 years," are not encouraging signs of an impending policy change or compromise. Moves to cause the United States to appear to be the supplicant, to portray China as the victim, to pressure "old friends" in the United States or at the conference to oppose or support a particular policy, to exploit differences among US politicians, parties and institutions, especially during political campaigns—these techniques that have been employed effectively to gain information concerning the US position. Sometimes employing the stoic's impatient silence, they are also masters of the dramatic monologue. Their speeches are prescriptive and thus often critical. In a hostile environment they abound with invective, which sometimes generates a helpful rebuttal from the United State. In the friendlier environment of Chinese hospitality, the host's deference to his guests and a patient, waiting silence puts the Chinese in the listening mode.

From their personal experiences, some Westerners interviewed believe that an examination of the historical record will show that the Chinese don't make concessions until the hard bargaining begins. Most of the Chinese interviewed argued strongly against this view. They argued that the Chinese make concessions throughout the process, "but not of principle." A somewhat biased but parallel evaluation is reflected in one KMT official's admiring remarks concerning Zhou Enlai's use of concessions during the CCP-KMT negotiations in March 1945:

> It's fascinating to watch Zhou...operate at a negotiation table.... He makes compromises, but only minimal and nominal at the very last moment just to keep the negotiations going. When you study his statements afterwards, you realize that he hasn't made any substantial concession on any important issue at all. . . . The Communists are winning the mainland not through combat, but across the negotiation table with Zhou sitting on the other side.[54]

While the length of this phase of negotiations is not necessarily determined by deliberate Chinese policy, China's leaders are disposed both ideologically and culturally to delay pushing for an agreement—including ceasing direct negotiations if necessary—until conditions are right, a factor which tends to favor retention of the initiative by the Chinese. Furthermore, in the Chinese experience the US side is impatient to begin bargaining long before the Chinese have completed their assessment, leaving the Chinese side to determine when conditions are ripe for the next phase.

Hard bargaining and closure. This final phase of direct bargaining tends to move very quickly. Conditions and expectations are similar to those the Chinese would expect to exist at the end of a successful pre-negotiation phase. The general framework for a solution is evident to both sides and both have made a decision to reach an agreement. The Chinese begin by restating their principles. They then state their agreed-upon position as if they had never shifted it or ever made a mistake. There are no apologies. The US negotiator must pay close attention to what is not said by the Chinese as well as to what is said. China's top leaders will be deeply involved in the details of the final settlement as if they were "just outside the tent." Where practical, after a settlement is reached, the US negotiators will usually have a departing session with the Chinese official upon whom the responsibility for the negotiations rest, one of those leaders from "just outside the tent."

Where the agreement does not completely satisfy the principles that guided Chinese participation, the resultant agreement will contain a means by which the negotiations can be reopened should objective circumstances improve. If no agreement appears possible, the Chinese will attempt to position themselves so that the United States can logically be blamed for the failure of the negotiations.

Postconference phase. Once direct talks have been completed, the Chinese begin unilaterally to impose their definitions on the agreement. From their meticulous records, unequaled by the United States, they cite remarks made during formal and informal conversations to show US agreement with their definitions.[55] The tone is moralistic, the language prescriptive. Mistrustful of legalistic interpretations of agreements, the Chinese press the United States to conform to the "spirit of the agreement," as they have defined it. Since intent is in the eyes of the beholder and the Chinese have seized the initiative, the US policymaker soon finds himself with an unexpected issue and the Chinese pressing the United States to change its policies. Such pressure is likely to begin as early as during the closing statement by the Chinese negotiator following an agreement.

Chen Muhua, Minister of Foreign Economic Relations and Trade signed two agreements on 9 May 1984 with Secretary Malcolm Baldridge implementing the PRC-US accord of January 1984 on industrial and technological cooperation. Ms. Chen concluded her press conference following the signing by stressing the importance of the next issue to be resolved, and implying an obligation on the part of the United States to seek a breakthrough in Sino-American economic and technological cooperation and trade relations:

> Currently all the restrictions and obstacles, whether imposed directly on Chinese trade with the United States, or existing in respect of technology transfers, credit, and transportation, are to a great extent directly related to the special provisions directed against China in US legislation.
>
> Therefore, to make a breakthrough in Sino-US economic and technological cooperation and trade relations, all those provisions which are not keeping with the times should be first abrogated or amended once and for all.[56]

Not only is the problem identified but the solution is specified. Similar action on the part of the United States would be objected to as interference in China's domestic affairs and classified in China's domestic media as an act of imperialism.

From the strategic perspective, the postconference phase is an important opportunity to make maximum use of the supportive emotions and momentum generated by the conference, render any concessions to the United States less damaging, and thereby enhance the positive impact of the direct negotiations on the objective conditions that shape China's negotiating strategy vis-a-vis the United States.

Negotiation Tactics

Chester Karrass divides negotiation tactics into two parts: maneuvers and techniques. By his definition, as modified to accommodate the Chinese style, maneuvers are composed of a series of related actions and techniques designed 1) to create attitudes and perceptions at the conference favorable to the Chinese negotiator; 2) to create a general attitude among parties interested in the conference that will be favorable to the Chinese position; 3) to increase US vulnerability to certain pressure; and 4) to facilitate the defense of China's bargaining position by eliminating or restricting the use of certain US techniques. Techniques are specific actions taken to secure an objective.[57] A broad range of maneuvers and techniques were observed in the case studies and discussed during the interviews. The maneuvers listed below were used in all cases examined and are briefly described, except for the agenda, discussed earlier. Many of the techniques tend to be more specific and are thus applicable only in certain phases, under certain circumstances or with certain maneuvers. China's techniques are described in the following discussion of maneuvers as well as in the earlier discussion of phases.

Maneuvers

- Agenda (discussed earlier)
- Principles
- Setting the pace
- Trust and equality
- Personalized relationships
- Decisionmaking authority
- Precedence
- Diversions

Principles. Negotiation principles are essentially objectives and generally fall into three categories: Principles the Chinese publicly announce must be met prior to any formal negotiations; principles that are Chinese objectives for the conference; and general principles. The first group consists of relatively firm objectives but fairly ambiguous in terms of a time by which they must be fulfilled. Seldom have these principles been fully achieved prior to the opening of the formal negotiations and often they are not even part of the final agreement. However, they tend to be enduring principles that the Chinese will continue to try to achieve as derivative of the "Five Principles of Peaceful Coexistence."

The principles of the second group relate specifically to the conference and are designed to fence off issues. They are thus harder to bend than the first category and are often completely inflexible.

The third category is the most general and includes such principles as independence, self-reliance, and the Five Principles of Peaceful Coexistence. These principles represent the broadest possible agreement within the central leadership and are thus the most enduring. The tactics employed to achieve these principles have varied with changes in the domestic and international environment, but because they represent fundamental policy guidelines, they have been remarkably consistent guideposts. As Zhou concluded in the lessons he drew from the negotiations with the KMT from August 1945 to the end of 1946, there can be no change or concession in a fundamental policy or principle. There is room for conciliation but, according to Zhou,

> It depends on tactics, which are determined according to circumstances. When the circumstances change, tactics too should change, but tactics are always employed to implement the fundamental policy...because of disparities between the objective situation and our subjective strength, our route too must sometimes zigzag. But our tactics should not go against our policy.[58]

Setting the pace. The Chinese attempt to retain or regain the initiative (*xianshou*) by controlling the pace of the negotiations. And they have been fairly effective against the somewhat more impatient "John Wayne style" of the United States.[59] Does this mean the Chinese are more patient? Not necessarily. The patterns of interpersonal relations in Chinese society tend to reinforce patience as a personal quality, or create the illusion thereof, more than in the West. Nevertheless, many Chinese are impatient. Zhou Enlai was internationally famous for his patience, at least when negotiating face-to-face. However, as several Chinese officials pointed out, he tended to be more pragmatic than patient. He had a temper of which his staff was well aware, particularly when dealing in the relative privacy of his office with apparent US decisions with which he disagreed.

One official felt that the emphasis in Western academic studies on Chinese patience is too strong. It suggests greater stability in the political system and in interpersonal relations than actually exists. For example, one Chinese interviewed suggested that General Teng Hua may have been reassigned from the Armistice Talk delegation at Panmunjom after less than 3 months in part because he lacked sufficient patience. The meaning for US negotiations with the PRC is that China's leaders recognize the value of being perceived as patient, especially in controlling the pace of the conference. An ability to endure while waiting for external events to change the negotiation situation can frustrate an impatient opponent who is governed by time constraints.

Some of the complementary techniques that the Chinese have used, either individually or in combination, to control the physical and psychological pace of the conference are listed below.

- Stoicism: Enduring physical discomfort longer than one's opponent. This technique was particularly effective during the early stages of the Panmunjom talks and has been used in varying forms, depending on the personality of the negotiator, in the early stages of subsequent Sino-American exchanges.

- Recesses: Called by the Chinese for an unspecified period of time, thus under Chinese control, create uncertainty and impatience among the Americans.
- Unexpected meetings: Called by the Chinese at unexpected times, particularly at night. Zhou Enlai in particular was well known for calling foreign guests to his office in the middle of the night, if only for a friendly conversation.
- Stretchout: Most effective when US negotiators are operating under the time pressures of a schedule (e.g., Presidential elections, legislated suspenses, publicly announced limits on conference or trip duration, airline schedules) or other similar constraints.
- Impatience: Often manifested by outbursts of angry criticism. Vice Foreign Minister Han Xu is well known in diplomatic circles for his very pleasant and friendly personality. He is also known to a small circle for his outbursts of angry criticism (similar to Zhou Enlai), such as he is reported to have showered on Ambassador Arthur Hummel during the course of diplomatic exchanges following the early 1985 breakdown of plans for US Navy ship visits.
- Pregnant pause: Waiting quietly until the other side speaks. The Chinese have often used this technique, sometimes in conjunction with stoicism, to pressure the US representative to present his position first. In general, Americans feel uncomfortable with a lengthy break in a conversation and will usually respond by filling the vacuum. Anxious to proceed with their business, the Americans find the lacuna an opportunity to present what they think every man will accept as the most "reasonable" or "rational" position. When the Chinese choose to respond, their response can range from an explicit or implicit endorsement of all, part, or none of the US position, to engaging in some degree of criticism or rebuttal or combination thereof.

An important variation of this technique is the insistence by the Chinese that their guests should present what is on their minds first. Interestingly, the reverse in not necessarily true when Chinese delegations visit the United States. General Vessey, who visited the PRC as Chairman of the Joint Chiefs of Staff in 1985, is one of the few senior American officials whose personal style was compatible with pausing until the Chinese felt compelled to present their position first.

Equality and trust. The "era of humiliation" that preceded and shaped the CCP's climb to power reinforced China's distrust of foreigners and imposed on the party a requirement to insure that China is never again controlled, exploited, or treated as less than equal. From the American perspective this emphasis on equality has often resulted in a disconcerting requirement by the Chinese during negotiations for similarity in actions, statements, and agreements where little if any parallelism was perceived to exist from the American point of view.

The Chinese feel that trust is the cornerstone of equality. Since there are few, if any, new political problems in a society as old as China's—although some problems may not have been seen in several generations—there are many ancient stories and maxims from which to draw inspiration for solutions and procedures. For example, during the "Warring States" period of Chinese history (402-221 B.C.), trust among states was insured by such rituals as the exchange of hostages through marriage, the exchange of hostage populations and territory, and the exchange of spies (the modern day attachés).[60] The losses of each state had to be proportionately equal or there was no basis for trust. This is similar to the frequent demand from the PRC's leaders for complete reciprocity, and thus equality, in Sino-American relations.

A variation on the use of hostages to overcome the problem of trust was described by one Chinese official whom I interviewed by the use of a popular tale from 283

B.C. The Duke of the powerful state of Qin coveted a jade treasure of the Duke of Zhao and offered a number of cities in exchange. The Duke of Zhao feared an attack if he didn't agree, but knew he couldn't trust the Duke of Qin to transfer the cities once the jade was delivered. He sent an emissary, Li Xiangru—a very resourceful man, loyal to his liege unto death—to visit the Duke of Qin. After delivering the jade carving, Li confirmed that the Duke of Qin did not intend to honor his bargain any more than his 20 powerful predecessors had honored their agreements with other weaker powers. Through clever manipulation of the Duke's greed and curiosity, Li retrieved the jade long enough to threaten to shatter it. Unlike gold and silver, a jade carving is fragile and if shattered, like a human life, it cannot be restored. Li then proposed a series of actions based on the accepted rituals of the time that resulted in the Duke of Zhao surrendering the jade to the emissary of the Duke of Qin only after the 15 cities had been transferred to Zhao.

The official being interviewed then pointed out that there is a clear parallel between the jade in the Zhao-Qin relations and American prisoners in the earlier stages of Sino-American relations, particularly at the Ambassadorial Talks in Geneva. The Chinese were willing to sign the agreement concerning US civilians imprisoned by the PRC, with the implied agreement that the United States would continue the talks and arrive at a settlement of other issues that concerned the Chinese. But like the Duke of Zhao, the Chinese did not trust the more powerful United States to live up to the agreement and thus dragged their feet on the prisoner issue.[61]

The high degree of distrust associated with the hostility of enemies was lowered by President Nixon's February 1972 visit to China, the signing of the Shanghai Communique, and the release of the last US prisoner in the PRC. Since then, the emphasis placed by the Chinese on trust and equality as problems in Sino-American relations has varied somewhat according to the situation. Nevertheless, these two interrelated problems have continued to permeate the language and assumptions used in every Sino-American bargaining situation to date. Nor have the Chinese forgotten the importance of holding "hostage" US values with the greatest popular appeal (e.g., importance of the individual, hence the emphasis on the return of prisoners; fidelity to commitments, hence support for Taiwan).

Personalized relationships. That most Chinese are inclined to deal with issues and problems through personal relationships is China's legacy from centuries of humanistic philosophies and conventions. The residual influence of such concepts as the Confucian five degrees of relationship is that personal relations still tend to be hierarchial, interdependent, based on reciprocal obligations, and governed by conventions. In any relationship, whether inter-family, between friends, or with authorities, there is always some degree of inequality, such as in power, age, knowledge, ability, or wealth, that sets one above the other. Depending on the nature of the relationship, this inequality obligates one party to assist the other to some degree, which in turn generates a reciprocal obligation of some sort. Failure to honor these obligations, whether to assist or reciprocate, can easily endanger the relationship and result in acrimony from the offended as well as a serious loss of face for the one giving offense. Even relations with enemies are prescribed to some degree, including the nature of the compensation required to restore a relationship. And of course all relationships, particularly friendships, are instinctively ordered and evaluated in terms of their impact on other relationships.

This focus largely explains the importance placed by the Chinese today on people-to-people relations as one of the categories of foreign relations. The other two are the impersonal concept of state-to-state relations as stressed in the West and party-to-party relations as introduced by the Communists. However, even these latter two have been sinicized to some extent by Chinese attempts to conduct party and state relations in a highly personalized manner, eschewing the more impersonal, legalistic approach of the West.

The importance of personalized relations is evident in the resources and effort expended on people-to-people relations through friendship associations and the amount of time senior officials devote to supporting such activities. These relationships are vital to the Chinese; Sino-American relations are classified as friendly only in the area of people-to-people relations.

This long history of managing interpersonal relations has produced instinctive and stylized approaches across the spectrum of relations, from enemy to close friend. Several Chinese interviewed were surprised to be asked why so much invective was used at Punmunjom by the Chinese negotiators: "Americans were enemies and that's how enemies are treated." As the relationship has gradually become more friendly, the appropriate traditional stylized approach had been dusted off and used. Prior to President Reagan's 1984 visit to China, Ambassador Chai Zemin evoked an old Chinese saying to describe the reception the President could expect in China: "Courtesy demands reciprocity"[62] suggested a cordial, friendly welcome that one might extend to a new acquaintance, but not the warm welcome for a trusted and valued old friend.

Chinese personalization of relations is also reflected in the degree to which they attribute US policy to specific individuals. During the early 1950s, Zhou Enlai focused his attention on Dulles as his adversary. Later, Kissinger, Brzezinski, and Haig were designated as "friends of China," or the individuals from whom the Chinese could expect the most successful results.

Friendship also brings obligations. "Old friends," having been cultivated through friendship associations or other means, are called upon during periods of change in Sino-American relations to present and support China's position.[64] Friends are called upon to be intermediaries because the Chinese generally prefer an indirect approach to another person for assistance or for an important decision, particularly when there is a possibility of refusal or contention.

As important and consuming as a friendship can be for the Chinese negotiator, it still must be kept in perspective. One ancient proverb, which was brought to my attention several times during the interviews, says: "Each person has his own ruler to follow." The proverb concerns a deep friendship between two warriors, each loyal to a different ruler, a fact that could result in them having to fight each other. A modern interpretation of this dilemma was given by Premier Zhao Ziyang who, in criticizing US policy, said:

> . . . relations between friends are different from those between states. They are totally different concepts. China always has faith in friendship, and never forgets its old friends. But we never place such friendships above relations between states. . . . "[64]

But even this concern for the sovereignty of the state does not equate fully in the mind of the Chinese to the nationalism of the West. Rather, they prefer to think of it in the more personalized terms of "Chinese culturalism."

Decisionmaking authority. The US negotiator will almost always find that no matter what agreement he reaches with his Chinese counterpart, it is subject to review by someone not present at the conference. Conversely, negotiations deadlocked by the Chinese provide the opportunity for a more senior cadre to break the deadlock, if desired.

Precedent. Western law relies heavily on precedent as the basis for agreement and universal application. The Chinese use the concept of precedent more selectively. For example, in negotiating normalization agreements with foreign governments, the Chinese insisted that the agreements reflect the acceptance by the foreign government of China's basic principles, but then allowed significant exceptions in implementation. However, when other nations argued for the same specific exceptions on the basis that China had granted such exceptions to another country, the PRC refused on the basis that in the implementation of the basic principles each country's situation is different.

As the US-PRC relationship has developed, the principles first agreed upon in the Shanghai Communique have provided the framework within which the Chinese have attempted to guide the relationship. However, the Chinese have been rather flexible about the initial terms in the actual implementation of the principles. Each variation approved does include the caveat that, in keeping with the spirit of the principles, every compromise must eventually be corrected. They have also selectively and cautiously used the West's argument that precedence is the basis of law to point out inconsistencies in the US position.

Diversions. Ethics have been a constant source of criticism from Western commentators on Sino-American negotiations. The withdrawal of commitments, deceptive facts and figures, add-ons to raise the cost of previous agreements ("low-balling"), endless negotiations, and a number of other practices considered questionable or unethical in the West have been attributed to the PRC's negotiators, particularly during the armistice negotiations. Only the unavailable Chinese written record, to the extent it shows the intentions of the senior leadership, could prove or disprove these charges. However, Chinese participants say they are false charges and accuse the United States of similar unethical practices. On the other hand, both the Chinese classics suggest and Lenin argues that under certain circumstances these practices are ethical. Chinese literature is replete with heroic tales that describe and by implication encourage deception when dealing with a hostile opponent, particularly a more powerful opponent. This, of course, points to probable societal differences over what is ethical under different circumstances and emphasizes one of the many amorphous societal intersections that are the bane of negotiators. Some Chinese interviewed felt that US interest in negotiation ethics was designed to manipulate American public opinion.

One interesting technique has been observed since 1978 that has the effect of a diversion, although it is probably not so intended. Anxious to agree with a particular US proposal, at least in principle, but limited in some way from full execution (e.g., lack of resources or a leadership consensus), the Chinese senior negotiator may appear to agree to a particular proposal, only to have a junior member of the delegation tell selected counterparts of the US delegation, possibly at a subsequent social event, that the agreement probably can not be executed as agreed. The reasons are unlikely to be explained or the ambiguity even confirmed by the delegation leader. The desired result appears to be to express the senior negotiator's belief that there will probably be institutional agreement or harmony over the principle, and to indicate there is not yet a consensus among China's top leaders over how to proceed on that issue. The frustration and hostility that often results among the US side over how to implement the agreement are not fully understood or appreciated by the Chinese who sent the mixed signal in the first place.

Techniques

A number of techniques have been discussed throughout the preceding sections at length. They are as rich in variety, application, and effectiveness as the negotiators and their superiors have been imaginative in using them. A list of these techniques, as well as those used by the Chinese in the case studies that follow, are provided below:

Add-ons

Agenda/rules

Anger

Blackmail

Concessions

Criticism

Deadline/time

Delays

Deletions

Denial

Equality

Escape clause

Hostages

Impatience

Informal discussions

Invective

Leaks

Listening

Low-balling

Media choices

Misleading statistics

Monologues

Nonnegotiable

Nonverbal communications

Not listening

Old friend

Parallelism

Patience

Promises

Questions

Recess

Reciprocity

Risking own position

Seating

Secrecy

Shame/sympathy

Statements of Principles	Take it/leave it
Stoicism	Threats
Stretchout	Trust
Surprise meetings	Victim

As techniques, there are no surprises in this list. They have all been used by US negotiators at one time or another. However, underlying many of these techniques are cultural factors that result in differences in timing, emphasis, etc. Consequently, for the experienced Western negotiator unfamiliar with Chinese culture, the techniques may go unrecognized and be more effective than they may have been if recognized.[65]

Summary

The key to understanding the Chinese approach to negotiations with the United States, according to one of China's former vice minister of foreign affairs, is to understand that the objectives of the negotiations must sustain the PRC's basic foreign policy principles. These principles are "predictable, credible, and represent an enduring consensus among China's central leadership, a function of China's century-long quest for independence and development as a socialist country. However, the strategy and tactics to implement these principles change to respond to China's perception of the world and its changes."[66]

Going to the negotiating table is a tactic, not a strategy. Formal negotiation is but one phase of a dynamic bargaining process that is continually at work. Negotiations are more than the formal finite process that concludes with a joint communique and a signed document. Bilateral relations are continuous negotiations, with a dynamic agenda in which all elements are subordinated to the achievement of China's national objectives. Diplomacy is a tactical means of influencing the milieu in which the negotiators must operate and which shape their perceptions of the process. War, or more precisely the fear of war, is but one tool of the negotiator. National objectives are not achieved by war; rather, war is a means to lower opposition to cooperation. Formal negotiations are a period of time in a negotiations process in which the intensity of exchange between nations is of such volume and potential value that a conference atmosphere is practical. The conclusion of formal negotiations does not mark the end of the negotiations, but simply recognizes that nothing more can be achieved at that time. Because the national objectives are enduring in nature, from the Chinese perspective, negotiations take on an indefinite character. They are a process that should not be hurried strategically, though there are occasions when tactics may dictate speed. The conclusions of today establish a plateau from which future negotiators can step to reopen the argument in the future, a springboard to further discussions on issues the US policymakers may have thought were settled.[67]

3.
THE CHINESE DIPLOMAT: MESSENGER, NEGOTIATOR, OR MEDIATOR?

The Communist system of negotiating does not depend on the individuals involved. Their method is dogma followed slavishly by each representative.[1]

—-Admiral Turner C. Joy
1955[2]

TO GAIN AN APPRECIATION FOR HOW experienced diplomatic negotiators assess their opposite numbers, Asian, European, and American diplomats were queried about how much influence they felt a negotiator might be able to exercise during any negotiation, and how they evaluated the opposition's influence. In general they agreed that the ability of any nation's negotiator to influence personally the progress of any negotiation with another country is largely determined by the authority he derives, and is perceived by the other side to derive, from his instructions. While international convention is also an element of his authority, it is less significant than it would be in a multilateral environment. The initial perceptions by the opposition of any negotiator's authority are influenced by such factors as previous associations or experiences by the opposition with the negotiator, the negotiator's international reputation as an authoritative representative of his government, the other side's familiarity with the national style of the negotiator, and the importance publicly and privately ascribed to the negotiator by his government. How these factors influence perceptions will vary among societies according to differences in culture, national style of negotiation, how much information is available, and whether it is received directly or through the lens of a third party.

As the negotiations unfold, each negotiator is likely to enjoy either an enhanced or reduced degree of authority and flexibility, depending on the application of his own skills and experience, his initiative and ambition, the degree to which he is included in his government's policy process, the efficiency of communications with his superiors, his opponent's perceptions of these actions and comparable input, and the reactions of and within each government to the suggestions of the two negotiators. From the initial perceptions to the end of the negotiations, the nature and importance of a negotiator's role are not likely to remain constant or be determined by a single factor like the slavish adherence to dogma that Admiral Joy ascribed to his counterparts.

In his analysis of how nations negotiate, Dr. Fred Iklé divided these variations in the role of a negotiator into three general categories of messenger, negotiator, and mediator. He defined the role of a nation's representative as that of a messenger when his power to negotiate is restricted to the presentation of prepared statements, to outlining his government's position, and to receiving and passing on messages from his opponent.[3] At the other extreme, a representative is a mediator when he becomes so consumed with reaching an agreement—whether for the common good or his personal glory—that he seeks to find and argue the merit of both sides of the issue, even if his opponent persistently pursues his own argument. When apparent, such a role is exploitable by the opposition. [4]

The characteristics of a negotiator fall on the broad continuum between these extremes. At the center, the ideal negotiator is defined by Iklé as a disciplined advocate of his government's position, though flexible enough to be accommodating, or to advise his government to be accommodating, when the occasion demands. He should inspire trust yet be able to bluff, dissemble, or use a threat effectively when necessary. He should have the confidence of his superiors and be involved in the policy process sufficiently to be authoritative during negotiations. And he should be patient enough to persevere and to maintain his will to win when the cause seems lost, as time and effort can change an opponent's views and objectives. Despite conventional wisdom, negotiations can be effectively conducted from a position of weakness.[5]

Dr. Iklé illustrates these three categories with examples drawn largely from the national negotiating experiences of the USSR and the United States. Consequently, the normative negotiating standards he recommends may not be valid universally. His descriptive typology, however, does provide a useful framework for cataloging the array of individual negotiating styles and techniques demonstrated by China's negotiators, and it facilitates the identification of role variations during the course of a single negotiation.

American Views of the Chinese Negotiator

In the past, American negotiators have frequently perceived the role of the representatives of the PRC in negotiations with the United States to be that of a messenger. Initially in 1951, however, Admiral Joy was impressed that the Chinese and North Korean representatives were negotiators who were prepared to get to the point without delay.

They appeared "willing and anxious to get down to business as if they wanted to show results or determine our position as quickly as possible." [6] His enthusiasm quickly evaporated with the lack of progress in the talks. The importance of the senior Communist representatives faded, and the role of the junior Chinese negotiator, Xie Fang, became dominant. Joy eventually concluded that all authority to make decisions was being exercised by the Chinese outside the conference tent, a development which he blamed in part for the erosion of his own influence on policy on the US side. Long before his 10 months were over, Joy was frustrated, convinced that his opponents, unlike his side, did not bargain in "good faith." Instead they "cavilled over procedural details, manufactured spurious issues, denied the existence of agreements made, made false charges, and indulged in abuse and invective." Furthermore, he believed they failed to exercise constraint, to offer constructive suggestions, or to demonstrate a willingness to be conciliatory and to compromise. Like the Soviet prototype, it seemed the Chinese negotiators were not critical elements in the negotiations after all. They were dogmatic Marxist-Leninist, disciplined to be mere obedient messengers for the leadership in Beijing.[7]

Kenneth Young drew a similar conclusion from his study of the Ambassadorial Talks in Geneva and Warsaw, 1953–1967. He felt that "the Chinese negotiator himself has little leeway in his actions or relationships. He is rigidly patterned by top authorities in Peking with just enough delegated authority to make limited decisions on technical points but none on major matters." Young contrasted the Chinese negotiator's role as a messenger with Washington's attachment of "considerable importance to the role of its diplomatic representatives." The US negotiator is delegated greater "initiative and discretion," involved more fully in the policy process, is nonpolitical in his diplomatic dealing, and more closely associated with his policymaker both organizationally and personally.[8]

From his study of the record of the Ambassadorial Talks conducted in the years just before and after the Cultural Revolution (1966–1967), Henry Kissinger drew the conclusion that the Chinese negotiators in Warsaw were mere messengers, but unlike Young believed the US representatives at Warsaw to be messengers and not negotiators. He noted that the "American ambassadors to Warsaw were generally not selected for their expertise in Chinese affairs. For each meeting, therefore, a middle level official had to be flown in with the text of a statement" to be read by the Ambassador, who then had no discretion beyond a "few clarifying questions." Kissinger concluded that the Chinese response was "produced by analogous procedures."[9]

Not all US participants at Geneva viewed the Chinese as simply messengers. Ambassador U. Alexis Johnson respected Ambassador Wang Bingnan, his counterpart (1957–1959), as an effective negotiator.[10]And it is clear from the official record that Ambassador Johnson was effective.

In the early 1970s American views began to change. During his July 1971 visit to Beijing, Dr. Kissinger found his Chinese counterparts to be exceptionally effective negotiators. They were so effective that he says he later emulated their style.[11] Those who have followed—Presidents Nixon, Ford, Carter, Reagan, and Bush and their respective senior officials—have likewise been impressed. The Chinese have been such successful negotiators since 1971 that some Americans have begun to wonder about the effectiveness of US negotiators.[12]

When the nature of Sino-American negotiations was hostile and agreement difficult, if not impossible, China's representatives were evaluated by Americans as messengers. When agreements are reached more expeditiously, suddenly the Chinese are effective negotiators. Is there that much difference between China's representatives of the 1950s and 1970s, two periods of similar policy orientation in China but periods separated by the Cultural Revolution decade?

The Chinese Negotiator

At first glance there is very little in the available biographical data of the Chinese participants in Sino-American negotiations to suggest that there is such a thing as a typical Chinese negotiator. The differences in their backgrounds, coupled with perceptions of an equal dissimilarity in temperament and personal negotiating techniques, led most of the Chinese interviewed to doubt that there is much in common between the Chinese negotiators who were directly involved in negotiations with the United States between the 10 July 1951 opening of the Korean Armistice Talks and the normalization of relations in 1979. However, when the traditional Chinese emphasis on personal associations and education is considered along with the Party's emphasis on experience, discipline, and proven loyalty, some patterns begin to emerge.

The number of Chinese who have negotiated with the United States is relatively small. At the armistice talks in Korea, there were two PLA general officer positions on the four-man North Korean-Chinese People's Volunteers (CPV) negotiation team. Only five officers held one of these two positions prior to the signing of the armistice on 27 July 1953. The senior members were Deng Hua, Bian Zhangwu, and Ding Guoyu. Junior members were Xie Fang and Chai Chengwen.

At the follow-on political talks in 1953, the PRC was represented by Huang Hua, who would later play an important role in the development of Sino-American relations while Ambassador to Canada and the United Nations and as foreign minister. In 1955, Ambassador Wang Bingnan opened the Ambassadorial Talks in Geneva and was followed first by Wang Guoquan in 1964 and then by Lei Yang. When the focus of negotiations moved to Beijing, the negotiators included Zhou Enlai, Huang Hua, and Qiao Guanhua. The following brief historical sketches of these men indicate some of their common and dissimilar experiences and characteristics.[13]

Deng Hua (10 July-October 1951): The first senior Chinese delegate a Panmunjom, "General" Deng Hua was a rising political-military figure in 1951 and a Long March veteran with many years of experience as a combat commander and a political commissar. He had been closely associated with Peng Dehuai, the commander of the Chinese People's Volunteers (CPV) in Korea, since at least 1928 and with Lin Biao since the early 1940s. Peng apparently was the more dominant influence in Deng's political career, for when Peng Dehuai was purged in 1959, Deng was transferred from his senior military post as commander of the Shenyang Military Region to the lesser post of vice-governor of Sichuan province.

Deng's assignment to the Armistice Talks was short, largely restricted to delivering short opening statements, and ended with his reassignment in October to be Peng's deputy commander of the CPV. Some Chinese observers say that he lacked the patience demanded by Zhou to deal with the Americans, an evaluation similar to that made by some Americans about Admiral Joy. An additional consideration might have been his close association with Peng, who had his own views on how to run the war. According to those interviewed, the Chinese armistice team received instructions directly from Beijing without any filtering or reinterpretation from Peng's headquarters. This procedure largely limited Peng's direct influence on the proceedings to that of his personal relationship with Deng Hua. Deng's promotion eliminated even this channel.

In assigning (General) Deng Hua to Panmunjon, Foreign Minister Zhou Enlai and the central leadership sent an officer of appropriate military rank and political importance to match that of his counterpart, Admiral Turner Joy, in expectation that they would expeditiously complete the military armistice, the framework of which China's leaders believed had been publically determined. When it became apparent that no agreement could be reached quickly, less senior military officers and foreign ministry officials were called upon to conduct the tedious task of exploiting the full range of negotiating tactics and techniques available to China. After Deng's departure in 1951 as the chief negotiator, none of the PORC's representatives who followed for the next 30 years would be of equal or higher political position, until Dr. Kissinger negotiated with Zhou Enlai in 1971.

Bian Zhangwu and Ding Guoyu: While Deng's contribution to the actual negotiations was largely ceremonial, the presence of his successors, Bian and Ding, was hardly noted at all by the UN delegation. They had neither the political or military prestige of Deng Hua for ceremonial purposes nor did they take a publically significant part in the negotiations.

Upon graduation from the Baoding Military Academy in 1923, Bian Zhangwu joined warlord General Feng Yuxiang as a battalion commander and then switched to General Sun Lianzhong's 28th Route Army until he joined the People's Liberation Army in 1931. There he was a combat commander, a political instructor, a guerrilla tactics instructor under Ye Jianying (the godfather in the late 1970s of Sino-American relations), and a rear corps commander prior to joining the Foreign Ministry in 1950. His first overseas assignment came in August 1950 when he was posted as a minister in the PRC embassy in Hungary. Just prior to being assigned to Panmunjom, he again put on his uniform to become the PRC's military attaché (1951) in Moscow. From there he reported to the Ministry of Defense through its Foreign Affairs Bureau, the military counterpart of the Foreign Ministry. A competent and loyal officer, he was certainly qualified to supervise, as the senior Chinese delegate, the bargaining process at Panmunjom, where apparently his full attention was given to carrying out his instructions from Beijing.

Ding Guoyu also had roots in the Foreign Ministry. After Panmunjom he remained with the Armistice Commission until assigned as the ambassador to Afghanistan in 1955 and then to Pakistan in 1959, where he negotiated the PRC-Pakistan border agreement. Following the Cultural Revolution he returned from Sichuan Province to be the ambassador to the Netherlands and then to Sweden. Although obviously considered a successful negotiator, like his predecessors, Ding does not appear to have contributed very much overtly to the Panmunjom negotiations other than the signing of the armistice agreement.

Xie Fang: Like Deng Hua, Xie Fang was an experienced combat commander and political commissar. In addition he had managed to acquire a foreign education, first at a Japanese infantry school in 1922 and then at the Sun Yat-sen University in Moscow in the early 1940s. As a result his military career reflected greater emphasis on the utilization of his educational experiences and powers of persuasion as an educator and a propagandist. Unlike Deng, Xie was not a rising political figure. What influence he might have derived from his association with Lin Biao in Northeast China during the mid 1940s did not prevent him from being accused of being a follower of He Long and purged during the Cultural Revolution.

Xie probably became known to Zhou Enlai about the time of his involvement in the December 1936 Xian Incident in which Chiang Kai-shek was kidnapped by two of his generals, Yang Hucheng, the Nationalist commander of the 17th Route Army (Northwest), and Zhang Xueliang, Commander of the Northeastern Army. They kidnapped Chiang in an effort to persuade him to strengthen his fight against the Japanese by accepting the assistance of the Communist forces. Xie was both a party member and a protege of the "Young Marshall" Zhang Xueliang, an important non-Communist political figure with whom Zhou worked closely at Xan. However, Xie was probably not well known to Zhou until he returned from school in Moscow around 1943 and began to work in the Central Party School in Yenan.

After returning to Beijing from Korea in 1952, Xie spent the majority of the 15 years prior to the Cultural Revolution in successive military training and education assignments as a close associate of General Xiao Ke. Following his rehabilitation after the Cultural Revolution, he returned to military education as the Deputy Director of the PLA's Logistics Academy in Wuhan until his death in 1984.

Admiral Joy considered Xie to be "the defacto chief of the entire Communist group of negotiators. He possessed a bitterly sharp mind and used it effectively. (He) rarely spoke from prepared material, as Nam Il (the North Korean representative) did invariably. His remarks were extemporaneous and fluent. (He) was markedly the mental superior among the Communist delegation. He conducted himself in a self- assured manner at all times. . . . He was the only member of the Communist delegation who seemed to be confident of his position with his Communist superiors in Peking."[14]

Chai Chengwen: Originally assigned to the armistice talks as the senior Chinese liaison officer, Chai eventually succeeded Xie Fang in 1952. Like most of the Chinese staff, Chai probably was assigned to the talks from either the Foreign Ministry or the PLA's Foreign Affairs Bureau. He was well qualified to be the senior liaison officer, being fluent in English and well versed in both diplomatic and military affairs. Albeit junior, his assignment to the talks as a PLA colonel assured equality with his US counterparts, who were all colonels.

Chai gained the begrudged respect of both the Americans at Panmunjom and of his superiors. The latter was evidenced by his selection to succeed Xie Fang in 1952 and

Courtesy Xinhua News Agency, Beijing

Chai Chenwen (left) and Ding Guoyu at Kaesong, 1951.

his subsequent appointment in 1955 as Minister Extraordinary and Plenipotentiary to Denmark. After his assignment to Denmark, Chai returned to duty in the Ministry of Defense where he was involved in intelligence work, negotiations with the Soviets following the 1969 border clash, and, from 1970-1982, the supervision of foreign contact by the PLA's military attachés and of contact by foreign attachés in Beijing with the PLA.

Huang Hua: The Korean Armistice called for a political conference to resolve the political issues not addressed by the military delegations. In October 1953 the United States, representing the United Nations, sent a representative to Panmunjom to meet with the Chinese to negotiate arrangements for a political conference. There on 26 October Arthur Dean, an experienced US negotiator, dealt with the Chinese for the first time. Conversely, the Chinese representative Huang Hua, while heading his first delegation to Sino-American talks, was very experienced in dealing with America's representatives.

As a student in Beijing at the Harvard associated Yanjing University, Huang Hua met a number of Americans, including the University's president, Dr. Leighton Stuart, later the US Ambassador to China from 1946 to 1949. In 1936 Huang followed Edgar Snow to Yan'an as his interpreter; by 1944 he was secretary to Zhu De, Commander of the Eighth Route Army and liaison to the US military "Dixie" mission to Yan'an. Later Huang worked for Zhou Enlai during the closing days of World War II in Chongqing, the wartime capital of the Nationalist government and headquarters for the US diplomatic and military presence in China. In 1946–1947 he served in the Peking Executive Headquarters as General Ye Jianying's secretary-interpreter and head of the Chinese Communist's press section. The headquarters had been established and staffed jointly by the Nationalists, the Communists, and the US to monitor the 1946 cease-fire agreement between the two Chinese parties following the mediation efforts of General George C. Marshall.

After a hiatus following the breakdown of the cease-fire, Huang's contact with Westerners continued first as Director of the Alien Affairs Office in Tianjin (March 1949), then Nanjing (May 1949) and Shanghai (1950). Nanjing in particular provided important Western contacts, including Huang Hua's often reported visit with Ambassador Stuart. Many foreign governments, including the United States, chose to have their ambassadors remain in Nanjing when the Nationalist government retreated, in order to position themselves for the eventual recognition of the People's Republic of China. Huang's office was their point of contact.

After Panmunjom, Huang's next exposure to the United States was while spokesman for the Chinese delegation headed by Zhou Enlai to the 1954 Geneva Conferences on Korea and Indochina. In 1958 he attended the Ambassadorial Talks in Warsaw as an advisor to Ambassador Wang Bingnan and in 1971 he negotiated with Kissinger during the latter's visit to Beijing. Shortly afterward Huang was posted first as China's ambassador to Canada for 4 months and then reassigned as China's permanent representative to the United Nations following China's admission in 1971. Later, as foreign minister, Huang and US Ambassador Leonard Woodcock negotiated the documents associated with the normalization of relations between the PRC and the US.

Huang Hua's arrogance and abusive language at Panmunjom have been credited with driving Ambassador Dean away from the negotiation table. However, Chinese who know him say that such conduct is not his nature. He is regarded as friendly, affable, and a devoted family man. Consequently some felt that his abusive behavior was directed from Beijing. Speeches at the Armistice Talks and later at the Ambassadorial Talks in Geneva are said to have been prepared in Beijing, with the style of delivery left to the negotiators. This process suggests that Huang Hua's abusive language probably was not directed by Beijing. Thus, if spontaneous expressions of anger do not reflect his personality, they probably were a deliberate expression of his anger toward China's enemy, the United States. Several of those interviewed felt that such behavior is common in China, particularly South China, where feelings toward an enemy often are released through loud, angry voices and abusive language as a surrogate for violence, unlike the West, where such language is more often a prelude to violence.

Huang Hua's arrogance was noted by several of those interviewed. One source remembered him from the days of the Peking Executive Headquarters in 1946 as usually pleasant but aggravatingly arrogant when involved in actual negotiations with the CCP's opponents. As the interpreter for General Ye Jianying, he often went beyond just interpreting for the general to lecturing the United States and KMT representatives and punctuating his remarks by wagging his finger at them. Thirty years later the arrogance of his finger-wagging lectures is said to have upset President Reagan during Huang Hua's 1983 visit to the White House.[15] As several Chinese interviewed commented, Huang Hua's resort to personalized, verbal abuse as a way to express his lack of respect for an opponent is a common response in Chinese society. Chinese expectation of interpersonal relations, whether between friends or opponents, tends to be more ritualistic in form than in the West. Thus Huang's arrogance merely exaggerated a rather common way of expressing a lack of respect.

Another explanation might be that offered by Wu Xiuquan, who has recorded that the anger with which he delivered his speech at the UN on 28 November 1950 was unplanned, unlike the speech itself, which had been approved in Beijing by Mao before Wu departed for the United States.[16] Wu's explanation of his anger is that "I did not mean to behave in an affected manner, but only felt that what I faced were the world's number one imperialists and their confederates. They were so wicked and detestable that naturally we would not be courteous in dealing with them."[17]

Others interviewed excused the excesses of Huang's public rhetoric as a means to compensate for the pro-American positions he often took within Chinese leadership circles, particularly after 1972. A complex political figure, Huang's actions probably can be explained in part by all of the foregoing observations.

After the failure of the political tasks at Panmunjom, it was not until a side meeting at the 1954 Geneva Conference on Korea between Wang Bingnan, Secretary General of the PRC delegation, and U. Alexis Johnson, Coordinator of the

US delegation, that direct contact was resumed. This meeting began the process that eventually led to the Ambassadorial Talks that Ambassadors Wang and Johnson began a little over a year later in Geneva.

Wang Bingnan: Ambassador Wang was the PRC's first Ambassador to Poland. In addition he was assigned the responsibility of being China's representative to the Sino-American Ambassadorial Talks that opened in August 1955. A hand-picked member of Zhou Enlai's foreign affairs elite, he was assigned to Poland from his post as Director of the Staff Office of the Ministry of Foreign Affairs. He was both experienced in dealing with Americans and a very knowledgeable foreign affairs specialist, particularly with regard to Europe. He was first introduced to the benefits of a foreign education at the Luoyang Military Academy. Following graduation he pursued first a year of study in Tokyo and then four years at the University of Berlin where he studied sociology. His close association with Zhou Enlai began during the Xi'an Incident, which occurred shortly after his return from Europe via Moscow. Wang played a key role in the incident both as a Party political organizer and propagandist and as an advisor to both General Yang of the Nationalist's 17th Route Army and Zhou Enlai. His competence in performing these many duties quickly lead to Zhou's increasing reliance upon Wang's organizational skills. By 1942 Wang was secretary and spokesman for Zhou Enlai in the Nationalist's wartime capital of Chongqing. Close at Zhou's side throughout the war years and the Marshall Mission, Wang not only became acquainted with many Americans but he also acquired some knowledge of English in addition to his knowledge of Japanese and fluency in German. He acquired a sense of the American approach to solving problems, and his experience with negotiations during the Marshall mission helped to prepare him for the negotiations in Geneva with Ambassador Johnson.[18]

Wang Guoquan: In July 1964 Wang Guoquan succeeded Wang Bingnan as the PRC ambassador to Warsaw and as the PRC representative to the Sino-American Ambassadorial Talks. A former PLA political commissar and political organizer in Northeast China, Wang had been an important party and government official in Jehol province. He was governor of the province until an administrative reorganization in December 1955 resulted in Jehol

Courtesy Xinhua News Agency, Beijing

Chinese representative Wang Guoquan reads a statement at the 131st meeting at the ambassadorial level between China and the United States, 7 September 1966, Warsaw.

being absorbed into three neighboring provinces. In June 1957 Wang was named Ambassador to East Germany where he remained until early 1964, when he was named to succeed Wang Bingnan. Although not as close to Zhou or as influential in the ministry as Wang Bingnan, he was a loyal party member, an effective propagandist and administrator, and an apparently successful ambassador. His new assignment came at the height of the Vietnam War, when the talks were seen as a potential relief valve for tension in Sino-American relations. It was not a negotiations assignment but rather that of a listening post or mailbox, where powers of observation and loyalty were important.[19] Recalled to Beijing during the Cultural Revolution, Wang reemerged in 1970 to work on the development of relations with Japan followed by an ambassadorship in Australia in 1973. In 1979 he returned to Beijing to be vice minister in another ministry until his probable retirement in 1982.

Lei Yang: When the PRC withdrew its ambassadors during the Cultural Revolution, a chargé d'affaires assumed the ambassador's responsibilities in most embassies. Lei Yang was chargé d'affaires in Warsaw in December 1969 when US Ambassador Walter Stoessel approached him at a fashion show at the Yugoslav Embassy. Lei attempted to avoid him by hastily retreating down the back stairs. Years later Zhou told Henry Kissinger that his chargé had nearly had a heart attack when Stoessel chased him because he had no instructions as to how to deal with such an event.[20] As essentially a messenger, Lei Yang later received Ambassador Stoessel and reestablished the Warsaw communication link.

Qiao Guanhua: According to Dr. Kissinger, "this impressive man was a lesser copy of Chou's charm, erudition and intelligence."[21] Qiao was a long-time close associate of Zhou Enlai. At the time he conducted the negotiations during President Nixon's visit to China with Kissinger over the final version of the "Shanghai Communique," Qiao probably reflected Zhou's negotiating style better than any other of Zhou's close associates in the Foreign Ministry.

After graduating at 19 from Beijing's Qinghua University in 1933, Qiao first visited Japan and France and then entered the University of Tubingen in Germany, from which he graduated with a doctorate of philosophy in 1936. Returning to China following the outbreak of war with Japan in 1937, he worked as a propagandist for the KMT in Wuhan until he joined Liao Chengchi in Hong Kong in 1938 as a journalist and propagandist for the CCP. With the fall of Hong Kong to Japan, Qiao made his way to Chongqing where he worked as a secretary to Zhou during the CCP-KMT negotiations and as a member of the Party's propaganda department. Qiao continued to work with Zhou through the Marshall Mission (1945-46) until assigned to Nanjing and Shanghai—centers of Western activity. Following the breakdown in KMT-CCP cooperation, Qiao again represented his party to the West in Hong Kong until he joined Zhou in Beijing in 1949. A member of the Foreign Ministry from its inception, Qiao was closely linked to Zhou's foreign policy.

From his initial assignment in 1949 as vice-chairman of the Ministry's Foreign Policy Committee, chaired by Zhou, and later as Director of the Asian Affairs Department (1950), he was closely associated with the Korean War and subsequent negotiations. Later, following his advancement to Assistant Minister in October 1954 and Vice Minister in April 1964, he was the key policy manager of the Warsaw Talks.

Zhou's confidence in Qiao's diplomatic skills, especially as a negotiator, and his linguistic skills (English, German, Japanese, Russian, and French) was amply demonstrated by the frequency of Qiao's overseas trips. He accompanied Wu Xiuquan to the United Nations in November 1950 to present the PRC's charges against the United States for its activities in Korea. He accompanied Zhou to the 1954 Geneva Conference, including a side trip to India and Burma and the trip home via East Europe and the USSR. He went with Zhou to the Bandung Conference in April 1955 and assisted him in the negotiation (April-May 1960) of border disputes with Burma, India, Nepal, Cambodia, and North Vietnam. He was a part of the team that participated in the Geneva Conference on Laos, May 1961-62, and then from December 1963 to February 1964 he toured 10 nations of Africa with Zhou and Chen-I. Qiao was a key player in these and many other visits and negotiations that Zhou initiated prior to the xenophobic years of the Cultural Revolution.

Following Zhou's recovery of the initiative in foreign affairs from the confrontational policies of Lin Biao, Qiao reopened the border negotiations with the Soviet Union on 20 October 1969, at the Deputy Foreign Minister level. In late 1971 Qiao represented the PRC at the United Nations as China's first delegate. Later during President Nixon's visit to China, he negotiated the final wording of the Shanghai Communique with Kissinger.

As pointed out by several interviewees, Qiao was more intimately involved in the history of Sino-American relations than anyone short of Zhou Enlai. Unfortunately he died at the early age of 69, a few months prior to a scheduled interview.

Collectively, the role of each of these representatives in the grand negotiation strategy of the central leadership varied, for the most part, between that of messenger and negotiator. According to some of the Chinese interviewed, a few of these men may have even taken on the role of a mediator, at least on selected occasions. However, to the extent that any of them assumed the role of a mediator, it was accomplished between themselves and the central leadership in such a manner as to never be apparent and exploitable by the Americans. Each of these men was a party member experienced in the art of persuasion. The farther the responsibilities of one of these representatives were from those of a messenger and the nearer to those of a negotiator or mediator, the more likely he was to be from Zhou's inner circle of lieutenants, to have a Western education, including fluency in one or more foreign languages, and to be experienced in dealing across the cultural chasms that complicated China's relations with the West. Behind each representative was the master strategist Zhou Enlai, who provided each with a degree of autonomy commensurate to the situation, his ability, experience, and closeness to Zhou. The following section discusses more fully the model against which these men were measured as negotiators.

The Ideal Chinese Negotiator

To the Chinese officials interviewed, the ideal negotiator would be another Zhou Enlai. When asked to list the characteristics of an ideal negotiator or to name the negotiator they most admired for his skill, the first response to either question was "Zhou Enlai." Everyone interviewed expressed respect for Zhou; a respect that in many cases could only be described as reverence or deep feeling of honor and respect mixed with love and awe. From these interviews and biographical information pertaining to Zhou Enlai and his principal negotiators for the three periods analyzed, the following list of ideal characteristics is drawn.

Disciplined advocate. Each of the negotiators mentioned was a seasoned party member, and most had suffered from the occasional breakdown in party loyalty and discipline that occurred during the Party's rise to power, especially during the civil war prior to 1949. Each knew firsthand that even small breaches in unity and discipline can lead to disaster. Each had close friends and family members who had suffered severely from breaches in discipline that ranged from the traitorous act of defection to the accidental or careless failure to faithfully execute Central Committee directives. Even seemingly minor deviations could be fatal. As a result, these men have been advocates of the Party's efforts "to persevere in its struggle to defeat the strong enemy" through a system of "Iron Discipline."[22] As the name implies, the standards are strict and require that once a decision is made, no exceptions can be made to the unity of effort and to obedience. "The individual is subordiate to the organization . . . the lower level is subordinate to the higher level, and the entire membership is subordinate to the Central Committee."[23]

The "Iron Discipline" that emerged from the Party's long years of struggle to power against extreme odds generated within the Party an outwardly focused unity, a state of mind similar to the "David and Goliath" wartime mentality of the modern state of Israel. The assumption of power in 1949 by the Communist Party in the world's most populous nation brought little relief as the Party turned its efforts to consolidating its position, to nation building, and to its quest to rectify "China's 100 years of humiliation" by the West. The repeated challenges by one or the other of the superpower "Goliaths" further reinforced the continued need for its externally oriented unity of "Iron Discipline" in order to exploit its limited strength to the fullest.

Strict discipline for China's diplomats was not an invention of the Communist Party. However, disciplined participation in the policy process by China's negotiators was essentially a Party innovation. Whereas compliance with Party decisions must be unconditional, the rights and opinions of all members are, at least, theoretically protected. "Before a resolution is passed, there is freedom to hold debates on the matter involved; after a resolution is passed there is the freedom to reserve one's differing opinions (but one has to comply with that resolution in action) [and] the right to appeal to the higher level, up to and including the Party Central Committee. Discipline and freedom from a unity of opposites."[24]

Party discipline means that any disagreement that the Chinese negotiator may have with his government's position is unlikely to result in his undertaking the semi-independent position of a mediator during the negotiation sessions. Most importantly, the Chinese negotiator is highly disciplined to achieve his government's objectives. However, he may, if persuaded, argue the case of his US opponent to his superiors rather than merely relaying it. Such interventions were difficult, a difficulty worsened by the difficulty of secure communications between Europe and Beijing according to those interviewed. On the other hand, it is unlikely that a Chinese negotiator's opponent would be aware of this action until either after the conclusion of the negotiations or at some future point during the negotiations where his support for his US opponent's position can be used to an advantage. Brzezinski has noted that "Ambassador Chai Zemin [was] an extremely skillful, persistent, and effective negotiator. [As the Chinese later revealed to Brzezinski] he not only faithfully reported my views to China but was quite prepared to urge accommodation and adjustment on some issues."[25]

Within the Chinese negotiation team there is room for the discussion of tactics and techniques. However, once the Chinese team engages its opponents, there will be virtually no evidence of any differences among the members of the team. Breaches in team solidarity are virtually unknown in negotiations with the United States. Where exceptions have been noted, they are likely to have been the result of a tactical maneuver. For example, during a meeting in the United States in the 1980s, a senior Chinese negotiator agreed with a US proposal, at least in principle. Subsequently a junior member of his delegation confided to his US counterpart that the PRC probably would not be able to implement the proposal. The result was the introduction of caution or fewer expectations of the agreement by the United States, leaving the Chinese with the initiative. In effect the two sides had agreed on a principle important to the United States but a concession was made to the PRC to delay full implementation because of an inability (e.g., for financial or domestic political reasons) or reluctance (e.g., for prestige, reciprocity, timing) of the Chinese based on the "realities of the moment."[26]

Confidence of superiors, or Guanxi. Each of the PRC's principle negotiators mentioned here has enjoyed the confidence of his superiors, especially that of Zhou Enlai, the principal architect of all of China's negotiations with the United States until his death in 1976. Having apprenticed under Zhou and, in most cases, worked closely with him just prior to assuming responsibility for a particular negotiation, each was a known entity to Zhou and selected or approved by him for the task. Reciprocally, each had a personal sense of obligation to Zhou and a keen awareness of the limits of his authority in implementing instructions from the Foreign Minister, later Premier. Contrary to the assertions of some Western observers, the Chinese interviewed argued that each negotiator exercised considerable latitude in deciding which tactics to employ in a given negotiating session.

Wu Xiuquan wrote that he was free to determine his manner of presentation at the United Nations and his response to subsequent developments.[27] Interviews with participants in the various Sino-American negotiations indicate that these Chinese negotiators were similarly free. Opening statements, particularly those involving changes in position, were usually directed from Beijing, but the tasks of communicating the meaning and the tactics of presentation were left to the negotiator and his staff—a process not too dissimilar from that used by the United States at Geneva.[28]

This operational procedure had been developed by Zhou by the time he conducted the talks at Xi'an in 1936. As events unfolded there, Zhou carefully kept the other leaders of the Party's Central Committee informed of developments and proffered his recommendations. In turn he received his instructions. Those talks depended upon a high degree of confidence and trust between the Party's leaders and Zhou. Communications were minimal, resources were scarce, and the potential danger for the individuals involved as well as for the Party was great. The leadership depended upon Zhou's accuracy in reporting, the quality of his evaluation of the opposition, his tactical judgment, and his faithfulness and resourcefulness in executing his instructions. In turn, Zhou had to be able to execute orders with which he may not have completely agreed, especially difficult in a crisis environment like that at Xi'an.[29] The major communication difficulties of that period meant that the process by which a negotiator was selected was very important to the Party's leaders. This problem with distance also has been present in nearly all Sino-American negotiations. As one interviewer noted, with the exception of the normalization process, which was essentially negotiated in Beijing, the long distances from Beijing to the Sino-American conference tables have made it very difficult for Beijing to maintain effective communications with its negotiators in comparison with the vastly superior capability of Washington—a capability Americans have not hesitated to point out. Zhou's confidence in the judgment and skills of his negotiators was a key ingredient.

Psychological initiative. Zhou Enlai has received accolades from friends and enemies alike for his effectiveness as a negotiator. The plaudits are most often for his statesmanlike view of the world and the persuasiveness of his argument. However, even more important was his ability to create the appropriate atmosphere or mood at any given point in the negotiations. He could inspire trust or anxiety, optimism or pessimism, the obligation of friendship or the hostility of an enemy by his own change of moods, by his tactics, the manipulation of the physical environment, and the use of language.

Henry Kissinger's account of his 1971 visit to Beijing is replete with references to his own mood shifts in response to the initiatives of his hosts. First, he was impressed and felt indebted to the Chinese for sending an escort 2,500 miles to accompany him from Pakistan. He then was placed psychologically on the defensive by his hosts when asked if his insistency on secrecy was because he was ashamed to acknowledge meeting Chinese leaders, as John Foster Dulles was at the 1954 Geneva Conference on Indochina. In Beijing, Kissinger responded positively to the elegant spaciousness of his guest quarters and "Marshall Yeh Chien-ying's [efforts] to make us feel at home and share tea with us." He says Zhou "set the tone within the first half hour of our encounter." He was unprepared for Zhou's frankness, and later he felt at "some disadvantage" when Zhou genially began to discuss and to agree with some of the concepts in a Nixon speech of which Kissinger "was unaware of either the fact or the content." At one point Zhou made a forceful presentation of the Chinese point of view. Kissinger responded in kind only to have Zhou stop him "after the first point, saying the duck would get cold if we did not eat first. At lunch . . . the mood changed and Chou's geniality returned." And so the Chinese orchestration of moods, whether conscious or instinctive, continued throughout Kissinger's visit.[30]

While China's negotiators have not always been as skilled or as sensitive to their opponent's moods as Zhou was, the wide range of assignments and experiences each has had in influencing the opinions and moods of others has prepared him for the task. In addition such key negotiators as Wang Bingnan, Huang Hua, and Qiao Guanhua apprenticed directly under Zhou and thus had observed closely "the master" during numerous multilateral and bilateral negotiations. They had honed their skills under his tutelage for many years, and judging from the remarks of the Chinese diplomats interviewed, they have in turn passed these skills on to their proteges, China's current negotiators, through similar apprenticeship-like relationships.

The collective knowledge within the Foreign Ministry concerning the West is impressive. Even through the external and self-imposed isolation of the 1950s and 1960s, according to both active and retired members of the Foreign Ministry, a determined effort was made to keep abreast of Western thinking. There was always the awareness that understanding the psychology of the West was a continuous learning process that required the efforts of at least a small group of specialists. Even so, plans did not always turn out exactly as expected. Wang Bingnan recalled with a chuckle his preparations as secretary general of the Chinese delegation for the Geneva Conference of 1954. "It was my opinion that the dress of the members of the Chinese delegation should be solemn and grave, so I selected some sort of black material, and had Chinese tunic suits made out of it for every member of the delegation. Later, when we appeared in those suits in the streets of Geneva, we found that passersby would stop, take off their hats, and salute us respectfully. We found out later that only priests wear black suits in Switzerland, so many people had mistaken us for missionaries."[31] Although a humorous anecdote in which the desired effect of "solemn and grave" was slightly over achieved, it also is suggestive of the detail with which the Chinese planned the psychological component of their approach to the negotiations.

Master of the record. It is often said that a cultural characteristic of the Chinese is their patience in dealing with others. Several of those interviewed, who had extensive foreign service, did not agree with this view and expressed their wonderment at frequent Western descriptions of the Chinese as a patient people. They felt that the Chinese are no more patient than any other people.[32] As an example, it was pointed out that, contrary to the Western sterotype, Zhou Enlai often expressed his impatience, through angry outbursts. Whereas he was careful and too polite by convention to allow himself to express his impatience publicly, his staff was well aware of the limits of his patience, particularly as one well informed individual remarked—when he was upset by an adverse policy decision in the United States. Consequently, those interviewed felt that what is misconstrued in the West as a sort of natural individual patience on the part of China's negotiators is really the product of the aforediscussed requirement for party discipline, the still strong social convention "to eat bitterness" or avoid the public expression of one's frustrations, and the longer term view of contemporary events that comes from mastery of the historical record. This combination of factors generates public action or inaction among China's foreign police negotiators and decisionmakers comparable to what one might expect from someone who is genuinely patient.

Mastery or a detailed knowledge by each of the PRC's negotiators of the PRC-US negotiating record is due in part to the extensive association with the subject of Sino-American relations each of the negotiators has brought to the table. Each of the negotiators from the Foreign Ministry began his association with China's US policy early in his career, with the experiences of the more senior members dating back to the Party's wartime interactions with the Americans at Chongqing. Each of the key negotiators was supported by a staff whose accumulated experience covered the spectrum of Sino-American relations in detail. And of course the staff of the Ministry responsibly placed the written record of previous PRC-US negotiations at the finger tips of China's negotiators.

Such mastery produces a persistence that often leaves Americans with the impression that they have entered into the dialogue somewhere in the middle and left before the conclusion. Admiral Joy's description of "dogma followed slavishly" and Kenneth Young's classification of the Chinese negotiator as mere messengers are interpretations, under negative or hostile circumstances, of the same phenomenon to which Kissinger, under more positive circumstances, reacted when he described his experiences:

> as if we were engaged in one endless conversation with an organism that recalled everything, seemingly motivated by a single intelligence. This gavc the encounters both an exhilarating and occasionally a slightly ominous quality. It engendered a combination of awe and sense of impotence at so much discipline and dedication.[33]

As masters of the record, Chinese negotiators are sensitive to the role of any given negotiation within the "endless conversation." Having been witness to the development of the "endless conversation" and increasingly more responsible overtime for the development of the PRC's end of the conversation, they are, as one former Chinese negotiator said, more concerned about the general situation and the achievement of goals through stages than immediate solutions. Each negotiation is a step in the process with goals to be adamantly pursued, but always with an eye to laying the foundation for the next stage. The combination of this long-term perspective, party discipline, and a cultural proclivity for internalizing frustration is tantamount to patience, at least in the eye of the foreign negotiator.

Being master of the record develops a dependency that causes a Chinese negotiator to feel uncomfortable when he lacks access to the record. He would much rather conduct the negotiations in Beijing where he can call upon the resources of the Foreign Ministry to research a point or provide additional details concerning an issue raised or that is likely to be raised. Because of Chinese perceptions of the superiority of the US system of communications, including the use of computers, there is a tendency to believe that apparent ignorance of the record on the part of US negotiators is trickery. When Americans make accusations or statements that can not be supported by the record, it must be calumny. No one, especially people with the technological lead in communications storage and retrieval, could be that ignorant of the record.

Familiarity with the record makes the Chinese sensitive to phraseology. The negotiator chooses every word carefully for effect and to agree with the record. His sensitivity to both reinforces the natural tendency in negotiations to be repetitive. He is also sensitive to changes in his opponent's terminology. For an American to change a phrase carelessly out of boredom will cause his Chinese counterpart anxiety until he can ferret out the purpose of the change. Furthermore, such a change is likely to be the source of considerable time wasted in potentionaly acrimonious exchanges.

Team player. The point was made several times during interviews that in China today, as in traditional China, a child learns early to think in terms of the collective instead of the individual. The Party has merely refocused a traditional value. Consequently, before an individual undertakes a new direction that might impact on others, the individual feels a need to obtain at least a tacit consensus. Collective judgment or consensus thus becomes a key element in decisionmaking. As several of those interviewed noted, this does not mean that Chinese decisionmakers are not willing to be responsible for their actions, although they acknowledged the Cultural Revolution drained the initiative of many. Instead, a decisionmaker would rather overcome opposition to a particular course of action before announcing his decision or taking action, somewhat the opposite of what is often done in the West.

For the chief negotiator this means that he will seek from the other members of his delegation their observations, opinions, and criticism of the negotiation's proceedings, his performance and that of his opponent, and the delegation's own performance. He will solicit their views on future courses of action, in addition to exploring his own with them. When satisfied with his conclusions, within the time available, he can then make his recommendations to his superiors. There a similar process may occur. The Chinese use of conferences, meetings, etc., is not necessarily to obtain a decision, but to provide information and to engage everyone in a consensus-building exercise. A Chinese decisionmaker exercises his authority not by battering down obstacles to the implementation of his decision but by insuring a consensus among his staff before committing himself to the decision. For example, at one point in the Geneva talks between Wang Bingnan and U. Alexis Johnson, Ambassador Wang wanted to accept Johnson's invitation to dinner; Johnson had requested permission from Secretary Dulles to extend the invitation.[34] After reflection Wang cabled the Foreign Ministry, which in turn referred it to Zhou. The initiative to accept the invitation was Zhou's; as such, any adverse consequences, such as unfavorable press coverage, would have reflected upon him. Rather than respond directly, however, Zhou took the request to the politburo—from whence policy emanated—for a decision. By taking the proposal to the Politburo, he co-opted criticism of the act and insured enough flexibility for himself to take full advantage of the opportunity.

Being an effective team player while retaining the initiative and authority of leadership requires a great deal of experience and skill, but the products of this process are negotiating policy and tactics that all members of the team understand and support. It is this kind of laborious process, coupled with discipline, that supports the Chinese negotiator's efforts to create an environment favorable to his initiatives.

The Negotiator's Staff

Interviews and conversations with Chinese diplomats pointed up the fact that the inculcation of the characteristics and skills of a successful negotiator in succeeding generations of diplomats was an important concern of Zhou

Enlai and has remained one for his successors. Even during the early years of the PRC, when the operational needs of the moment greatly overshadowed almost any career need or personal consideration of China's diplomats, training of the next generation, albeit not necessarily systematically accomplished, was still a salient concern of the Foreign Ministry's senior decisionmakers. For example, diplomatic delegations, were generally larger than necessary in order to take advantage of their educational value. Ambassador Wang Bingnan has written that one of the reasons for China's large delegation to international conferences was to "let more comrades go abroad in order to expand their vision and increase their experience."[35] Throughout his memoirs, Wu Xiuquan emphasized the importance of emulating Zhou Enlai's work style and extolled the educational value to himself and others of having worked for the Premier on the various diplomatic delegations Zhou led out of China. Although the Foreign Ministry had little in the way of a structured career development program through which to manage its officers from recruitment to retirement, a major effort was made to provide following generations with an opportunity to observe and emulate the PRC's model diplomats.

As Premier, Zhou was occupied in the early 1950s with the endless tasks of supervising the creation of a government to rebuild and manage war-devastated China. But he was probably best known outside China for another and presumably a lesser responsibility, that of Foreign Minister. The diplomatic reputation he acquired by the mid-1950s was possible largely because of the effort he exerted during the PRC's initial years in recruiting officials and in organizing and leading the Ministry. Although the focus of Zhou's efforts was the recruitment of a diplomatic corps and the building of an organization and staff to deal with the press of emerging foreign policy issues, he was always mindful of the more distant future. He both instinctively and from experience considered in his decisions the effect of precedents and the need to lay the foundation for China's diplomacy of the future. For example, party members with diplomatic experience were few and excess war heroes were many. The Foreign Ministry had to absorb its share. Consequently, a number of ambassadors were chosen who had extensive experience among the senior ranks of the PLA's politician-soldiers. These were officers who were successful propagandists, leaders, and demonstrably loyal and disciplined team players, though largely as yet unproven in foreign diplomacy. Some, like Geng Biao, proved to be effective diplomats, while the ambassadorships of some others can only be described as relatively brief sinecures.[36] However, in staffing the Foreign Ministry, where policy, processes, and organizations were being developed, Zhou significantly concentrated men and women with extensive exposure to foreign education, language, and culture, men who had pre-1949 diplomatic-type service with him in such places as Xi'an, Chongqing, and Beijing during the Marshall Mission. These were the people who would set the standards and practices for the Foreign Ministry that would be carried into the future, where many of them, and their proteges, would be China's country directors, ambassadors, vice-ministers, and foreign ministers. To transfer these standards and practices to the next generation, Zhou intuitively relied upon the ancient cultural norm of model emulation.

Model Emulation. Judging from the perceptions of those interviewed, the Ministry's professional staff was heavily recruited in the early years from among those who had acquired a foreign language capability, either overseas or from foreign operated universities in China, notably in Shanghai and Beijing. For Zhou Enlai and many of his key advisors, themselves returned students, fluency in a foreign language was the key for several reasons.

First, in rebuilding China's foreign service from the ground up, the development of a linguistic capability was a basic requirement if the PRC was to communicate effectviely with other nations. The Chinese have long been aware of the value of providing translators in an exchange with the foreign "barbarians." In China this middle man is more than a translator. He is held responsible for providing advice and assistance to the Chinese official concerning the antecedents to almost any event that might be discussed in the exchange. Often referred to by Westerners as the "barbarian handlers," these specialists are much more than just translators, escorts, or protocol officers. They are key players in the exchange, sometimes influencing the pace and direction of the exchange and inserting actions, remarks, innuendoes on their own authority. Of course, sometimes these additions are made at the behest of their principal, who is always free to endorse, ignore, or refute any of the initiatives of their intermediaries.[37]

Second, linguists have an area specialist's background, especially those who have studied abroad, in which they have developed an insight into how the people of another society think, their value structure, and the influence of their historical experiences. They have a sense of the major differences that might develop between the two societies over a particular issue. In this regard, the Chinese have a very impressive group of "Americanologists"—foreign affairs specialists who have spent all or a significant portion of their careers associated with China's US policy. Many have also had functional or other area assignments that have tended to strengthen and broaden their ability to deal with US and European problems.

Third, fluency in a foreign language signals an exposure to non-traditional ideas and knowledge, the catalytic agents of change needed in the revolution not yet completed in the 1950s. Such new knowledge is a mixed blessing. Even in the 1980s, when China's leaders were pushing the acquisition of foreign knowledge, many of the students interviewed felt apprehensive about their acceptance in China. Although they knew they would be welcome and respected in China for their accomplishments, they also sensed that there would always be an element of suspicion among their countrymen that somehow they were no longer fully Chinese. Somehow they are tainted and not completely trustworthy. To some extent this is intuition, but it is also based on their own observations of the alienation that many of China's foreign-trained officials—particularly those trained in America and Europe—endured during the anti-rightist activities of the "Hundred Flowers" campaign (1956–1957) and again during the Cultural Revolution. Like the humiliation of America's China specialists during the McCarthy era, many of China's American specialists suffered at the hands of their countrymen who questioned their loyalty, largely because of past foreign associations.

The greater a recruit's academic and language capability, maturity, and experience, the greater his potential for immediate utilization by the Ministry. Yet irrespective of his qualifications and entry level, years of experience under the tutelage of more senior and experienced Ministry-Party officials were necessary to instill in these young intellectuals a correct pattern of analysis. A time honored belief in China is that it is the "nature of education (that) people learn through the emulation of models; the best way to inculcate any behavior in them is to introduce a model for them to emulate; and to be a model is the legitimate goal for men to seek" (respect is preferable to material reward).[38]

Zhou himself was the role model for the senior Ministry officials, particularly those who had served pre-1949 under his tutelage, acquiring his style and techniques. These men in turn became role models for succeeding generations of negotiators, perpetuating and spreading Zhou's style throughout the foreign service, a style that, according to those interviewed, remains dominant today.

Cut off diplomatically from the West after 1949, the Ministry's recruits increasingly included fewer "returned students" and more graduates of such domestic language schools as the Beijing Language Institute Number One. In general, such "home grown" language graduates are less prepared to enter the foreign service than the returned students in two ways. First, China's institutes essentially have provided graduates of middle schools (foreign language training generally is not part of middle school education) with 4 years of language training, whereas the returned students had college educations, many with graduate degrees, in disciplines other than language, greater fluency in one or more foreign languages, and practical experience in one or more foreign cultures.

Second, traditional Chinese philosophy advocates that men learn best through the emulation of models. As was repeatedly pointed out during the interviews, China's schools continue to emphasize strongly rote learning of mountains of facts and acceptable patterns of analysis through which all problems can be examined and solved. Some interviewees felt that this traditional approach to learning, particularly as stressed at both the middle school level and in the language institutes, resulted in potential recruits from the institutes being less flexible and ingenuous in their approach to analyzing and solving foreign affairs problems than if they had had a more Westernized education. The Foreign Ministry's entry training course compensated to a small extent in the eyes of a few interviewees, at least until the Cultural Revolution intervened and further reduced the educational experience of new recruits.

After the Cultural Revolution the Foreign Ministry restored and reassigned most of its professionals, but with proportionately fewer resources. The "farmer, worker, soldier, student" accessions of the "lost decade" of the Cultural Revolution were unprepared to assume the rapidly growing responsibilities of the "open door" diplomacy of Deng's administration, and the pre-Cultural Revolution generation were too few to cover fully all of these expanded responsibilities.

Since 1978 there has once again been a strong emphasis, according to those interviewed, on raising the quality of recruits through education. For some, the reopening of the foreign language schools and the reestablishment of the language emphasis of the 1950s is adequate. Others are concerned that the few foreign service professionals are still not exposed to a wide enough spectrum of learning, especially analytic skills, to meet the ever expanding requirements of the PRC's "open door" policy. They advocate that language training be required in middle schools, as well as at the university level, and not be the exclusive focus of study. A knowledge of political science, economics, law, and philosophy is as important to a foreign service official as a language. Yet, even for those that advocate a more western style of education, the emulation of a "virtuous model," such as Zhou Enlai, is still an important component of the education of the whole man.

Translators. The translator in any given Sino-American negotiation appears to be assigned because of his skill with the language, his area expertise relative to the importance of the event, and the rank of the negotiator. Lesser qualified linguists are often thrust forward to both spell the more experienced and to gain experience in the presence of the better qualified linguists. This is particularly true for lengthy negotiations conducted in China and for delegations that travel abroad. The less experienced linguists sit in on the negotiations, take notes, translate the conversations, and transmit both the English and Chinese texts back to the Foreign Ministry. This attention to records has been required of each Chinese delegation that negotiated with the United States. In addition, until the early 1970s, Chinese and English versions of each negotiating session were sent back to the Ministry. The two text submissions were stopped about that time because of a shortage of staff, possibly because of the impact of the Cultural Revolution. These texts were studied very carefully in the Ministry, by Zhou Enlai, and often by Mao, for nuances that might indicate a change in the US position, as well as any misunderstandings by the United States of the PRC's position. This translation work was hard and guaranteed to improve significantly not only the language skills of the junior linguists but also their detailed knowledge of the history of the negotiations and their knowledge of correct negotiating style and skills. The effort exerted far exceeded that expended by the US side in any case examined.

The higher the rank and authority of the negotiator, the more often he used a young person with essentially a native fluency in English as a translator during meetings away from the negotiating table. The honor and prestige of such a responsibility insure a degree of discretion, as well as role modeling, which would be less likely if a more senior but equally able linguist were used. One well-known example is Ji Chaozhu, who frequently translated for Mao and Zhou, including the 1972 Nixon visit when Ji was recalled from banishment to the countryside (a function of the Cultural Revolution) to translate and then return to the countryside. Ji learned English during his youth when he lived for more than 10 years in the United States, including a little more than a year at Harvard. He later developed his skill as a translator at Panmunjom and, except for the period spent in the countryside during the Cultural Revolution, has been essentially an area specialist associated with China's US policy. He served in Washington, DC, in the PRC Liaison Office (1973-1975) and later as a counselor in the PRC Embassy (1982-1985). Even as Ji has advanced in responsibility, he has continued to be called upon to translate for senior officials or to backstop more junior interpreters. He was Deng Xiaoping's interpreter during Deng's visit to the United States.

Less senior officials are not necessarily saddled with less qualified interpreters. In fact, they may be assisted by officials within the Ministry who are also outstanding linguists. For example, when Wu Xiuquan went to the United

Nations in December 1950, his chief interpreter and assistant was Dr. Pu Shan, a Harvard Ph.D. in economics with an excellent command of English. Dr. Pu was later given the rank of colonel and assigned as a liaison officer for the Korean War negotiations at Panmunjom. An extremely capable man, he retired from government service as the Director of the Institute of International Economics of the Chinese Academy of Social Sciences.

Huang Hua's assistant at Panmunjom was Dr. Pu Shouchang (albeit reported by Arthur Dean to be Huang's interpreter, a lesser position).[39] The older brother of Pu Shan, Pu Shouchang also has a Ph.D. in economics from Harvard. A very competent individual, he served as Premier Zhou's personal secretary through the Cultural Revolution and as a Vice Minister of Foreign Affairs under Huang Hua until his retirement. Another example is Qiu Yingjue, who was Wang Bingnan's interpreter at Geneva. He grew up speaking English in Malaysia and like so many, returned to China shortly after the formation of the PRC. He was a translator at Panmunjom; subsequently served in the Ministry under Wang Bingnan for a several years; and, in 1955, became Wang's interpreter at Geneva and later at Warsaw, staying on long after Wang Bingnan returned to the PRC to assume his new assignment as Assistant Foreign Minister.[40]

Each of these men has been associated with Sino-US negotiations throughout a large part of his career in the Foreign Ministry. Their value to their principal as a source of institutional memory has often been as important, if not more so, than their linguistic skill. They served as confidant, adviser, a double check on statements made by the negotiator, and a buffer when the negotiator needed extra time—a knowledgable extension of the negotiator's own self.

Other members of the negotiator's staff were also important if not as intimate. They also were extensions of the negotiator's knowledge of the record because most of them had, at different times, been assigned to the various Foreign Ministry offices associated with the development of Sino-American policy. They offered the negotiator a sounding board for his views of the negotiations and they were able to provide insights into the effect of the negotiations on other important relations. A typical example of this last point is Li Huichuan, who was Wang Bingnan's number two man at Geneva in 1955. Li was a talented diplomat and a specialist on the Soviet Union who was assigned directly from his post in Moscow to Geneva. Coupled with his knowledge of English, he was able to interpret the American positions for Wang in terms of the Sino-Soviet relationship. Huang Hua acted similarly. He was temporarily assigned to Geneva in 1958 as a special assistant to advise Wang Bingnan on policy developments in Beijing, as well as to take a firsthand report on the negotiations back to Zhou and Mao.

In Beijing, the appropriate offices of the Foreign Ministry were likewise staffed with men who had an English language capability and who had matured professionally in the Ministry alongside developments in the PRC's US policy. A notable example is Zhang Zai, who is know to many Americans as one of China's most knowledgable men concerning development of China's US policy. Like so many others, Zhang began his career as an area specialist at Panmunjom. He was assigned to Washington, DC, in 1984 as a counselor to replace Ji Chaozhu. Both have since served overseas as ambassadors.

Is Chinese Method Dogma?

To conclude, as Admiral Joy did, that the PRC's negotiators can be anyone, since anyone can be a messenger, is to greatly underestimate the ability and importance of the men assigned to the negotiations by the Chinese. A great deal is communicated about the Chinese view of the negotiations just by the qualifications of the individual assigned.

In the sense of Dr. Iklé's definition, a few have been messengers, although possibly only from a lack of opportunity. In the early days of the negotiations in the 1950s at Panmunjom and Geneva, and of course later in Beijing in the 1970s, those Chinese assigned to the negotiations came as negotiators. For a number of reasons the Chinese, like the West, misjudged the situation and arrived at Panmunjom and Geneva with unfulfillable expectation; however, the results of these negotiations should in no way detract from the unique qualifications and the importance of the individual assigned to the negotiations.

China's negotiators are the product of their culture, the training they received as apprentice translators and officials from veteran diplomatic negotiators, their own experiences as Communist Party members, and their study of English and the American society, either overseas or in China. They come from diverse origins and have equally diverse experiences, yet they can all be said to be highly disciplined party advocates, who enjoy the confidence of their superiors. As such they are active but disciplined participants in the collective decisionmaking process from which China's negotiating positions are developed. As tacticians they are adroit in seizing and maintaining the psychological initiative. Their individual mastery of the negotiating record between China and the United States tempers the likelihood of any individual becoming a zealous advocate for any solution or becoming overcommitted to the results of any single formal negotiation. They are keenly aware that going to the negotiations table is a tactic, not a strategy, and that it is but one phase of a dynamic process that is continually at work between China and the United States. As masters of the record, they recognize that bilateral Sino-American relations are continual negotiations with a dynamic, everchanging agenda in which they are but one element, never *the* element. Their utility as formal negotiators will last only as long as a formal conference is useful. While the negotiator's skills are critical to the successful conclusion of the formal talks, the conclusion may not mark the end of negotiations, but rather establish a plateau from which future Chinese negotiators could conduct further discussions on issues Americans may have thought were settled.

China's negotiators generally have been a vital, although not the determinant, factor in China's policy process. They have been able negotiators, who are also impatient to show results, as Admiral Joy early found, but who are also less prone to be trapped by a schedule. Not without their weaknesses and mistakes, Chinese negotiators are nevertheless substantial opponents at the negotiating table.

4.
CASE I: PANMUNJOM

Nowhere in the record is there a single action of your side which indicates a real and sincere desire to attain the objective for which these conferences were designed . . . you (the communist delegation) did not enter these negotiations with sincerity and high purpose, but rather that you entered into them to gain time to repair your shattered forces and to try to accomplish at the conference table what your armies could not accomplish in the field.[1]

—Admiral C. Turner Joy
65th Plenary Session
May 2, 1952

After ten months and twelve days as Senior Delegate of the United Nations Command delegation, Admiral Joy was hopelessly frustrated. He was departing Korea without having accomplished his mission. There was no armistice and the fighting and attendant dying continued. His enemies were to blame. A little over a year later, his successor, Major General William Harrison, succinctly expressed similar frustrations when he responded to a query from Arthur Dean for advice as to how he should negotiate with the Communists. Harrison's written response was "Don't."[2]

Ambassador U. Alexis Johnson was the Deputy Assistant Secretary of State responsible for the negotiations at Panmunjom during this period. While he also acknowledges that the Chinese Communist approach to the negotiations wore his patience thin, he points out that it was as much the Chinese negotiator's mission, as it was that of the US negotiators, to secure his country's objectives to the maximum extent possible. From his experiences, Ambassador Johnson attributes part of the frustration expressed by

Courtesy National Archives

Admiral Turner Joy, Panmunjom, 1951

Joy and Harrison to their lack of experience as negotiators— particularly in comparison with their counterparts—and the extra burden each carried by having his instructions delivered as orders via military channels. These factors introduced an inappropriate degree of tactical rigidity in the implementation of their instructions at the negotiations table.[3] When Joy's remarks and their attendant frustrations are examined from the perspective of these factors and the implied institutional differences between the two sides, one is led to the conclusion that Joy's frustrations also stemmed from the fundamental differences between the political cultures of China and the US. The importance of a negotiator understanding these differences is described by Dr. Henry Kissinger as follows:

> If the domestic structures (of nations) are based on commensurable notions of what is just, a consensus about permissible aims and methods of foreign policy develops. When the domestic structures are based on fundamentally different conceptions of what is just, the conduct of international affairs grows more complex. Then it becomes difficult to define the nature of disagreement because what seems most obvious to one side appears most problematic to the other.[4]

Neither the US negotiators at Panmunjom nor the PRC negotiators, as will be shown later, were atune to these differences. Furthermore, any interest in understanding the fundamental differences referred to by Kissinger were exacerbated by the hatred and distrust that flowed from the violence of war, blocking any efforts made by either side to bridge the chasm of misunderstanding.

In retrospect it is easier to see that the Chinese and American "notions of what is just" were not commensurable. The aim or objectives of the Chinese in going to war in 1950, as well as in seeking the negotiations that ended the war, were different in many ways from what the Americans expected. Furthermore, the Chinese style or method of negotiations made comprehending the nature of the disagreement even more problematic. Although a better understanding by the two sides of the differences between the objectives of each side for the war, the purpose of the negotiations, and their respective negotiating styles would not necessarily have resulted in any major changes in the final solutions, understanding possibly would have enabled the two sides to find those solutions acceptable to both sides with far less conflict and in a much shorter period of time with fewer lives lost.

Objectives of War

The objectives of both sides changed several times during the course of the Korean War. Initially US objectives were focused on the preservation of South Korea, motivated in large part by the political concern that either a forced or a voluntary American withdrawal would weaken other American alliances, especially NATO. Either way a withdrawal would strengthen communist political influence and undermine confidence in the foreign policy and military capability of the United States.[5]

For their part Beijing's leaders initially were not overly concerned about US objectives in Korea, despite Russian pressures. However, the destruction of the North Korean Army following the Inchon landing of 15 September 1950 and the ensuing advance northward transformed Chinese opinions. The United States appeared to be attempting the forced reunification of Korea and, if successful, would threaten the existence of the newly formed government of China. Chinese warnings and concerns increased rapidly. The UN resolution of 7 October 1950, which established the United Nations Commission for the Unification and Rehabilitation of Korea, only served to further reinforce Chinese fears that the United States had adopted an aggressive policy of forcibly reunifying Korea.[6]

In opposition to US policy, China's volunteers entered the war in October 1950 and by the year's end pushed the forces of the United Nations Command back to the vicinity of the 38th Parallel and beyond Seoul by mid-January, by forcing the US—from Beijing's perspective—to change its objectives. US fears outstripped Chinese capabilities as the US objective of unification by force was replaced by that of just maintaining a toehold on the peninsula.[7]

This fear was relatively short lived as in the months that followed, UN forces gradually pushed the Chinese, who had out run their logistics capability, back to the vicinity of the 38th Parallel. There a stalemate developed that neither side could break without risking general war.[8] Eventually the need for a political settlement was forced into the consciousness of US leaders. By the spring of 1951 support for the war was becoming increasingly difficult to maintain, both domestically and among the UN allies. The US had to find a way to end the war. Because an imposed military solution was no longer possible, politics would necessarily play a larger role, but America's leaders had no confidence that the other extreme, a political solution, could be achieved or relied upon. An armistice, with its emphasis on institutionalizing the military status quo and, by inference, the accompanying political realities, was to be the extent of America's concession to the pressure for political solutions.

Chinese objectives also changed. Having barely begun the consolidation of their newly won authority to rule China as the People's Republic when the war erupted, Beijing's leaders were anxious to avoid being drawn into Korea. However, the United Nations Command's march in the fall of 1950 to the Yalu in an attempt to unify the peninsula forced China's leaders to reconsider their priorities. The aforementioned internal vulnerabilities of China were transformed in a matter of a few days from being the main deterrent to Chinese acquiescence to Soviet and North Korean pressures for the PRC to become involved in the war into the primary motivation for involvement. As the powerful American forces moved further into North Korea, the greater became the fear of China's leaders, that the extreme domestic vulnerability of the new government might be exploited by the United States.[9]

The farther US forces moved, the greater became Beijing's vulnerability to Soviet pressures for China's involvement in the war, the greater became the political importance to the PRC's national security of communist North Korea's continued existence as a buffer state, and the greater became the need to prevent the emergence of a unified Korea under UN supervision with the concomitant concerns about a possible US-Japan-Korea coalition. And finally there was the benefit that would accrue to the prestige of the PRC, particularly with its Asian neighbors and with foreign communist revolutionary parties.[10]

Despite these pressures, the decision in Beijing was not unanimous. Although the discipline of the Chinese Communist Party kept this dissent from being apparent externally, there was concern among the PRC's leaders as summarized by China's ancients, that "When the army marches abroad, the treasury will be emptied at home."[11] These men were concerned about the impact that the war would have on the recovery of the economy, devastated by more than a dozen years of war, and the impact on China's war weary populace. And true to their prediction the economic pressures of the war were great and a major determinant in Chinese decisions throughout the war, as Mao was to later acknowledge.[12] Considering the costs of concluding the civil war with the "Nationalist" remnants, of gaining control in Tibet, and of rebuilding the nation, the PRC had enough debilitating internal problems without going beyond China's borders to fight the United States.

US leaders assumed that the objective of the Chinese upon entering the war was to destroy the UN forces or drive them from Korea—the same as that of Moscow and Pyongyang.[13] However, from those interviewed, it would appear that the Chinese neither began or ended their campaign in Korea with the expulsion of the United States as an objective. There were hints during the interviews that some of China's military leaders differed with Beijing, as MacArthur did with Washington, over the military objective of the war. There undoubtedly was a period in December 1950 and January 1951 when these leaders, as well as the Soviets according to one interviewee, argued that China's volunteers should take advantage of the speed and magnitude of their successes. Nevertheless, the Chinese interviewed argued that Beijing recognized not only the military and economic limitations of China, especially in the area of logistics, but also the risks of expanding the war if they pushed the Americans off the peninsula.[14]

Furthermore, both the amount of Soviet assistance necessary to overcome limitations of the Chinese Volunteers (and the PLA) and the even greater assistance that would be necessary in the event of an expanded war would be in either case an intolerable increase in the dependence of the PRC on the Soviets. This argument suggests that the strategic objectives of the PRC and the US in Korea were far more complementary than either side perceived. The lack of trust and understanding on both sides, the emotions of war, and the alternating periods of success and failure on the battlefield prevented each side from fully recognizing and effectively capitalizing on these complementary, though not coincidental, interests.

Purpose of Negotiations

By the spring of 1951, both sides were ready to negotiate. However, this congruency of interest in opening negotiations tended to conceal the fact that the intended purpose of these negotiations differed for each country. The Americans perceived the negotiations foremost as a means to end the fighting, essential to dealing with such growing political problems as domestic and allied pressures to end the war.

As a result of their experiences with the Soviets, the Americans believed that a mutually acceptable political settlement with the communists would be difficult to find, if ever. As a result attention in Washington was narrowly focused on a predominantly military solution, that of obtaining an armistice agreement.[15]

Following the decision to seek an armistice, there emerged a reluctance on the part of the Joint Chiefs of Staff and the UN Commander, General Ridgway, to commit troops to a major offensive. Believing that both sides wanted to end the hostilities, the Americans assumed that both sides had a common interest in reaching an armistice agreement quickly. Because the possibility of a ceasefire existed, US military leaders were unable to justify to themselves the casualties that a major offensive would involve.[16] The intensity of the narrow focus on the termination of hostilities and the building pressures to end the fighting in order to prevent casualties became apparent to the Chinese early in the negotiations. They soon factored these American views into their efforts to influence the negotiating environment.

For the US the armistice agreement was the vehicle for institutionalizing the status quo, as in a legal contract. Only through a legal framework could the West's concept of justice and fairness be assured. The emphasis was less on co-opting an opponent's view to insure compliance with the agreement than on actions to insure enforcement.

Finally, the attitude of Americans at this time toward the Chinese suggests the ethnocentricity that underlay these purposes. In 1950 Americans were disposed to think of the US as being the invincible power it was at the end of the Second World War, irrespective of the stalemate. There was a tendency to look down upon the Chinese rather than deal with them as a worthy, if not equal adversary, a slight still keenly remembered by the Chinese interviewed.

China's leaders also were under pressure to end the war and thus were interested, as the Americans correctly assumed, in a quick settlement. According to those interviewed, the Chinese came to the talks prepared to reach an armistice agreement in order that both sided could move on to more difficult political questions. However, when it became apparent to them that the Americans were not prepared to reach an agreement under the conditions that the Chinese expected, the talks then became a means to influence the American view of the situation. The Chinese had little faith in the efficacy or justness of international law, assuming instead that any long term solution depended on changing the attitudes of the Americans toward the issues.[17]

In most of the classical military writings of China, as well as among most of those Chinese interviewed, war does not possess the finality that it does for the West. Although "war is the highest form of struggle for resolving contradictions," war is not viewed as the final arbiter of the argument nor does it provide a long-term solution to the argument.[18] Influenced by the philosophies of China's ancients concerning war, particularly as they have been reinforced by the Marxist-Leninist view of the role of war in history, the Communist Chinese view war as a means to reshape "objective reality." War reshapes and reorders the factors that its participants must consider in reaching a settlement. The Chinese see war as a means of making an opponent more susceptible to persuasion. They place greater emphasis on war or the threat of war as an instrument for converting their opponent to the Chinese viewpoint than on its inherent nature as an instrument of coercion. "Those skilled in war subdue the enemy's army without battle. They capture his cities without assaulting them and overthrow his state without protracted operations. Your aim must be to take All-under-Heaven intact."[19] Thus war and formal negotiations are but two complementary tactics available to China's leaders for managing the strategic dialogue, or more accurately the strategic negotiation, that is continuously at work between the PRC and the US.

This does not mean that war is easily used as a tactic. Philosophically the Chinese are not insensitive to the loss of human life, that combat causes; however, their emphasis is less on the individual and more on the collective than in the US. Consequently there is relatively less motivation to endanger the many for the few and more acceptance of the sacrifices of the few for the many. This difference between East and West is relative—a matter of emphasis. The importance the Communist Chinese placed on the welfare of their troops in Korea is not doubted by the Chinese interviewed, a number of whom fought in Korea. Indications of this concern was also strongly pointed out to the author during interviews with South Koreans who had fought against the Communist Chinese while serving in the Japanese Army from 1937-1945.[20] However, equally true is the fact that many of China's senior leaders became inured to mass casualties during China's civil war and faced with no alternatives, endured them in Korea. More pragmatic than idealistic in the resolution of such opposites, the China's leaders were relatively invulnerable to having the question of casualties used as a lever—either domestically or internationally—against them during the negotiations at Panmunjom.[21]

Such different purposes for entering negotiations help explain the seemingly less hurried approach of the Chinese to the negotiations, an approach which not only exasperated many Americans at Panmunjom, but also confirmed the American perception that the communists were indifferent to how many battlefield casualties they received. From the Chinese view, endurance—not indifference—is a powerful ally. This view is illustrated by a speech that Mao made to a domestic audience in August 1952 concerning the costs of the war. In his speech, Mao conditioned his optimism about the eventual outcome of the war upon the Chinese being able to outlast the Americans:

> Just how long will the fighting go on, and just when will the negotiations draw to a close? I say negotiations will continue, fighting will go on but there will be a truce.
>
> Why is that there will be a truce? A thirty years' war or a hundred years' war is highly improbable, because a long war is very much against the interests of the United States.[22]

Mao then enumerated these interests of the US as the cost in lives, the cost in money, the "insuperable contradictions" or opposition to the war at home in the US and abroad, and the Europe first strategy of the US. While he recognized that the PRC faced the same or similar pressures, he argued that the Chinese were better able to handle these pressures and could outlast the Americans.

Negotiating Style

The road that the Communist Chinese followed to Panmunjom was not difficult for the Americans to understand, or so they thought. It was believed that the Chinese, as communist clones, merely followed the Soviet's lead, even to the extent of mimicking the harshness of the Soviet negotiating style. Because of this perceived oneness, the United States showed little interest in differentiating the objectives and style of the Chinese from those of the Soviets. Time has revealed this to be a mistake, for the Chinese were different from the Soviets in many essential ways, not the least of which was their negotiating style.

From the Chinese perspective the PRC-US relationship is a continuous negotiating process. It is a process in which they have felt disadvantaged, a process from which the Americans have often gained the most. They acknowledge that mistakes have been and will be made, on both sides, but a great deal of effort is devoted to learning from their mistakes. In this process formal negotiations are used when the activity in the relationship is of such intensity and potential value that a conference is useful. However, as part of a larger process, the value or purpose of the conference normally transcends the stated purpose of the conference. From this perspective the range of activities considered by the Chinese during the pre-negotiation phase exceeds what Americans might consider as germane. "Linkage" at a complex level of analysis is fundamental to the Chinese thought process.

Pre-negotiation Phase—Prelude to Panmunjom

To the leaders in Beijing enmity between the Chinese Communists and the United States did not begin with the Korean War or the placement of the Seventh Fleet in the strait between China and Taiwan. The war was just the latest manifestation of the enmity that had been building from the Party's earliest association with the United States. There was a great deal more to be dealt with by the armistice negotiations than just the fate of Korea.

From the Communist perspective, the US had consistently behaved as an imperialist power in China. During World War II and the Communist Party's Second United Front with the Nationalists, the United States refused to assist the Communist Chinese in their fight against the Japanese, despite the efforts of the Party's leaders to court the United States and the supportive efforts of a few US military and foreign service officials.

After the war, the Communists suffered from the continued alignment of the United States with the Nationalists during China's civil war (1945-1949), even during the mediation efforts of the Marshall Mission (1946-1947) when the United States was ostensibly neutral. Following these experiences and given the hostile political climate developing in the United States in 1949, China's leaders decided following "liberation " that there was little, if any, prospect that the United States would provide any assistance. Conversely it was almost certain that the USSR would. In addition, if the Party was to consolidate its authority and regenerate China as a nation, China must be purged of the malignant forms of foreign influence. As several Chinese interviewed pointed out, China and the West—the United States in particular—had to go separate ways in order for the Chinese to have time to reestablish their identity as a people and as a nation. This argument was reinforced by another interviewee's account of Zhou Enlai's conversation with a group of "what if-ist " scholars from the United States who were asserting that the United States was responsible for the failure of the US and China to establish relations in 1949. Zhou told them that while there certainly was fault on the part of the United States, China had its own agenda that prevented normalization.

With the establishment of the PRC in October 1949, China's new leaders formally began managing their relations with the West by controlling the process by which relations with foreign countries were established. Rather than seeking recognition, Beijing awaited its suitors. As public policy, the principles of equality, mutual benefit and respect for territorial integrity and sovereignty provided a framework within which all countries were theoretically welcome.[23] Practically, each nation's sincerity with respect to these principles was measured against a criterion that only the Party knew at the time and which varied according to the Party's view of each supplicant's history of exploitation of China. The effect was a self-imposed quarantine behind which the communist could reeducate the Chinese populace. Foreigners would be reeducated during the process of re-entry; the more pernicious their colonial influence had been, the more difficult their re- entry. Of the West European nations, only Sweden Denmark, Switzerland, and Finland were able to quickly reestablish relations.[24] From the perspective of the Chinese, the process provided equality; from that of some Western nations it appeared to discriminate against those who had the most to lose.

This process was interrupted, but also enhanced by the Korean War and US pressures on its allies, particularly the European nations, for unity in their approach to China. Western perceptions of what concessions were required to reestablish relations with China had already been shaped by the Chinese. The war heightened the pressures for concessions, particularly on the British. These perceptions later generated disagreement on the part of the allies from Europe with the US approach to the negotiations at Panmunjom. Once the wartime pressures for unity were lessened by the prospect of peace through negotiations, other interests—such as investments and trade—revived to generate pressure for the rapid conclusion of the peace process.[25]

As the war proceeded, China's leaders increasingly sought to communicate to the West, particularly to the United States, their interests, concerns, and probable actions to deal with these concerns. In part attributable to the absence of diplomatic relations with the United States but more importantly because of the Chinese preference, at least as volunteered by many interviewed, the Chinese chose to deal with the United States—their principal rival—indirectly, often through a third party. As foreign minister, Zhou issued public statements and warnings, sent cables and emissaries to the United Nations, received UN officials and sent messages via intermediaries. Of these indirect approaches, Zhou tended to put greatest emphasis on third party intermediaries to insure that his message was received and understood by the United States. For example, before China entered the war, Zhou called upon representatives of India and two European nations to warn the US against crossing the 38th Parallel. The US record shows that at least India delivered this warning, although the Indian warning was not taken seriously.[26]

Still reluctant to become militarily engaged, an even firmer warning was issued by the initial contact the Chinese People's Volunteer Army made with US forces shortly after crossing the Yalu in October 1950. After a brief encounter the Chinese forces broke contact, and in so doing provided the US with another opportunity to accept China's warning.[27] Unfortunately the meaning of the temporary withdrawal was not clear to the Americans, for according to US reports the CPV forces "mysteriously" disappeared for nearly a month.[28]

China's step-by-step approach to war still left the United States surprised when the Chinese attacked in November. In part because of the past record of the Chinese, the United States was reluctant to believe that the Chinese weren't bluffing. The United States was not yet very good at distinguishing between Chinese statements for domestic consumption, statements designed to test the waters, and firm policy commitments. Paradoxically, once the Chinese attacked, there was never any consideration given among American policymakers that the PRC might not share the Soviet and North Korean stated goal of driving the Americans from the peninsula. Washington never considered that the Chinese objective, as described during the course of the interviews, was to pursue the war only until they could negotiate a mutually agreeable settlement, possibly the antebellum status quo.

Korea was an imposition, an interruption. National unification and reconstruction were the priorities. Chen Yi was preparing his forces to seize Taiwan, while others prepared to bring Tibet back into the fold. Economic reconstruction and the pacification of South China were also at the top of the agenda of daily crises in Beijing. The effect of the "imperialistic" action of the US in Korea and in Taiwan was to thrust national security into the foreground alongside unification and reconstruction. The war was an unwelcome intrusion that both interrupted the Taiwan campaign and severely strained the national economy. However, once committed, China's leaders pragmatically reassessed their strategy for achieving their long term objectives or principles, and proceeded to take advantage of the effect of the war where possible.[29]

With respect to unification the late November 1950 visit of Wu Xiuquan to the United Nations marked, in his words, the temporary shift of the "struggle against the imperialist ... from battlefields full of gunfire to a platform where people were engaging in battles of words. We (the Chinese) would directly face the number one imperialist (the United States) over the question of Taiwan."[30]Although the immediate effect of his harsh presentation was to temporarily generate a degree of unity among the western nations, the longer term effect was to reinforce the division of opinion between the United States and others, particularly Britain and India, over how to deal with the PRC and Taiwan.[31]

In January 1951, Zhou essentially turned down a UN cease-fire proposal at the height of the PLA's victories because it was clear to Beijing that the United States was not yet ready to deal with China as an equal member of the international community with legitimate security interests. Instead he responded with a cable that charged that the United Nation's purpose was "merely to give the United States troops a breathing space." There was no change in the objectives of the US and thus a cease-fire followed by negotiations "could never lead to genuine peace." He then reiterated his December statement of the PRC's "principles" for the withdrawal of all foreign troops from Korea and the settlement of Korean domestic affairs by the Koreans themselves; the United States armed forces must be withdrawn from Taiwan; and that the representatives of the People's Republic of China must assume their rightful place in the United Nations."[32]

The escalating pattern of signals, third party interventions, and warnings that had preceded China's entry into the war was comparable to the patterns of actions that typically preceded clan wars in China. Likewise a similar parallel was evident in the manner the Chinese approached the termination of hostilities. As the military stalemate developed and China's leaders perceived via third parties and other means that the United States was amenable to a solution acceptable to the Chinese, Beijing initiated efforts through third persons to arrange a meeting whereby the representatives of the United States and the PRC could meet and finalize the emerging agreement.

Several of the Chinese interviewed pointed out that Beijing followed closely the mounting pressures in both the United States and at the United Nations to end the war, though possibly with too much of an Indian and European bias in their source of information. Consequently a lot of emphasis was placed on the implications for US policy of Dean Acheson's June 1951 statement concerning the acceptability to the United States of ending the war on the 38th Parallel and of the acceptability to the US of the contingent withdrawal of UNC forces from Korea.[33] These conditions, to the Chinese, reflected a fundamental change in American perceptions of reality and approximated the conditions China could accept for an armistice. These developments opened the way for the PRC to agree to having the USSR—as a more credible third party—propose a negotiated settlement. To the Chinese these conditions suggested a willingness to accept the principles in Zhou's January cable that were directly related to Korea and a more reasonable attitude in the United States about negotiating with the Chinese. Of course the war also had reshaped the Chinese view of what was achievable at that time.

The interviews pointed out that the Chinese went to Panmunjom with the perception that the essence of an agreement was at hand, albeit only a small step toward their ultimate goals or principles. As in settling a clan war, they believed that all that was needed was a limited amount of negotiations to finalize the armistice agreement. That the

Chinese half expected the negotiations to be semi-perfunctory was indicated by the fact that the initial Chinese military negotiators, Deng Hua and Xie Fang, had both the political and military stature necessary for them to conclude an agreement and to represent the PRC in any attendant ceremony. However, neither of them had the foreign affairs experience one might expect for extended negotiations, as did their successors. Conversely their foreign affairs oriented successors had neither the political stature or military expertise of either Deng or Xie. Supporting China's military negotiators was a staff recruited principally from the staff of the Foreign Ministry.[34] Since the armistice talks were expected to end quickly, the staff was said to have been organized to support the more important mission of the team of Foreign Ministry negotiators that was standing by in Beijing to replace the military negotiators as soon as a military agreement was reached. These individuals were not identified during the interviews, but it is logical to assume that Huang Hua and his Harvard educated assistant Dr. Pu Shouchang, the political negotiators of 1953, were probably the stand-bys for at least the latter part of the military negotiations.[35]

Opening the Conference

As the military stalemate emerged the United States tried to convey to its opponents the interest of the United States in a negotiated settlement in Korea. There were approaches to the Soviets, through the United Nations and other third parties, and approaches to the Chinese through their embassy in Moscow and through contacts in Hong Kong.[36] Although both the Chinese and the Soviets were approached, the United States—unlike some others countries—expected the USSR, as the architect of the problem, to take the lead. Consequently, US leaders were momentarily confused when the Soviets passed their lead by recommending during the 23 June 1951, UN-sponsored radio program that the two sides in the Korean War seek a cease-fire and an armistice.[37] The indirectness of this third party recommendation expressed interest without a commitment. It was a maneuver designed to elicit a substantive proposal from the United States to which the Chinese could respond. In this traditional Oriental waiting game, US impatience favored the Chinese, allowing them their preference of commenting on an opponent's entreaty. A direct overture by the United States, from the Chinese vantage, was an important element for setting the stage psychologically.

Soviet Foreign Minister Gromyko told US Ambassador Kirk on 27 June that the USSR envisioned in the Malik speech of 23 June, a meeting between the two opposing military commands "to conclude a military armistice ... which would be limited strictly to military questions and would not involve any political or territorial matters. As to assurances against the resumption of hostilities ... this would be the subject of discussion between Commands. ... (The) conclusion of a military armistice would be 'entering on the path of peaceful settlement'." Gromyko said his government did not know the view of the Chinese on Malik's statement and that the United States may ask them.[38] The United States subsequently adopted a position similar—from the US perspective—to Malik's recommendation. Since the USSR, and by extension the PRC, proposed the idea originally, China's negative reaction to the US approach only increased the US distrust of the Chinese.

During a State/JCS meeting on 28 June, General Vandenberg, USAF Chief of Staff, argued for a less direct approach to the Chinese than a message from Ridgway to his opponents concerning a meeting between the two military commands since that "would in effect mean that we are asking for peace, instead of the Communists." General Bradley noted his point as well as the argument that a cease-fire might allow the enemy to build-up while draining US resources, but counterargued that "we could not ignore the effect on the will of our people and other contributing UN member nations to continued support of the hostilities if we in effect turned down what appeared to be an opportunity to end the hostilities."[39] Subsequently General Ridgway was directed to send a message to the Commander in Chief, Communist Forces Korea offering to hold a meeting between the two military commands on a Danish hospital ship in Wonsan Harbor.[40] While the ship was viewed by the United States as a neutral location, the Chinese felt disadvantaged. US naval dominance gave the US control of the local environment and a propaganda advantage. Would a picture of the communist negotiators boarding the ship resemble another Tokyo Bay surrender? The Chinese countered with the suggestion that the location should be in the city of Kaesong, between 10 and 15 July.[41] Kaesong was on land where the armies were evenly matched and the local setting was oriental. The communists would be the hosts. The initiative would be in their hands.

The fact that the Chinese did not accept the hospital ship as the meeting site has been cited to support the idea that communists never accept any proposal in total. However, the acceptance by the United States, without any further bargaining, of a site that so obviously favored the Chinese surprised them. Kaesong favored Chinese interests just as the ship favored US interests. A more neutral site would have been agreeable. Panmunjom was easily agreed upon as a new site, once the Americans realized the advantage of Kaesong to the Chinese and insisted upon a change.

Kaesong was an interesting choice for the negotiations. Physical considerations were relatively important to the Chinese as a location within their lines facilitated communications rearward to Beijing. According to those interviewed, the Chinese maintained telephone contact with the Foreign Ministry in Beijing throughout the negotiations. This would have been virtually impossible—certainly more difficult and less secure—if the site had been aboard a neutral ship or in US held territory. Ease of secure communications with Beijing was critical to the Chinese pattern of operations and decisionmaking during the negotiations.

The psychological value of meeting in Communist controlled Kaesong, the former imperial capital of a united Korea, was also an important consideration. Although the Americans were not overly sensitive to the symbolism, Koreans who were interviewed felt strongly that both the possession of Kaesong by the communists and the holding of the armistice talks there had a significant psychological value. It was valuable to the Communists, particularly the North Koreans, in generating morale among their respective populations and as a negative influence on the South.

When the liaison representatives from the two sides met at Kaesong to make arrangements for the talks, the US representatives were nervous and distrustful. They were

Courtesy National Archives

Lt. Underwood, US Army translator, en route to the inn at Kaesong, July 1951.

met cordially when they landed, but then visibly reminded of their anxieties by their heavily armed escort from the helicopter pad to the inn at Kaesong. In a photograph it looks like a surrender procession.

When the representatives reached the inn, the communists again attempted to be cordial, inviting the UN representatives to sit and have an informal conversation over tea and cigarettes before beginning the negotiations over conference arrangements. The Americans refused these amenities and pressed to get the formal discussions started in the next room. Whereas the Americans tended to view cordiality as fraternization with the enemy, the Chinese preferred to recognize the duality of the situation. Albeit currently enemies, hence the visible reminders, the objective is to find agreement, hence the cordial atmosphere. Rejection of their hospitality suggested to the Chinese an arrogant, hostile and uncompromising attitude on the part of the Americans.[42] (As addressed in an earlier chapter, Kissinger also found the dual nature of his reception strange but was better able to handle the ambiguity.)

When the two delegations moved to the adjoining room, the UN team deliberately took the chairs on the north side. The UN representatives were aware that by eastern tradition the honored seats in a meeting are those that face south.[43] Furthermore tradition holds that the military victors sit in the northern chairs facing south and the vanquished in those facing north. By taking the northern chairs the Americans felt they visibly discomforted the communists.[44] At noon the liaison team turned down the lunch offered by the Communists. Then, while resting after eating their own "brown bag" lunch, the Americans rejected an offer of cold watermelon. Chinese meals, especially where guests are present, are concluded with fresh fruit.

During the liaison meeting the Americans also turned down the Communist's offer to provide accommodations at the Kaesong site for the UN delegation to the forthcoming armistice talks and the "Communist offer to provide all food and supplies required for the meeting, stating that the UN delegation intended to provide for its own needs."[45] Throughout the initial liaison meetings and the early plenary sessions of the armistice talks, the communist officers were "courteous" and conducted themselves with "marked dignity," yet the US representatives rejected or mocked the small but nevertheless proffered amenities and informal contacts in an effort to avoid any evidence of fraternization.[46] This rejection reinforced communist evaluations of the uncompromising attitude of the United States and contributed to their subsequent "harshness" or adversarial style. US negotiators were later to bemoan the absence of these informal contacts without which it was impossible to develop the personal side conversations that both Western and Eastern negotiators have traditionally used to overcome some of the communication limitations of the negotiation table.[47]

At the first plenary session the communist delegates recreated the dual sensations of hostility and cordiality that had marked the liaison meetings. Just prior to arriving at the negotiation site, the UN convoy was suddenly joined by a heavily armed communist escort, which together with the white flags of truce gave the impression of a surrender delegation, an impression of some propaganda value for use with Chinese and North Korean audiences.

For the Chinese delegation another product of the creation of an atmosphere of both hostility and cordiality was the confusion and uncertainty created among the Americans as to what to expect from the Chinese. This characteristic use of opposites (like sweet and sour) to simultaneously emphasize and soften the extremes of opposites distracted the US delegation, causing them to expend a lot of time and effort responding to these small incidents instead of taking the initiative themselves. Momentarily US attention was redirected to peripheral actions on the "*weiqi* board" and away from the main effort. The Chinese had the psychological advantage, the Americans were on the defensive.

Furthermore, American complaints about those incidents they perceived to be particularly disagreeable gave them a value in the negotiations beyond their propaganda and psychological importance. US reactions put the Chinese in the position of being able to negotiate an accommodation with the Americans over issues that began with incidents of marginal intrinsic value to the Chinese. By accommodating US demands, the Chinese could point to their concessions and logically expect some consideration in return. The movement of the negotiations site from Kaesong to Panmunjom and the renegotiation of the security agreement was such a strawman.

As the negotiations over the agenda opened, Admiral Joy's initial impression was that the communists were prepared to negotiate, a correct impression according to those interviewed.[48] As the negotiations proceeded, Joy changed his mind. He began to see the five-point agenda of the communists as a maneuver to gain advantage. As structured it left very little to negotiate but the details of how to implement the agenda.[49] According to those interviewed Joy's observations were again correct, he merely failed to recognize it as a two-step process. Joy's opponents saw the agenda as the basic outline of the agreement that had been worked out via third parties during the pre-negotiations phase. Consequently the next steps for the delegates were to clarify any ambiguities, to define the implementing details, and to affirm the agreement. The Chinese did not expect that this would be an easy task, but they certainly did not expect the three-year marathon that occurred. When the United States began to dismantle the PRC's agenda it gradually became clear to the Chinese that there was no basis, or at best a very limited basis, for the agreement they had anticipated. There was a sense of betrayal within the

Chinese delegation that suggests some of the bitterness that remained so close to the surface throughout the talks.

As it became clear to Beijing that the United States was not prepared to reach the agreement expected, the Chinese moved to develop the agenda as a means for controlling the pace and direction of the negotiations. The negotiations were to become an instrument of education, a means to cause the United States to change its position. Those subjects that the Chinese felt had the least long term significance, and about which agreement could be reached rather quickly without betraying the PRC's principles, were placed first and those that could be more controversial were placed last. The Chinese recognized that an early agreement on an agenda item, or several quick agreements on sub-issues, tends to generate expectations and, in turn, pressures on an opponent for continued, rapid progress. This is especially true for Americans who are extra sensitive to domestic and international opinion. These pressures can be particularly useful when there is a need for greater concessions on the part of the United States concerning later and more difficult issues.

With the shift in strategy came an emphasis upon the time honored practice of "Fight, Talk, Fight, Talk." Although Americans criticized this practice as debased and typical of the Communists, it is neither from the Chinese perspective. Having roots in ancient oriental warfare, the concept is conceptually more humanitarian and saving in resources than the Western concept of entering negotiations or talking after one side has been beaten into submission. While "fighting while talking" can take a heavy toll of the military and economic resources of an opponent, the greatest impact is intended to be psychological. It can be particularly effective in influencing the relative balance of power in favor of the belligerent with the greatest endurance, not necessarily the one with the greatest physical power.[50] Albeit critical of the Chinese, the US also adopted essentially the same policy prior to entering the negotiations by deciding not to permit a cease-fire until an armistice agreement was reached.[51] It is interesting to note that this is the same position Zhou Enlai took in his cable of 17 January 1951, a position that Secretary Dean Acheson then denounced.[52] While this policy took a heavy toll on both sides, from Beijing's perspective the net gain fell to the PRC.

Zhou's January cable was a declaration of the principles or objectives that guided the Chinese in their thinking about how to resolve the issues that underlay the war. According to those interviewed the Chinese were surprised by the failure of the United States to respond with a counterproposal. Beijing wanted, but realistically did not expect, the United States to accept its principles in total. The denunciation was an education for Beijing. With respect to future negotiations, it was clear to the Chinese that Americans were focused on immediate, short term goals and had little patience for dealing with long term goals or principles. Mechanisms had to be found whereby in any dialogue with the United States the Americans could be kept interested in the discussions long enough for the Chinese to take a step, however small, toward their own longer term objectives.

In deciding in the summer of 1951 to go to the negotiations table, the Chinese temporarily laid aside that portion of the principles outlined in January 1951 that they believed the US was not ready to negotiate. Although derived from the basic foreign policy principles of sovereignty and territorial integrity, the return of Taiwan and the related issue of the admission of the PRC to the United Nations were not raised. Nevertheless, the fear of their being raised continued to influence US decisions throughout the negotiations.[53] The withdrawal of foreign military forces from Korea, a stated objective of both the United Nations and the PRC, then became the key principle upon which the PRC focused its proposed agenda.

The negotiation of the differences between the proposed agendas of the two sides resulted in a five point agenda that deferred discussions of the withdrawal to some vague future time. The five points agreed to were: (1) the adoption of the agenda, (2) fixing a military demarcation line and demilitarized zone, (3) arrangements for a cease fire and armistice including a supervisory organization, (4) arrangements relating to Prisoners of War, and (5) recommendations to the governments of countries concerned on both sides. (See Appendix for original positions and final agreed agenda.)

Only those political issues about which the Chinese believed the US had indicated the possibility of a compromise were included in their initial agenda. These included the restoration of the 38th Parallel and the withdrawal of foreign forces. Placing these items on their proposed agenda as the second and third items suggests that the Chinese began their agenda with those items with which the agreement with the US was thought to be the greatest and continued to those with the least common prior definition. By the time the final negotiated agenda was agreed upon, China's two political objectives had been subsumed under item five, the most ambiguous and thus potentially the most difficult item to resolve.

The Chinese were not prescient with respect to the position the US would take on each issue during the negotiations nor even with respect to their own reactions to issues, as subsequent events revealed. However, they knew the importance they attached to each of the principles involved in their agenda items, and had fairly accurately assessed the importance the Americans attached to each of their agenda items. This assessment was based on their previous experiences with the Americans, the initial agenda of the United States, and subsequent discussions. Among the more salient experiences was the concern the Americans had demonstrated over their captured troops earlier in the Korean war as well as in China during the civil war

(1945-1949). By strongly arguing for the placement of visits to POW camps second on the agenda, the US delegation reinforced the earlier experiences of the Chinese with the priority Americans placed on the early return of captured personnel, and the leverage their impatience gave the Chinese. These experiences later heavily influenced the Chinese approach to the Ambassadorial Talks.

With the agenda completed, the boundaries for the dialogue were established. From the US perspective the talks would focus only on military matters. For the Chinese the distinction was not so clear as war is only a more violent form of politics. Bringing a halt to the fighting was a common objective, but an armistice would be acceptable to the Chinese only if it contributed to an acceptable political situation. For the United States the concern was less political and more focused on securing an armistice that could be guaranteed by keeping the balance of military power favorable to the United States.

The agenda was negotiated and adopted in a little over 2 weeks (10-28 July 1951), rather quickly considering the unexpected lack of agreement Beijing found in these initial sessions. In agreeing to the agenda, Beijing temporarily lowered its expectations for the conference in terms of the immediate gratification of its foreign policy principles, and instead took a step back and focused its efforts on using the conference as a means to change perceptions of the PRC, principally among the Western nations.

Evaluating Possible Outcomes

If during the process of setting an agenda with the United States it had become clear to the Chinese that an agreement was in fact within reach, this period might have been brief. Some of those interviewed even argued that the Chinese would have preempted the US and moved rapidly to their bottom line, as Zhou Enlai did in 1971 with Dr. Kissinger. Instead China's leaders misjudged the United States. They overemphasized the importance of selected US public statements as a result of the synergistic influence of domestic pressures to end the fighting, optimistic judgments by the Indians and other third parties, and an inadequate understanding of the US political system. However, once it became clear that they had misjudged the situation, the Chinese stepped back to probe the range of possible US options, while at the same time attempting to conceal their own options. While probing they also sought to reshape American views of reality so as to cause US policy makers to expand their range of options to include those acceptable to the PRC.

In partial response to these added objectives, the negotiation of each of the next four agenda items, to some degree, became a separate, miniature version of the five-part negotiation process *. Because of the long periods of time involved in negotiating each item and the creativeness of each side, most of the eight maneuvers ** commonly observed in Sino-American negotiations were employed in each. Likewise, a wide range of techniques were also used. The following examples are neither comprehensive in their presentation of Chinese negotiating tactics nor a history of the negotiation; however, they are representative of the negotiations and reflect what stands out most about the talks in the memories of those interviewed.

Agenda Item 1. The first agenda item to be negotiated after the agenda itself involved the 38th Parallel. Initially American expectations for progress were high, until the Chinese responded to what appeared to them to be an unequal and demeaning proposal. The UN proposal called for a demilitarized zone twenty miles wide with its southern boundary to be the current line of contact. This would have required the Communist forces to retreat twenty

* Pre-negotiation phase, opening the conference, evaluating possible outcomes, hard bargaining and closure, and the postconference phase.

** Setting the pace, trust and equality, personalized relations, agenda, decisionmaking authority, precedence, diversions, principles.

miles. The US justification for this request was that in ceasing air and naval attacks, UN forces would make a greater concession than the Communists.[54] The Chinese saw the war as a stalemate at the current line of contact, in spite of the United Nation's superior naval and air power. In fact, one interviewee argued that the communist forces had withdrawn from Seoul and not attacked again, despite the replenishment of their forces, in order to show a willingness to compromise. The United States never recognized the signal.

The Chinese counterproposed the 38th Parallel as the demarcation line. Paradoxically this proposal would have denied them Korea's ancient capitol Kaesong, which US negotiators perceived in subsequent negotiations that the communists wanted as badly as the United States. The United States argued that the 38th Parallel was not defendable, to which the communists responded that both sides would have to rely more on trust than might.[55] The obvious difference in focus was that the US considered military factors to be the key to the preservation of peace after the armistice and the Chinese, while not indifferent to military considerations, were more concerned over the longer term political viability of the settlement. In a political settlement trust eventually becomes the key factor.

Agenda Item 2. The negotiations over the second agenda item began 13 August 1951. By mid-October there had been relatively little progress toward an agreement, each side adhering to its basic position in an effort to convince the other of the non-negotiability of its demands. This lack of progress coupled with several lengthy breaks that resulted from more than a dozen "neutrality violations " generated considerable concern in the West that the talks might breakdown. The ability of the Chinese to wait out their opponent was telling. Control of the pace of the negotiations was passing to Beijing.

Nearly 3 months after discussions of the second agenda item began, the United States advanced a proposal that reflected to the Chinese a change of attitude by the United States. Accepting the Chinese argument that the battleline reflected the net resultant of each sides efforts, the United States proposed a four mile wide demilitarized zone that centered generally along the line of contact, although deviating enough to include Kaesong. The move toward equality was sufficient for the Chinese to compromise by dropping their insistence on the 38th Parallel and accept the line of contact as the demarcation line. The American proposal did not specify a demarcation line. In their response the Chinese proposed that the line of contact be the demarcation line; however, when the two sides compared their respective map plots of the line of contact, the Chinese version was well south of the US version. Nevertheless, despite the fact that the atmosphere between the two sides had recently degenerated over a US neutrality violation, it only took the staff officers of the two sides two days of meetings to resolve the differences once the principals agreed to use the line of contact and turn it over to the staffs to define.

Clearly part of the problem with the different front line map plots was the comparative communication advantage the United States had over the communists. Besides the obvious advantage in speed via radio communications due to the larger number of radios at a lower level in the command structure, the United States also had maps in greater quantity at lower levels with people able to use them. This technical advantage created two problems for the Chinese. First, they were unwilling to admit their inadequacies by either asking for more time than the United States or by using US information. Consequently there was a need to stall until the information could be obtained or at least the US data could be verified.

Second, the Chinese were constantly concerned about some advantage, big or little, that technology—particularly any of which they were unaware or knew little about—might have given the Americans. Where the technology was known, but not available to the Chinese, they tended to believe that the United States was using it as the Chinese anticipated they might use it themselves. An example was their unwillingness to allow the United States to use a wire recorder during the conference. The Chinese kept meticulous records of everything said in the three original languages of Chinese, English, and Korean as well as a version translated into Chinese from English and Korean. The originals and translations were sent to Beijing as well as kept locally for study. The Chinese perceived that the recorder would give the United States an advantage both in speed and in the accuracy of this process as well as in the recall of conversations, an important factor in the way the Chinese develop their negotiation arguments.

Then, of course, there also was the problem of the potential propaganda usage of the recordings, a problem of no small concern to the Chinese. The United States, on the other hand, never tried to keep the same multi-language verbatim record that the Chinese did. The English language version was the official record, never mind the difficulty of conveying concepts through languages ill-equipped to handle the differences in political culture. Nor did the United States attempt to provide Washington a timely transcript of every spoken word. Instead an extensive summary was sent at the end of each day.

From the 26th of October through 27 November 1951, at the initiative of the United States, the negotiations were conducted in the more informal atmosphere of a sub-committee. There the communist spokesman was the Chinese general Xie Fang. On 31 October he proposed that both sides pull back four kilometers from the DMZ and that no subsequent adjustments be made. Interestingly his proposal placed the city of Kaesong on the north side of the DMZ.[56]

The proposal was attractive to many in the West who felt that there was little to be gained from arguing over small amounts of terrain. The pressure from the press mounted.

The problem with the proposal for the US government was the creation of a defacto cease-fire, which would make the application of pressure on the Chinese via the battlefield difficult during later phases of the negotiations.[57] After more attempts by both sides to find a formula, the United States proposed that the line of contact, as jointly determined, be the demarcation line and that if within thirty days the other items on the agenda are completed this line would become the final agreement. The communists accepted this proposal in toto and the subcommittee sent the agreement to the plenary session for ratification on 27 November. The US proposal of a 30–day limit provided, for the moment, the flexibility of implementation essential to all Chinese agreements that don't fully conform to the PRC's principles.

Incidents during the negotiations were usually judged by the United States to be diversions to permit the communists to adjust their negotiating positions or to be efforts to try the patience of the United States. In many cases these evaluations were accurate. In addition there was the influence of a largely unnoticed element involving the Chinese demand for equality, which often took the form of a demand of parallelism in the wording of agreements where no parallelism existed, a problem that later sorely challenged US negotiators at Geneva in 1955. Furthermore, because the Chinese didn't trust the motives of the United States, on occasion they unwisely put themselves in the position of trying to match or outdo the United States with respect to a particular agreement.

On 16 July it appears that partisans, not under the control of the United Nations or the Communists, fired from within UN lines into the neutral area. On 21 July the Communists said UN planes attacked the supply trucks of their delegation. The trucks had been marked with white crosses as required, although their movement had not been reported to the UN team as required. [58] The United States ducked responsibility for either incident and offered no reassurances for their stoppage.

On 4 August, a company of Chinese combat troops marched through the Kaesong neutrality zone, the only incident, of more than a dozen, for which the Communists were clearly responsible. Whether originated by the Chinese in response to the incidents of UN origin or by accident, the Chinese were unprepared for the unilateral recess of the talks by the United States and the strong demands for an explanation, actions far in excess of the Chinese reactions to the US violations. After several other somewhat ambiguous incidents of partisan firings and the strafing of communist supply vehicles, a Chinese military police platoon leader was killed in the neutral zone in an apparent partisan ambush. The next day the US negotiators refused to attend the funeral for fear of the implication of responsibility and of the propaganda value to the Chinese.

Then on 22 August the first of three incidents occurred in which the Communists asserted that UN planes violated the neutral zone, though the United States could find no evidence that US aircraft had been in the vicinity. Following the 22 August incident the Chinese, not to be outdone, unilaterally recessed the talks until 25 October. During this hiatus there were liaison officer meetings concerning violations of the neutral area, most notably those by US aircraft and a South Korean medical team. Following the strafing of Kaesong by a US plane on 20 September, Admiral Joy sent a letter of apology which impressed the Chinese. When the United States requested on 19 September that the liaison officers be allowed to settle the conditions for the resumption of talks, to discuss a new location for the talks and the details for neutralizing the site, the Communists agreed.

At the first liaison meeting the Communists appeared anxious to resume the talks, but the United States hesitated, preferring to focus on the details of a new site. The talks were delayed while negotiations were conducted by the liaison officers over a smaller side agenda. Accidents involving US pilot error continued to plague the talks with the most serious occurring the day after the liaison officers began to negotiate for a new location. A 12–year–old Korean boy was killed and his 2–year–old brother wounded by an F-80 pilot who cleared his machineguns over the neutral zone on his return to base. Although the United States accepted responsibility for the incident, the atmosphere for the liaison meetings was tense. Still, the meetings over a revised site security agreement continued until a settlement was reached and eventually ratified by Admiral Joy and General Nam Il.

Both the agreement over the revised security arrangements and the second agenda item reflect considerable compromise on the part of both parties, considering their initial negotiating position. However, the final agreement over the demarcation line and the demilitarized zone resulted in the virtual cease-fire that both sides had early declared they could not accept due to the advantage it gave the other. Even after the 30–day period, there was a reluctance on both sides to conduct a full-scale offensive. The longer the existing line of contact held, the more acceptable it was as a demarcation line. In the following two years both the PRC and the United States proved unwilling to commit the men and materiel necessary to make any major changes to the line of contact.

Agenda Items 3 and 4. The next two agenda items involved ceasefire arrangements and prisoners of war. The Chinese did not expect either of these to be particularly difficult subjects in light of the apparent change in attitude the United States had demonstrated during the later stages of the negotiations of item two. In fact the initial intensity with which the negotiations on item three began was of itself encouraging. Within 2 weeks of beginning the negotiations on item three, the communists agreed to open subcommittee talks on 11 December about item four concerning prisoners of war. Then on 6 February 1952 concurrent discussions began on the fifth and final item concerning the "recommendations to the governments of the countries concerned on both sides."

Not long after the negotiations over item three began, the lack of trust or confidence the United States had shown earlier in the communists reappeared and once again became the single biggest obstacle to a settlement. The United States demanded guarantees from its opponents that the United States was not willing to provide itself. For example, one of the biggest sticking points with respect to cease fire arrangements had been the US demand that airfields in North Korea not be repaired during the armistice. The purpose was to prevent the forward deployment of combat aircraft by the North. Yet the United States, sensitive to its own limited manpower resources, was unwilling to agree to a similar limitation on the rotation and replacement of its manpower—the Achilles' heel of the United States. That the United States eventually yielded on its unequal demands during the negotiation generated a cautious optimism among the Chinese concerning item four.

From the Chinese vantage, the US position on item four concerning POWs should have been straight forward since the US was the principal architect of Article 118 of the "Geneva Convention Relative to the Treatment of Prisoners of War, 12 August 1949." Article 118 requires that "Prisoners of war shall be released and repatriated without delay after the cessation of active hostilities." All prisoners are to be returned to their homeland and no circumstances justify any delay.[59] On the other hand, because of Chinese distrust of Western international law, that which justified the imperialist's exploitation of China, some of China's leaders focused on the potential for conflict in the POW issue. They doubted that the United States, an advocate of western international law, would easily allow for the application of Article 118 to include the PRC. Still the Chinese were unprepared for the defacto reversal by the United States of its stand on the Geneva Convention when it refused at Panmunjom to return all of its prisoners of war in exchange for the POWs held by the North.

After accepting "Western infidelity and while considering accepting a modified version of the US proposal, China's leaders were psychologically assaulted by the news that a large percentage of the Chinese prisoners held by the UN command were unwilling to return home. Unable to accept the "loss of face," disturbed by the "inequality of the US position," and recognizing the propaganda leverage they possessed given the focus in the United States on the worth of the individual, the Chinese felt compelled to use as many ways as possible to convince the world of the correctness of their position and to persuade the United States to change its policies.[60]

The variety of tactics employed covered virtually every conceivable option. Those emphasized by the West in describing the negotiations focus on the harshness of language and some of the less honest efforts by western convention, to generate a sense of shame on the part of the Americans. Because of cultural dissimilarities, these tactics were not as effective as they would have been in China; however, with respect to many of the allies and nonaligned nations, they created long-term attitudes more supportive of China.

Throughout this phase of the negotiations, the most effective levers on the United States were those involving manpower. Proposals and actions that appeared designed to weaken America's already vulnerable manpower capability were viewed by the United States as particularly dangerous, the most notable being the Communist proposal to put off replacements. Similarly the Chinese recognized the value of American prisoners as a bargaining chip and the pressure on Americans to avoid further casualties after the beginning of the Armistice talks. The concerns of the Americans about casualties and prisoners of war greatly enhanced the leverage potential of Chinese endurance.

Hard Bargaining and Closure

After two years of negotiations, intermittently conducted across the table in nearly 160 plenary sessions, an armistice agreement was signed on 27 August 1953. The later part of 1952 had been largely non-productive as the Chinese waited to see which US presidential candidate would win and if a change in presidents would mean a change in policy. The Eisenhower Administration, despite campaign rhetoric, didn't change the Chinese view of the situation much.

Courtesy Xinhua News Agency, Beijing

Liaison officers from China and the United States exchange documents of the Korean Armistic Agreement, 29 July 1953, Panmunjom. Final signing by commanders was held 27 August 1953.

With US concessions on cease-fire arrangements, and some adjustments on the POW issue, the Chinese finally agreed to the exchange of wounded and on an arrangement for the handling of prisoners after the armistice. The last few months moved fairly quickly after a solution was evident to both sides.

Yet as one Chinese interviewee noted, the PRC always retained a lever (similar to the use of the jade hostage in the example from the Warring State period in chapter 2) by which to insure compliance by the United States with the agreement. In addition, compliance with some aspect of each agreement was measured by how well the United States conformed to the "spirit of the agreement." Since the Chinese held the interpretive key, this criterion left the Chinese in the position to reopen the negotiations at any point during implementation that they felt it necessary to secure their interests.

Postconference Phase

Each of the first four articles of the Armistice Agreement resulted in virtually a separate regime to manage implementation. In working out the solution to agenda item five, it was agreed that in Article IV of the Armistice Agreement the military commanders of both sides would "recommend to the governments of the countries concerned on both sides that, within three (3) months after the Armistice Agreement is signed and becomes effective, a political conference of a higher level of both sides to be held."[61] This conference was to be assembled to work on a settlement of the political issues raised but set aside at Kaesong and Panmunjom. The United States expected that there would be a conference by October 30 and proceeded to consider various alternatives for the date, place, an acceptable agenda, participants, and the duration.[62] The PRC soon made it apparent through such third parties as Sweden and India that a conference was not automatic. Who attended must be determined first. The Chinese wanted a multilateral or roundtable arrangement that included neutral nations, whereas the US assumed a bilateral arrangement involving those nations that had participated in the war. Suddenly China had the initiative and the United States found itself renegotiating what was assumed to have already been settled.[63]

Ninety days after the signing of the Armistice, representatives of the United States and the PRC met at Panmunjom on 26 October, not to hold a political conference, but to negotiate the arrangements for such a conference. The Chinese representative was Huang Hua and the US representative was Arthur Dean. The talks were conducted using the same adversarial format as the armistice talks.

Huang Hua was skilled in dealing with Westerners while Arthur Dean was experiencing his first such exchange. The match was uneven, despite Dean's skills as a negotiator. The United States was determined not to legitimize the PRC. The PRC was even more determined not to be denied, especially in light of the efforts of the war. The subsequent failure of the talks to produce a bilateral political conference appears to have been foreordained, but for the Chinese the talks were necessary to (1) ascertain US resistance under the direction of Eisenhower and Dulles, (2) to enable an alternative to be found, and (3) to continue efforts to legitimize the PRC's claims in the eyes of others at the international level.

The conference failed to produce a bilateral meeting, but it did enable the Chinese to test the resolve of Dulles to not deal bilaterally. Second, an alternative arrangement was worked out through the Soviets in Berlin by which the political issues of the Korean War would be dealt with on a multilateral basis in an international conference in Geneva.

In Retrospect—A Chinese View

Chinese evaluations of the negotiations at Panmunjom have a lot in common with their evaluations of the war. The PRC was much more successful strategically than tactically. Marshall Peng Dehuai speaks of "victory won by our troops [because they] forced General Mark W. Clark [to say] 'In carrying out the instructions of my government, I gained the unenviable distinction of being the first United States army commander in history to sign an armistice without victory.'"[64]

Peng was right when he said that in "signing the armistice, I thought that the war had set a precedent for many years to come—something the people would rejoice at."[65] The war was an affirmation of Mao's assertion that China had stood up. The world knew that in Korea the Chinese had fought a powerful allied army, representing the most modern and best of the West, and had not lost. China could not be ignored. However, tactically the war revealed to the PLA's leaders just how weak their forces were and just how thin the line that separated success from failure. The victory had been nearly Pyrrhic in nature.[66]

The negotiations were likewise successful—at considerable cost. The international community was forced to accept China as a major international actor that could no longer be ignored. On the other hand, the United States successfully avoided any formal actions that might have legitimized the government of the PRC, including membership in the United Nations. Still it was clear to all of Asia that China would play a major role in their future, a fact which worried many.

In terms of accomplishments, the war and the subsequent negotiations enabled the Chinese to forge, in the eyes of those interviewed, an internal consensus around a set of foreign policy principles that have provided a strong thread of continuity and sense of direction in China's foreign policy ever since then. The negotiations did not accomplish many of the stated objectives, such as admission to the United Nations or the return of Taiwan. Rather they set the stage for a step-by-step (*yibu yibu*) achievement of a few small successes at a time—the practical strategy of the weak against the strong, providing there is consistency in objectives and constancy in effort.

The negotiations opened the door for Chinese participation in future international conferences, such as the Geneva Talks of 1954 and the Bandung Conference. China had earned its spurs as a major power in the Pacific. Others now demanded China's participation.

Other lessons learned were that the traditional reliance in China on a third party as a mediator was not very practical in the international environment. The cultural demands of face that insured that the mediator had a stake in a solution acceptable to both sides were not operative in the international context. Other nations had their own interests that often made them poor mediators, no matter how good their intentions. Both India and the USSR as the principal third parties did not meet Chinese expectations. In future negotiations the Chinese relied heavily on third parties in order to avoid direct approaches, but never again did China put much faith in a third party as a mediator.

To some extent the Chinese experience with the technology of the West in Korea was at the expense of their own self-confidence. Most of those interviewed felt that the United States knew more about China than the Chinese knew about the US and that the US had the technological capability to exploit this knowledge. Of course the Chinese have had a few specialists who were very knowledgable about the United States, people who on a man-for-man basis are probably better than the China specialists of the United States. However, general ignorance among China's leaders has greatly hampered the effectiveness of China's Americanologists. The result is a great deal of suspicion about American intentions in any particular negotiation. Meaning is given to actions far beyond that intended by the responsible American because of Chinese fear of the technological capability of the United States to coordinate the implementation of policy.

Lastly, there were techniques that were used that have been perpetuated. For example, when representing China in a negotiation type forum, a Chinese diplomat speaks in Chinese and provides a interpreter to enable his guest to understand. Having stood up the Chinese people should be proud of their language and as Chinese use it when officially representing their country. Of course there are also certain tactical advantages that result from this procedure. Many Chinese diplomats understand English and thus gain the extra time during the Chinese translation to think through their response. The process is tiring and thus allows the Chinese negotiator to have an edge in manipulating his opponent both physically and mentally.

With the passage of time the vituperation, rage, and violence of the insults that were so common at Panmunjom have been tempered. However, the humiliation that inspired these violent emotions is still there, especially among the older generation that personally experienced the second class treatment of the Chinese by the West, whether in China or abroad as students. Actions by Americans that stir these submerged feelings bring a rapid and sure response that surprises most Americans in its intensity and moralistic tone.

Panmunjom was the first major and probably the single most important set of experiences of the Chinese in instilling in China's foreign policy community what has become the PRC's approach to Sino-American negotiations. Many of the tactics and techniques employed at Panmunjom have changed or evolved, either because of the change in the overall nature of Sino-American relations or because of the greater sophistication and experience that has been accruing within the foreign policy community in dealings with Western cultures. These changes have led many of the Westerners interviewed to believe that there is no relationship between the Chinese approach to the Armistice negotiations and negotiations conducted in the 1970s and 1980s. However, in summarizing the Chinese perspective discussed in this chapter, the strategic approach of Beijing to Sino-American negotiations that guided China's negotiators at Panmunjom, as well as many of the tactics and techniques they employed, remain fundamentally unchanged.

5.
CASE II: GENEVA AND WARSAW

The talks' accomplishments, though significant, were considerably more modest than had been hoped. In retrospect I can see that the two countries were just too far apart and too deeply wary of each other as to permit major progress. Neither side would make the concessions considered by the other as prerequisite to healthy relations.

—U. Alexis Johnson, 1984

FROM THE VANTAGE OF HINDSIGHT both Ambassadors Wang Bingnan and U. Alexis Johnson have recorded in their memoirs their opinions of the "specific conditions" or "fundamental realities" that delimited their talks in Geneva. Like the difference between describing a half glass of water as either half full or half empty, their descriptions differ little in fact but suggest significant differences in what motivated each side to enter into the talks, in their negotiating styles, and in the perceptions of each concerning the results of the talks.

The PRC Prepares

When the talks began on 1 August 1955, Ambassador Wang was one of the PRC's most experienced diplomats in dealing with Americans. He had been a close assistant of Zhou Enlai's throughout the 1940s and the early 1950s, including the talks with General Marshall and Ambassador Leighton Stuart and the Geneva Conferences on Korea and Indochina.

In assessing Ambassador Wang's many qualifications for the job, English could not have been at the top of the list of requirements, because as he and others have noted, his "English was not so good."[1] Rather he says that he was selected over several other candidates because he "had experience in maintaining contacts with different types of Americans and because Premier Zhou knew me and trusted me very much."[2]

The selection of Wang Bingnan meant that the Ambassadorial Talks were to reflect more of Zhou's personality and his more traditional style than did the negotiations at Panmunjom. There Zhou's influence had been diluted by competition and his absence from Beijing for several months to convalesce at Luda during the formative period of preparations for the Korean talks.[3] Under Zhou's leadership the Ambassadorial Talks were to enable the Chinese to exploit more fully international convention, the views of other nations, the American perspective and differences in American views.

Following receipt of the telegram notifying him of his responsibilities, Wang Bingnan says he felt a great deal of stress. He worried about failing. As the PRC ambassador in Warsaw, he was a long way from Beijing, communications were difficult and sluggish, and during his previous diplomatic experiences he had relied on Zhou's "teachings and direct instructions." He would have to make many "decisions, analyses, and judgments ... with regard to many things, [as well as make] suggestions to the government.

The situation was complicated, and . . . was a matter of prime importance, to which the whole world paid close attention."[4] He was greatly reassured to learn that a task force or "guiding group" composed of many old friends had been set up directly under Premier Zhou (who was concurrently Foreign Minister) to "devise measures to be taken at the talks." Qiao Guanhua, a "talented scholar" and friend for whom Wang Bingnan had the highest regard, was the key member of this group as well as the official through whom Ambassador Wang reported.[5] As an extension of this talented support structure and with much personal preparation Ambassador Wang went to Geneva well prepared to accomplish his task in the "several meetings" that he and the leadership in Beijing expected would be necessary.

By 1955 the leadership of the PRC was sufficiently confident of its domestic position and of how well its basic policies with respect to the country's fundamental interests of security, development, and independence were being implemented to be more flexible tactically. World revolution, for example, remained an important objective, but one for which a variety of less radical and often conventional tactics now also became applicable. As Ambassador Wang has said, "the new period of unfolding work in foreign affairs in an all-round manner had arrived."[6] This flexibility, born of confidence and pragmatism, included an initiative to develop relations with the US.

Although this initiative was potentially beneficial to all three of the PRC's fundamental interests, independence was the principal objective. As one senior Chinese official remarked when interviewed, "If the US could have been convinced to accept the PRC as an independent equal, the rest of the Western world would have followed suit." It was a policy designed to reinforce the growing national and international awareness of China as a major, independent power free of external domination.

Until 1954, violence had been the principal means by which the PRC had been able to gain respect for its policies.

According to Wang Bingnan "The United States (had been) compelled to make contacts with us and to acknowledge the fact that New China had stood up."[7] Yet compelling contact was a long way from being able to compel the US to accept the PRC as a sovereign equal. Acceptance required a change of attitude that could only come about through the development of agreements in principle at the policy level and the development of interest and understanding on a "people to people" basis. But to do so required a change of tactics.

As the contrast with "sour" enhances the pleasure of "sweet", the still fresh memories of World War II and Korea and the renewed possibility of Sino-American conflict enhanced the appeal, particularly at Bandung, of Zhou's proffered principle of "seeking a community of views while preserving points of difference."[8] It was with this principle in mind that the Chinese determined that the Ambassadorial Talks "had to emphasize discussing some substantial problems such as the Taiwan issue, make arrangements for direct talks between Secretary of State Dulles and Premier Zhou Enlai, and the establishment of cultural ties between the two countries."[9] This was a step-by-step agenda, not one designed to solve all the problems at once. While discussions of contentious issues were necessary to find the common ground, only practical results were sought that could be accomplished in "several meetings" and set the stage for the next round of negotiations.

The United States Prepares

Conversely Secretary of State Dulles was more defensive of the status quo. He "did not expect much substance to take place, (although) he did approve of the idea of the talks."[10] Dulles had been an early advocate of the admission of the PRC to the United Nations, but China's entry into the Korean War changed his mind. The "Formosa crisis" that emerged in the fall of 1954 convinced him of the implacable nature of that issue. To him the PRC obviously wanted the United States out of the Western Pacific altogether, an area of major interest to the US. Therefore, to Dulles, recognition of the PRC should be withheld so long as the PRC's policies reflected this objective of expulsion. His response to the PRC, as a perceived expansionist power, was reinforced by vigorous domestic opposition to any efforts that appeared to favor Beijing over Taipei and by the anger of the American people over the imprisonment of Americans in the PRC, the Korean War and the loss of China. Dulles was also concerned that US recognition would encourage others to do the same and would raise the question of recognition for East Germany.[11] At the same time Dulles was under a lot of counter pressure from the international community to negotiate with the Chinese. Many nations felt that world peace required a Sino-American rapprochement.

The talks provided Dulles with a means to open a dialogue with the PRC concerning American citizens imprisoned in China, thereby offering hope to the international community and, by negotiating for the release of American prisoners, not offending domestic interests. He was able to shunt aside both the domestic and the international pressures for behavior that he felt was too extreme, behavior that he thought sacrificed US interests.

His immediate goal for the talks was to obtain the release of all of the American citizens held as prisoners in China. His longer term hope was to continue the talks as long as possible in an effort to develop an acceptance by the Chinese of the need for a peaceful solution to the Taiwan problem. The emphasis in the West on law and Dulles' own successes as a lawyer translated this second objective into a US requirement for the Chinese to formally renounce the use of force in solving the Taiwan problem.

What appeared logical and reasonable to the United States was received by the Chinese as an insult to their newly won independence. To renounce any portion of the revolution's costly won sovereignty, especially at the demand of a western imperialistic power, was unthinkable. This conflict with new China's concept of sovereignty increasingly became intractable during the negotiations. The absence of reciprocal trust precluded the compromises essential to a mutually beneficial agreement. Both sides misread the intentions of the other. With their focus on agreements in principle, the Chinese initially believed there was more common ground for agreement than existed. For the US progress meant legal agreements, the unattainability of which lead to the United States underestimating the common ground.

More the exception than the rule for US and PRC negotiators, U. Alexis Johnson and Wang Bingnan were in many ways a matched pair. Like his counterpart, Ambassador Johnson relied heavily upon his interpreter during the talks. He had begun his foreign service career as a Japanese language student in Japan about the same time Wang was studying in Germany. Also like Wang his long association with Sino-American relations began prior to World War II, though in Johnson's case more at the fringes. From language training he made his way through consular posts in Seoul, Korea, Tientsin (Tianjin), China and Mukden (Shenyang), China during the early years of Japan's occupation of North China to internment by the Japanese following the bombing of Pearl Harbor. Following repatriation he returned to the Far East when MacArthur's forces entered the Philippines and continued with them on to the occupation of Japan. Returning to Washington in 1949 he was soon caught up in the Korean War, eventually becoming the "highest-ranking person in the Department to have sustained involvement with Korea through both the Truman and Eisenhower Administrations from the beginning of the war in June 1950 to the signing of the armistice in July 1953."[12]

He first met Wang Bingnan when they were both serving as the Secretary-General of their respective delegations to the 1954 Geneva Conferences on Korea and Indochina. His first negotiations with Ambassador Wang also occurred during this period in a series of private meetings concerning US citizens interned in China and Chinese citizens detained in the United States.

However, Ambassador Johnson was never as closely associated with Sino-American policy as Ambassador Wang was nor as close to Dulles as Wang was to Zhou Enlai. While the relationship may have appeared similar to the Chinese, Johnson never enjoyed the intimate knowledge of Dulles that long years of close association enabled Wang to enjoy of Zhou.

In terms of staff, the excesses of the McCarthy era had deprived Dulles of the services of those China specialists with unique insight into the thinking of the new leaders of China. There was relatively little advice to balance the insights of those more knowledgeable of the Nationalists. Whether because of his own management style or because of these shortages, Dulles tended to manage the development of policy toward the talks through staff competition rather than by a task force. During the early months of the talks he generally arbitrated the differences, including the use of input from Johnson, himself. Only months later did he delegate these responsibilities to others. As a result Dulles' initial guidance to Ambassador Johnson may have been a little less finite than that given to Ambassador Wang, Johnson's preparation a little less thorough, and a bit more may have been left to Johnson's judgment in execution. However, the differences were relatively small and not noticeable across the table to Ambassador Johnson, who remembers Ambassador Wang as a very effective and worthy adversary.[13]

Prenegotiation Phase—Panmunjom to Geneva

Even as Huang Hua and Arthur Dean sat down to talk at Panmunjom in October 1953, Zhou Enlai was considering the next step in dealing with the United States. Domestically the Party's progress in consolidating control and establishing effective government provided a foundation for China's "new period in foreign affairs." The major obstacle to achieving the "fundamental interests of the people" was the United States. "Since it lost China, it turned Japan into its major strategic base in the East, armed Taiwan, established a foothold in Vietnam, and increased its control over other Asian countries. The United States established battlefields encircling the PRC in a planned way, simultaneously blocked China's entrance into the United Nations, and implemented an economic blockade against China."[14]

Zhou's challenge was to guide, with relatively little apparent negotiating leverage, the development of an independent foreign policy in the face of a wary and overbearing ally, the USSR, and a powerful adversary, the United States. However, the success of the PLA in Korea had provided an unexpected windfall. According to Ambassador Wang, "The United States, through its defeat (in Korea), came to realize New China's strength." So did the other nations of the region, including the USSR. From a national security viewpoint the Chinese felt more secure, "The general situation in Asia was relaxed due to the Korean war truce."[15] However, the greatest significance of the "victory" in Korea for Beijing, particularly from Zhou's vantage, was the change in the political realities of East Asia that would eventually insure a greater role for China at the expense of the US and the West.

Several other events occurred in the next 2 years that also had a significant impact on the "specific conditions" that led to the Ambassadorial Talks. Through these events the Chinese further probed and attempted to influence the interests, intentions and perceptions of Americans. Chinese experiences with these events likewise shaped their own views. The first of these events was the pre-political conference talks between Ambassadors Huang Hua and Arthur Dean at Panmunjom. These were followed by the 1954 quadripartite meeting in Berlin, the Geneva Conference of 1954, the first Taiwan Strait crisis, and the Bandung Conference.

Dean-Huang Talks at Panmunjom, 1953-54

A political conference was to have convened within ninety days from the signing of the armistice agreement on July 27. However, China and the United States couldn't agree on who should attend the conference. The PRC wanted to move away from a bilateral conference format by inviting neutral nations to attend. Zhou argued that "there appeared no possibility of a conference being held in a more friendly spirit of having any change to succeed unless neutrals participate."[16] The neutrals which China preferred were "non-Communist Asian countries with which Peiping had diplomatic relations."[17] This short list included India, which President Rhee of South Korea adamantly opposed as being too close to the Communists.

The United States sought to keep a bilateral format and wanted the USSR invited as a belligerent. The PRC countered that the USSR should be a neutral. During the course of this exchange, in an early September conversation with Indian Ambassador Raghaven concerning the PRC's response to the UN General Assembly resolution of 28 August 1953, Zhou applied a little pressure on a friend by remarking about Liu Shaochi's opposition to sending a reply.[18] Zhou was suggesting that he was concerned about the effect on his own position "if, in an effort to keep negotiations open and notwithstanding the fact that the Chinese had, from their own viewpoint, already made substantial concessions to meet the United States stand, the

Chinese reply would lead to no modification [of the] US position."[19] Such pressure applied to a "friend" ideally encourages them to work harder for a desired result in order to protect their Chinese "friend."

In a private conversation with Arthur Dean in early October, the Indians suggested that an emissary might be sent for preconference discussions with the Chinese. Dean's favorable response apparently triggered a message of 10 October from the PRC reiterating that the political conference should include neutrals and that the PRC was ready to meet with the US representative to discuss arrangements for the conference.[20] The United States responded favorably through the Swedish Government on October 12.[21]

Courtesy Xinhua News Agency, Beijing

Arthur Dean, center, at the Dean-Huang talks, Panmunjom, 26 October-12 December 1953.

The talks between Arthur Dean and Huang Hua began on 26 October 1953. they discussed arrangements for the political conference called for in the Korean Armistice Agreement, including Communist insistence that the conference must precede the release of the POWs who had refused repatriation. They continued until Dean walked out on 12 December 1953 at the end of an "uninterrupted 5-hour and 45 minutes meeting" involving an "increasing tempo of rude, arrogant intemperance and increasingly insulting abuse" from Huang Hua, including his now famous comment about the "perfidy" of the United States in "conniving with Rhee to release 27,000 prisoners after General Harrison had signed terms of reference in June," and the US had guaranteed that Rhee would abide by the agreement.[22]

Although Dean returned to the States, his deputy, Kenneth Young, and the Chinese delegation remained at Panmunjom, where both sides continued through a series of liaison meetings to seek a formula by which to reconvene the preconference talks. Dean's demand for a retraction of the term "perfidy" eventually involved a reciprocal demand from the Chinese concerning Dean's description of the PRC as an "agent" of the Soviet Union. He made this remark on 28 October (the PRC took formal exception the next day) during his argument that the USSR should participate in the conference in order to carry out the obligations toward Korea it undertook at Cairo, Potsdam, and Moscow.[23] The Chinese were insulted by his remark, both because the PRC is an independent power and because the PRC should be the key Communist power, not the USSR, in the resolution of the Korea issues.[24] In effect both sides demanded concessions, essentially on the grounds of honor, that the other was unwilling to make—at least until other objectives were achieved.

This channel of communications remained open until the fifth meeting of the liaison secretaries held on 26 January 1954. After delivering a letter for Arthur Dean and a brief summary of their position on the talks, the Chinese requested a recess. They then unilaterally implemented their own request by walking out, as Dean had done.[25] At least in theory the fate of the talks was left open, although in practice the foreign ministers meeting in Berlin soon ended the utility of the talks.

As the talks progressed and the impossibility of Korea becoming unified became even more apparent, there was an increase in value of the talks to the United States as a vehicle for preventing the Chinese from achieving their objectives and a decrease in the value of the talks as a tool for the creation of new relationships. The talks were useful in helping to "prevent damaging actions in the UN General Assembly" concerning "Chinese representation in the United Nations, China trade, etc." Furthermore it was important to continue to talk because the "Imminence of a [political] conference [would] help counteract Russian pressure at Berlin for a Five-Power Conference and for a discussion of other Asian questions as a means of relaxing international tensions."[26]

The talks at Panmunjom were more important to the Chinese as an opportunity to influence the international alignment of political power as it then affected China and as a means of communications with Washington. To the international community the assertiveness and hostility of Beijing, as exemplified by Huang Hua's strident and demanding style, reinforced the opinion of many, notable the Indians and the British, that if progress was to be made over the Korea issue and peace maintained in East Asia, the US would have to try to wean the PRC away from the USSR and be more accommodating to China's demands for a greater role in East Asia. These growing differences over China policy added to the existing strain in British-American relations over Asian policy. Because of the importance of Europe to Americans, these differences aggravated similar strains among the foreign policy elite of the US.[27] For the Indians, who like the Chinese were also seeking to refurbish their national identify after a hundred years of Western influence, the talks provided another opportunity to enhance their role in Asian politics. From the perspective of Dulles the efforts of the Indians, especially those of Krishna Menon, were abetted by the Chinese and tended to produce results largely at the expense of the United States. Without the pressures of an alliance with the US as the British had, the Indians were not hesitant about taking positions openly antithetical to US interests.[28]

Second, the talks provided Beijing with a means to judge reactions in the United States to changes in the Chinese position and to explore variations in the American position. In the Armistice Agreement both sides agreed that the purposes of the political conference would be "to settle through negotiations the questions of the withdrawal of all foreign forces from Korea, the peaceful settlement of the Korean question, etc.,"[29] and the disposition of unrepatriated prisoners of war.[30] However, absent a conference, unilateral actions began to erode these purposes and to elevate others. In the months following the armistice agreement, the Chinese aggressively strengthened the bonds between North Korea and the PRC through economic assistance and reconstruction.[31] Defenses were greatly enhanced and some Chinese troops were withdrawn.[32] Apparently with these ongoing changes in mind, Huang Hua told a member of the Indian delegation that the Communist delegation was prepared to keep Dean in preliminary talks well into May 1954.[33] With the release of 22,000 Korean prisoners of war to civilian status on January 23, 1954, the US announcement of the withdrawal of two divisions, and the decreasing probability of a unilateral ROK attack on the North, the objectives of the armistice were slowly taking on a de facto existence. On the other hand, unification of the type sought by either side was increasingly apparent to all to be impossible.[34]

The talks apparently were as frustrating for the Chinese as they were for the Americans. They told the Indians that they found the Americans to be "the 'trickiest,' most difficult people in the world to deal with," including the Russians.[35] The cultural barrier to understanding was high, in spite of the expertise on the PRC's various staffs. Nevertheless there were signs that the PRC's leaders had begun to develop, as the result of nearly 3 years of talks, an appreciation of some of the factors that influenced the development of US policy. It had become increasingly clear that the President and the Secretary of State were not as powerful as the Chinese might have assumed. In addition to the pressures from allies, the President had to contend with the Congress and the American public in the development of foreign policy far more than they would have assumed from experiences in their own system. However, as experiences in latter years were to indicate, their understanding of the relationship between the President and the Congress does not appear to have been very well developed or accurate. Still, from their observations they fairly accurately deduced that the United States would avoid a political conference until the POW problem was resolved and that the US primarily wanted a conference in order to shunt aside pressures to convene the General Assembly over Korea and to minimize demands by the USSR at Berlin for an American acceptance of a Five-Power Conference.[36]

Berlin, 1954

Dulles wanted the talks at Panmunjom to resume prior to the beginning of the January 1954 quadripartite meeting of the Foreign Ministers of the United States, the United Kingdom, France, and the USSR. The German and Austrian questions were a full agenda without giving the Soviets the subject of East Asia as a divisive issue with which to manipulate the three Western powers. Indochina had become the biggest crisis in Asia and each of the Western powers had a different solution. Korea was already a source of contention between the US and its allies, a fact which the

Soviets were sure to use as a lever. Dulles would have difficulty in deflecting any Soviet initiative concerning Korea without demonstrating some progress at Panmunjom toward a political conference.

The meeting convened in Berlin on January 25 with no political conference on Korea in sight. This fact left the United States vulnerable to the USSR's proposal for a five-power conference, which would include the PRC, to deal broadly with world peace. Further weakening the US position was the fact that US policy did not preclude negotiation before recognition (the United States had been negotiating regularly with the PRC at Panmunjom since 1951). Furthermore, the French position in Indochina was rapidly deteriorating, forcing the French to seek negotiations if anything in Indochina was to be salvaged. Finally since France, Britain, and the USSR all accepted and argued that the problems of East Asia could not be worked out without a greater role for the PRC, the United States acceded to the inclusion of the PRC in a multilateral conference, but only as it concerned Korea and Indochina.[37] Secretary Dulles attempted to minimize the significance of the participation of the PRC by insisting that a disclaimer be accepted by the other three powers to the effect that such a conference would not constitute recognition of the PRC by the United States and that the conference would not be a five-power conference with a worldwide agenda.[38] As a result the conference communique proposed a conference at Geneva to deal with the problems of Korea and Indochina. Interested parties, including the PRC would be invited, but "neither the invitation to, not the holding of, the above mentioned conference shall be deemed to imply diplomatic recognition in any case where it has not already been accorded."[39] These restrictions had more domestic political significance than international. Due to the tensions in Asia, the narrow focus of the two conferences and the list of invited parties had the effect of raising, not lowering, the importance of the conferences for the international community. Second, the recognition formula merely stated the obvious, that each state reserved unto itself the right to extend recognition to another. In seeking protection behind such a statement, the United States passed the propaganda advantage to China. Third, formal avoidance of the description of the conference as a five-power conference was fairly easy. But avoiding the appearance of a five-power conference was hard, especially when the Chinese referred to it as a five-power conference and appeared at the conference with a delegation as large as or larger than the four other major powers.[40] The Geneva Conference was, according to Foreign Minister Molotov, a step up from the "low level" negotiations at Panmunjom.[41] Molotov's perceptions reflected those of the Chinese, for they also anticipated that the PRC's "first international conference as a big power" would be "a turning point for New China's playing an important role in world affairs."[42]

Geneva, 1954

Zhou was instructed by the central committee that his delegation should "strengthen our (PRC) diplomatic and international activities in order to counter the US imperialist policies of blockade and embargo, arms expansion, and war preparation, and promote relaxation of the tense world situation. At the same time, [the delegation should do its] utmost to reach some agreement, so as to help open the road to solving international disputes through negotiations by the big powers."[43] As during the Dean-Huang Talks, Beijing placed greater priority during the Geneva Conference on changing the conditions that determined China's relations with the United States and the West than on the specific subject of the conference. While Korea's future was important and an agreement was actively pursued, the conference subject was more a means than an end. The "correlation of forces" in Korea did not favor a unified

Korea on the terms of the Communist Party, so unification would have to wait. The process was more important than the written result.

Zhou Enlai's tactical interpretation of these instructions to his staff was that "it was necessary to open up a new situation in our country's diplomatic front through this conference, so that more countries would understand New China, and [that China] should strive to establish diplomatic relations with them." The feeling was that "Many countries dared not recognize China because of their lack of understanding or because they were subjected to pressure by the United States."[44] The observations of both attendees and observers suggest that the Chinese were reasonably successful in dealing with the problem of understanding.[45] Clearly the views of other countries about the PRC began to change or to be attenuated. Perceptions of Zhou Enlai changed even more, with the majority of the observations being very complimentary of him, even from among some of the US delegation.[46]

A good impression was important to Zhou. Wang Bingnan was assigned to organize and prepare the delegation. Planning was done in great detail, down to "solemn . . . tunic suits . . . for every member of the delegation." The delegation was large, both for purposes of training and "to demonstrate New China's strength in foreign affairs." It included two chefs that Zhou specifically requested in order that the delegation "could invite guests to dinner and make friends during the conference."[47]

To the Chinese appearance and impressions were important, they set the tone, a sort of moral righteousness. In the same vein they closely observed their opponents. To them Secretary Dulles, with his glasses and perennially taut expression, appeared "stern and grim." "He spoke insolently" and "his language was vilifying and his attitude arrogant." By contrast Zhou delivered his speech "sternly with a sense of justice and dignity."[48] Attitudes are very important. In another incident Assistant Secretary Walter

Robertson made a speech that the Chinese interpreted as an unfavorable reversal from the position that Deputy Secretary Walter Bedell Smith had taken the day before. Zhou reacted strongly, reminding Robertson, who was "left speechless and flush with embarrassment," that he had known him when Robertson had been a member of the Marshall mission in China and that his attitude, which Zhou resented, had not improved.[49]

The conference as it pertained to Korea opened on 26 April with 19 delegations and closed on 15 June 1954. Despite Dulles' success at Berlin in avoiding the designation of the Geneva meeting as a five-power conference, the Chinese treated the conference—according to Wang's memoirs—as if it was a five-power conference involving a bilateral confrontation between East and West.[50] The USSR, PRC, Korean, and Vietnamese delegations were "closely united," meeting frequently outside the meetings and coordinating with each other during the meetings. Since the "Military Demarcation Line was already settled, the . . . problem was to ensure our [the communist powers'] political power."[51]

Despite the lack of a conference agreement, for the Chinese the conference did "help open the road to solving international disputes through negotiations by the big powers." The conference was a watershed in terms of the ease with which the United States had formerly obtained international support for its policy toward China. From now on US views would be more easily challenged, as indicated by the ease with which a few mistranslated words nearly destroyed, in the last moments of the conference, the unity that the United States had maintained among the Western nations throughout the conference.[52] The difference in Western views was made even more evident during the conference by the dramatic establishment of diplomatic relations between Britain and China at the level of chargés d'affaires.[53] To make matters worse, within a few days after the close of the conference Dulles found himself making a frantic effort to shore up the French lest they also recognize the Chinese.[54] Negotiations with the United States were the keystone of the Chinese objectives, and now pressures on the United States to negotiate would increase even more rapidly in the months and years ahead. Over the next decade an average of three countries per year would normalize relations with the PRC, including three Korean War allies, two of whom were major powers—Britain ('54), Netherlands ('54), and France ('64)—and more than half of the newly independent African states.[55] Accompanying this shift would be a less easily quantified but nevertheless an ever greater disagreement over US policy toward Taiwan.

As the meeting on Korea approached the end without any "fruitful agreement," Zhou proposed a "fair and reasonable suggestion" for resuming the talks in the future that the United States "refused to accept."[56] Despite this failure to keep an opening by which to resume the conference at some future date, a means of continued contact with the US was eventually established.

On May 26, Huang Hua, Counselor in the Ministry of Foreign Affairs and spokesman for the Chinese delegation (and Arthur Dean's counterpart at Panmunjom), indicated in an off-the-record press conference that the Chinese were prepared to meet with the US delegation to discuss the problem of each country's nationals retained in the other country. The following day Huan Xiang, Director of the West European and African Affair Department of the Foreign Ministry, met with Humphrey Trevelyan, British Chargé d'Affaires in Beijing (both members of their respective delegation to the conference) and confirmed that the Chinese were prepared to meet if the US representatives made a direct approach or if they were introduced by Trevelyn. Huan made it clear that the Chinese were unwilling to discuss further with Trevelyn that which should be discussed directly with the United States.

The Chinese refusal to continue dealing with the British as a go-between forced the United States to decide between either meeting with Trevelyn and the Chinese or dropping the issue.[57] Dulles' initial response was to drop the issue for he feared that such a meeting would be construed as an opening step toward diplomatic recognition.[58] However, his cable crossed one from Under Secretary Smith, now head of the delegation in Geneva, recommending the meeting be held for humanitarian reasons. In the ensuing exchange Dulles reversed himself and concurred in having representatives from the US delegation accompany Trevelyn to one meeting with the Chinese.[59] The sequence of events left some of Dulles' staff believing that the British abetted the Chinese in this maneuver in order to get the US to negotiate directly with the PRC.[60]

U. Alexis Johnson was selected to represent the United States, as Wang Bingnan has observed, "only after careful consideration as to what signals would be sent by the selection of a specific representative.[61] Under Secretary Smith initially recommended Edwin Martin, Deputy Director of the Office of Chinese Affairs for his country expertise, but switched to his deputy, Assistant Secretary of State for Far Eastern Affairs, Walter S. Robertson, when Trevelyn pointed out that the Chinese wanted the name and rank of the US participants in advance, as they are "obsessed with equal footing." Trevelyn recommended that the US representative be at least equal to a Chinese department head as they have direct access to Zhou.[62] Dulles may have vetoed Robertson because his position was higher than Trevelyan's recommendations, but more probably because of his strong and rather inflexible anti-Communist stand. Instead, he selected Ambassador Johnson, Secretary–General of the US delegation. He reasoned that Ambassador Johnson was "accredited to a Communist country [Czechoslovakia] and had had experience in negotiations with Chinese re Korea." Reading between the lines, Dulles also judged Johnson to be a more imaginative and flexible negotiator than Robertson.[63] The US selection prompted the Chinese to send Ambassador Wang Bingnan, Secretary-

General of the Chinese delegations, after Zhou obtained approval from the Politburo.[64]

The first of a series of four meetings between Wang and Johnson was held on 5 June and the last on 21 June.[65] For the first and second meetings Johnson accompanied Trevelyn. The first was administrative because the Chinese had conflicting plans and only met to take advantage of Trevelyan's presence before he returned to Beijing.[66] At the second meeting Wang both rewarded the United States for the direct contact and raised hopes about future cooperation by unilaterally stating that the PRC would arrange the exchange of mail, heretofore prohibited, between American civilians imprisoned in China and their relatives. Wang noted that military prisoners were a separate matter to be discussed later. Before the meeting ended Wang expressed his appreciation for Trevelyan's help but added that since he would soon leave Geneva and there would be "many more meetings," he need not attend anymore. Wang's timing was excellent. Secretary Dulles had instructed Johnson to try to have the British present at all meetings to minimize the direct nature of the contact, but he had also decided to have at least three meetings, depending on the progress on the meetings, in hopes of "obtaining the release of at least some Americans" before cutting off the contact.[67] The establishment of direct, bilateral contact with the US over the objections of Secretary Dulles was a small victory in terms of principles for the Chinese, and an important step toward their goal of recognition.

During the course of these meetings Wang tried to get Johnson to accept several other proposals of a political nature that were designed to move Sino-American relations a little closer to recognition. There was a proposal for joint records, one for a joint statement that the "nationals of each in [the] territory of [the] other be allowed to return to their homeland," and one for a third party to represent each country's interests (a protecting power) in the other country. All were rejected for the reason they were perceived to have been requested, they were political steps toward recognition.[68]

At the last meeting, Johnson provided Wang with the names of 15 Chinese students whose cases had been reviewed and were now free to leave the United States. After raising the question of a joint communique for the second time, Wang raised for the first time the topic of third party representation. He pointed out that in 1950 the United States asked the UK to take charge of US interests in China, but that conditions at the time made this impossible. Now the PRC was ready to consider this on a mutual basis. The United States could ask a third country with diplomatic relations with both Beijing and Washington to take charge of American interests in China and the PRC would likewise request a third country with diplomatic relations with both parties to take charge of the interests of Chinese nationals and students in the US. Although the United States had decided before the meeting to end the Wang-Johnson talks, Johnson used the fact that Wang had raised a subject beyond the scope of the talks to point out that further discussions were no longer necessary. Since their remaining business now consisted of exchanging information, staff officers could be designated to pass the information. Johnson further recommended that after the Geneva Conference both parties use the services of Trevelyn in China. Wang only agreed to the exchange of information at the staff level during the remainder of the conference, of which there were subsequently two such exchanges.

At the second staff meeting, the Chinese announced that six Americans' exit permits had been approved (in an effort to generate a sense of obligation on the part of the United States to reciprocate) and then raised again the question of third party representation. The United States would not discuss the question nor would the Chinese consider using Trevelyn, the British Charge in Beijing, since it was not proposed on the "basis of equality and reciprocity." Dr. Pu Shan was prepared to depart when Alfred Jenkins suggested that the information could be exchanged between their respective consulate generals in Geneva.[69] Pu Shan took note of the comment. A week later the first meeting to exchange information took place in Geneva on 29 July. Ten more meetings of this kind followed during the next twelve months.

The administrative details for the private meetings between Wang and Johnson reflect an often repeated scene in Sino-American negotiations. When there is an issue to be discussed, there is a clear preference on the part of the Chinese for conducting the talks across a conference table. The arrangement of the two parties on opposite sides in orderly rows conveys an appropriately solemn and dignified air with the table in between formally demarcating space and thereby symbolizing the conflict of interest to be discussed. When the subject for discussion is more congenial, whether after the completion of a successful negotiation or to exchange information, the meeting will probably take place in a reception room where the seating arrangement usually calls for the senior person of each side to sit in adjoining chairs with the US guest on his host's right. Their respective delegations are then seated in rank order down their principal's side of the U or V pattern of chairs.

```
   oo            oo
 o    o       o      o
 o    o    o            o
```

Although these arrangements depend upon the facility, it appears that the more open the arrangement, the more social and less substantive the discussion in terms of details. Nor should the senior US participant be surprised if he finds the two senior participants facing a southern exposure.

Johnson arranged the first meeting and, desiring to establish a congenial atmosphere, arranged to have only soft chairs in the room. Wang Bingnan felt that the room "had the feel of a reception room, rather than a conference

Courtesy Xinhua News Agency, Beijing

An example of the U-pattern of chairs, with senior participants facing "south." Chou Enlai, Mao Zedong, Richard Nixon, and Henry Kissinger meet in Mao's famous library, Beijing, 1972.

room," so he arranged for the second meeting to have a table across which to conduct the discussions.[70] Johnson logically interpreted this to be somewhat of a return to the confrontation tactics of Panmunjom although that was not the exact intent.[71]

Zhou achieved a number of big successes at the Geneva Conferences, but with respect to progress toward recognition of the PRC by the United States, he had to be content with some rather hard to measure steps in that direction. The international community had perceived some movement and the private meetings between Wang and Johnson had resulted in direct contact and in an agreement, at the last minute, to maintain a more limited form of this contact through the United States and PRC consulate-generals in Geneva. Though not very visible to the public and at a lower level of contact on a very narrow subject, it was nevertheless a means of communications with the United States on very nearly a normal diplomatic basis as opposed to the military commission in Korea or special conferences. From the perspective of Beijing and many of the world's observers, step-by-step progress was slowly being made.

Even as the Geneva Conference meetings were being held, events were taking place in the Taiwan area that were indicative of the frustration over the slow pace of change. Conflict in the Strait between the Communists and the Nationalists would eventually lead to the crisis of 1954.

Taiwan Strait, 1954-55

The shelling of Quemoy on the third of September refocused the world's attention on an old problem that had been reemerging over the past year. With the signing of the Korean Armistice in August 1953, anxieties in the United States had increased in anticipation that the PLA's resources would now be used in Indochina and against Taiwan. However, according to the Chinese interviewed, it appears that in mid-1953 there were a variety of opinions in Beijing as to the immediacy of the Taiwan issue.

While the objective of "liberating Taiwan" was accepted in principle, a consensus had not been reached on priority, methodology or timing. A lot had transpired since the invasion preparations of 1950 that had changed the nature of the problem.

From a military viewpoint, the United States blocked the invasion of Taiwan in 1950 by the People's Liberation Army (PLA) and prevented the resolution of China's civil war. Shortly thereafter General MacArthur, who spoke of the Nationalists attacking the mainland and of Taiwan as an "unsinkable aircraft carrier," sent a team to evaluate the capabilities of the Nationalist forces. Within the next few years an enormous improvement in the capability of these forces occurred as US economic and military aid very quickly approached a billion dollars and the number of advisors grew from a few dozen to over a thousand.[72] Then in 1953 the United States established an operational command on Taiwan to provide the tactical planning and operational requirements for US air, naval, and logistical support for the defense of Taiwan.[73] However, like a two-edged sword, to Beijing such a command could just as easily coordinate an invasion of East China.

During the course of this buildup, as one of the conditions for the sale of advanced equipment like the F-84 jet aircraft to Taiwan, the United States required the Nationalists to agree to not engage in offensive military operations against the mainland of China inimical to the best interests of the United States. [74] Yet at the same time the effectiveness of Nationalist raids against the mainland improved as did their ability to interdict seaborne traffic. And then there was the planned use of Nationalist forces by the United States as a strategic reserve in Asia.[75]

By 1953 it was clear to the PRC that the United States was committed to the defense of Taiwan. Furthermore, Taiwan's forces, if released and logistically supported by the United States, were a serious military threat to the PRC in the event China's defense resources are drained by such events as a renewed Korean conflict, a failure of the economy or a succession crisis. A solution involving either offense or defense—to attack Taiwan or to improve East China's defenses—would be very expensive. However, the latter also offered partial solutions to a wider range of economic development and domestic security problems.

The rejuvenation of the Nationalist Party was another major concern. Domestically it was a source of inspiration from counter-revolutionaires, particularly in South and East China where pacification was still a problem, and a symbolic alternative to the Communist Party in the event of a major domestic crisis. Furthermore, US aid was responsible for recreating on Chinese territory (Taiwan) the same kind of colonial dependency and "warlordism" that the revolution had sought to eliminate. Internationally, the Nationalists challenged the PRC's claim to be the sole representative of the Chinese people and blocked its admission to the United Nations and other world organizations. To many foreigners the obvious solution was two Chinas, but nationalism made that an unacceptable solution to all Chinese, at least in principle.

For others, Taiwan was a source of both local and national economic stress because of the blockade of key ports on the East China coast, the interruption of coastal traffic, civil disorder, and the military expenditures needed to improve the East China defenses to cope with Taiwan's military improvements. Yet the costs of an invasion and the damage from Nationalist strikes on the mainland would be even more expensive. It's easy to imagine leading members of the Politburo, particularly those concerned with the economy like Chen Yun and Kao Kang, searching for an alternative to an invasion that would have imposed on China the kind of costs suffered in Korea.[76] Still the revolutionary and nationalistic pressures to "liberate Taiwan" were very strong.

Internationally among the third world nations, there was a growing sentiment for the collective advancement of the national independence movement. During the June recess of the Geneva Conference, Zhou had visited India and Burma where he told each prime minister that he supported the call of the Colombo Conference (April 1954) for an Afro-Asian conference and the advancement of the national independence movement.[77] In principle many agreed with the PRC's stand on Taiwan. Conversely there was an overriding fear that a military solution would bring war with the United States, which in turn meant world war.

An important factor in finding a solution was the fact that the United States had defined the off-shore islands as being outside the perimeter which it was willing to defend. Despite the presence of the Seventh Fleet in the Strait and Nationalist troops on these island, the US did not appear to have the resolve to directly engage in the defense of these islands. Furthermore, the US had announced that it was withdrawing forces from Korea and had resisted using ground forces in Indochina in support of the French.

This combination of conflicting domestic and international opinions provided Zhou, the consummate strategist and negotiator, the maneuver room to develop a domestic consensus, as needed, to take advantage of events as they occurred. In this environment he was able to push the US to the brink of war and then back away without losing face and thereby enhance his influence domestically, his reputation internationally and his bargaining position vis-a-vis the United States. Some Chinese interviewed believe that the central leadership, with Zhou's inspiration, had intended originally for the PLA to capture the off-shore islands, beginning with the Tachens, but that the leadership sought to retain the flexibility of stopping at any point where the counter pressure became too threatening, such as a counterattack against the mainland. The disadvantage of this concept, which one mainlander interviewed said Beijing finally realized during the 1958 crisis, was that the capture of the off-shore islands without Taiwan proper would mean the diminishing of contact between the mainland and Taiwan and thus the hastening of the evolution of the undesired two-China solution. This weakness in Beijing's logic does not appear to have ever been realized and intentionally exploited by Washington.

The integrity of China's territory, or the Taiwan issue, thus became the second lever by which Zhou could gain the initiative in the development of Sino-American relations.[78] Or from the perspective of Ambassador Johnson, some of the "accelerating tensions over Taiwan" were "contrived by the Chinese to induce us to negotiate" or as he shorthandedly says today, Taiwan in the Sino-American relationship is the "control rod" (as in a nuclear reactor) that the PRC has repeatedly used over the years to either dampen or accelerate the relationship to its advantage.[79]

The "accelerating tensions" were also a negotiating process, in which violence and threats of violence were used to bargain over the fate of the off-shore islands. It was a PRC-ROC debate that gradually became a PRC-US debate.

In the summer of 1953 the PLA captured some small islands in the Tachen area, possibly as a response to ROC raids on the mainland. In response the US persuaded a reluctant Chiang Kai-shek to put a division, which had been trained and equipped by the US, on the Tachen Islands to buttress its sagging defenses.[80] In early 1954 the PLA began a build-up on the mainland and on the islands near Tachen and Yushan. Artillery attacks between 11 and 15 May on several small Nationalist held islands forced the relocation of some Nationalist guerrillas. Several aerial and naval engagements occurred with some losses to the PRC.[81] As a deterrent against further such actions, President Eisenhower ordered the Seventh Fleet to routinely visit the Tachens.[82]

On 23 June 1954, the Nationalists seized the Soviet tanker, Tuapse, on the high seas midway between Luzon and Taiwan, took it to Taiwan, unloaded its cargo, and began encouraging defections among its crew, similar to the earlier seizure of Polish ships.[83] Since the ROC had virtually no capability to locate shipping on the high seas, the PRC undoubtedly assumed that the US directed or at least gave approval for these acts.[84] The PLA began to escort Communist bloc ships. In this hostile environment, a Cathay-Pacific airliner was shot down on 23 July in the vicinity of Hainan Island by two PLA fighters, killing three of the six Americans aboard. Two US aircraft carriers were sent to the area to protect further search and rescue efforts.[85] On 26 July, while looking for survivors, two US Navy carrier-based planes shot down two PLA "patrol aircraft." The Chinese argued that the incident was between themselves and the British, paid the indemnities, and rebuffed three US protests and other actions as being unwarranted.[86] In doing so they avoided the precedent in which the British represented US interests.

In late June the PRC began a major propaganda campaign promising to "liberate" Taiwan and denouncing US "occupation." [87] Propaganda from the ROC was equally intense. In early August President Syngman Rhee complicated the issue in a speech to the US House of Representatives by calling on the US to join the ROK and the ROC in an invasion of the PRC.

In a speech on August 11, Zhou Enlai strongly denounced the ongoing security negotiations between the Americans and the Nationalists, and US efforts to surround China with its alliances.[88] On August 26, forty PLA special operations troops killed ten nationalists on Quemoy. Then on 3 September, the shelling of Quemoy began.[89] On 6 September, Secretary Dulles met in Manila with representatives of the nations that were to sign the Manila Pact and bring the Southeast Asia Treaty Organization (SEATO) into existence. On November 1, the PLA bombed the Tachen Islands and on 23 November, the Chinese sentenced thirteen Americans to prison terms (ranging from four years to life) for espionage.[90] The mood of much of the Congress was bellicose. Senator William Knowland's call for a naval blockade was representative of some of the more extreme feelings. The Congress generally reflected the mood of the electorate to whom they would have to answer shortly in mid-term elections. On the second of December the US-ROC Mutual Defense Treaty was signed. More than a hundred PLA planes raided the Tachens followed on 18 January by a well-executed attack by the PLA on I Chiang Shan Island, near the Tachens.[91] In initiating the Formosa Resolution, which he signed on 29 January, President Eisenhower stated he planned to evacuate the Tachens and implied the US would insure the protection of Quemoy and Matsu. On 4 February the US began the evacuation of ROC troops.[92]

In an effort to convince the PRC of his determination, the President responded to a question in his 16 March press interview that in the event of general war in Asia, the United States would use tactical atomic weapons.[93] The tensions mounted until late March, just prior to the Bandung Conference when the "liberation" propaganda in the

PRC press began to subside.[94] Both the PRC and the United States had pressed hard against each other, attempting to influence the implicit negotiations that were taking place by testing the other's resolve. From President Eisenhower's perspective, which probably expressed Zhou Enlai's thoughts fairly well also, "we refused to retreat, and the enemy, true to his formula, for a while tried harassment but refused to attack. The crisis had cooled. . . . The hard way is to have the courage to be patient."[95]

Even as the tensions subsided, the United States found itself wondering, and to some extent worrying, about what was happening at Bandung. The crisis set the stage for the PRC, now it had the negotiating initiative. A number of changes in the international environment had again been effected by force. The Western allies were split over policy toward the off-shore islands. All were convinced of the dedication of the PRC to its claim to Taiwan, but there was little agreement over what the PRC would do. The term "liberation of Taiwan" caused leaders to shudder over the prospects of a world war. The trend was toward the isolation of the US and the consolidation of opinion on the side of the PRC. The stage was set for Bandung.

With regard to Taiwan the seizure of one third of the off-shore islands sowed the seeds of doubt among the 700,000 soldiers in the Nationalist army about the ability of the government to return to the mainland, a step toward the destruction of the Nationalist threat from within.

Bandung Conference, 1955

The Asian-African Conference (better known as the Bandung Conference) was the perfect forum for Zhou Enlai's political skills. The following remarks in a note to his wife, Deng Yingchao, on the eve of the conference provide some insight into his frame of mind. "Dear Chao, . . . A diplomatic war can be as dangerous as actual combat on the battlefield. Likewise, we should not fight it without good preparations. We should take everything into consideration in all our undertakings, and adopt action only after collective discussion and decision."[96]

On 18 April, President Eisenhower attempted to influence the Conference to pressure China by publicly expressing the hope that the Conference would "seek agreement to a general renunciation of force with respect to the realization of national claims and objectives."[97] And, Asian concerns about war did generate pressures, such as the Prime Minister of Ceylon's proposal for an immediate cease-fire in the Taiwan Strait and a 5-year international trusteeship for Taiwan followed by a plebiscite—a formula for independence.[98] However, during the course of the conference, in a brillant performance by all accounts, Zhou deftly turned the force of these pressures to the support of his position, which he consolidated during a 23 April meeting with the delegation heads of eight key countries, including India, Indonesia and Burma. After the meeting he had Huang Hua distribute to the press a statement on the issue of Taiwan:

> The Chinese people are friendly to the American people. The Chinese people do not want to have a war with the United States of America. The Chinese government is willing to sit down and enter into negotiations with the United States government to discuss the question of relaxing tension in the Far East, and especially the question of relaxing tension in the Taiwan area.[99]

Zhou's statement took the pressure off the PRC for the ceasefire the United States had sought. The PRC had avoided such a commitment since it would lend credence to the idea that Taiwan was not a domestic issue. Zhou was arguing that a ceasefire was not necessary since there was no war between China and the United States. His position avoided the question of whom the Chinese considered the belligerents to be. Furthermore, his statement offered peace negotiations that tended to discredit US claims that the PRC intended to "liberate" Taiwan by force. These efforts raised the PRC's standing among the third world nations, even among some of those allied or friendly to the United States. Among the NATO countries, particularly Britain and France, the effect was no less troublesome.

Initially the US essentially rejected the offer in a 23 April State Department press release that made any such formal negotiations dependent upon the inclusion of the ROC as a participant and a formal ceasefire. Both terms were unacceptable to the PRC because of their implications for PRC sovereignty and the nature of the conflict. Dulles reversed the decision in 26 April news conference and accepted the offer, but with the caveats of no implied recognition and no discussions of Taiwan's "rights and claims in their absence."[100] The President reaffirmed this position in his press conference of April 19.[101]

Zhou gave his report on the Bandung Conference to the National People's Congress on 13 May in which he said the "Chinese people are willing to strive for the liberation of Taiwan by peaceful means so far as possible."[102] Then on May 30 the Chinese, encouraged by the Indians as an interested third party, released four US airmen as a first step. In the following months there were numerous other offers and efforts by third parties, particularly leaders from India, Indonesia, Lebanon, Burma and Pakistan (all leading conference participants with Zhou Enlai at Bandung) to help facilitate contact between the US and the PRC.[103]

In early July, Prime Minister U Nu of Burma, one of those who took upon himself to provide his services as an intermediary between the United States and China, visited Washington. Near the end of his visit Dulles told him that time was needed to manage the problems between the United States and the PRC, but that "sooner or later American recognition (of the PRC) must be granted." In addition U Nu has written that in the course of the discussion he suggested to Dulles that the consular talks in Geneva be raised to ambassadorial level.[104] Both of these points were undoubtedly conveyed to Beijing. As a result when the United States did propose ambassadorial talks, there was a suggestion that Dulles was prepared to be more flexible about relations with the PRC.

Two other prominent diplomats involved in this cumbersome version of shuttle diplomacy were Dag Hammarskjold, Secretary-General of the United Nations, and Krishna Menon, personal representative of Prime Minister Nehru. In response to a resolution initiated by the US and adopted by the United Nations in early December, Hammarskjold actively pursued with Zhou Enlai in Beijing and through subsequent communications the release of the 11 US airmen and 2 civilians that the Communist Chinese had sentenced on 23 November 1954 in Beijing. Although no one was released as a result of his efforts, Hammarskjold's efforts opened a dialogue that was helpful to the United States. The Chinese welcomed Hammarskjold but treated his efforts more as those of an emissary or appellant for the United States than as an independent third party.[105]

Krishna Menon worked the hardest of any third party to get the two sides to negotiate. As a part of his efforts he also addressed the release of detainees; but, being more sensitive to the scars left by the influence of colonialism, he thought more like the Chinese in terms of reciprocity. For example, he felt that the United States should have reciprocated when the PRC released the four airmen in May 1954. While not particularly laudatory of the efforts of any of the third parties, both Eisenhower and Dulles tended to be more critical of Menon, viewing his efforts as the source of much confusion in the emerging Sino-American contacts. In addition his apparent egotism and a penchant for preaching about such issues as sovereignty, independence, and reciprocity detracted from the worth of his efforts.[106] There were other intermediaries, such as the Soviet Union, which advocated a multinational conference approach, as well as Sweden, Pakistan, Indonesia, and the Philippines, but their involvement was not as extensive.

In early July Dulles decided to propose to the PRC through the British, the idea of elevating the talks in Geneva to the ambassadorial level in order to aid in the repatriation of civilians desiring to return home. This in turn would facilitate the discussion and settlement of "other practical matters now at issue" between the United States and China.[107] The specific proposal was relayed through the British Foreign Minister to the British Chargé d'Affaires, Walter O'Neill in Beijing, who then discussed it with Zhou on 13 July. [108]

The Ambassadorial Talks, 1955

Once again, after using a combination of diplomatic and military pressures to probe and shape US perceptions, the Chinese had sounded out the United States through a third party and were now the recipient of a specific US proposal. Conditions once again appeared to be right to try to sit down and formally negotiate with the United States. The proposal appeared to reflect a change of heart on the part of Dulles. (From the perspective of the Chinese, the struggle between China and the United States was personalized as a struggle between Zhou and Dulles. The talks would "measure Zhou Enlai's strength with Dulles'."[109] Elevating the talks to the level of ambassadors was helpful but in itself did not reflect a change in attitude by the United States. On the other hand, the willingness of the US to discuss practical matters at issue between the United States and China did appear significant. There were few if any practical matters that in some way or another didn't lead to such broader questions as the PRC's sovereign right to Taiwan or the recognition of the PRC by the United States. Zhou thus responded favorably with a draft communique that would have had China and the United States announce that the meetings would begin towards the end of the Geneva Summit Conference that was to be held 18–23 July.

One of the factors that had precipitated Dulles' decision to press for the talks had been the desire (once again) to preempt Soviet pressure to place the Far East on the summit agenda. With tensions in the Far East on the minds of all the Summit participants, it's doubtful that either the announcement or the first meeting would have gone unnoticed.[110] It's not clear what the effect of beginning the talks during the Summit would have been, but from Dulles' response he didn't consider it likely to be favorable. Instead he proposed 1 August for the first meeting, allowing a week to prepare himself and Ambassador U. Alexis Johnson for the talks.

In his response Dulles also substituted the words "Peiping and Washington" for "China and the United States." From Zhou's perspective such a change was certainly not conciliatory and was a serious problem. It was finally resolved by both sides accepting a British proposal for each side to use its preferred spelling. To Dulles it was just an excuse by the Chinese to avoid the negotiations—until Johnson explained that "in Chinese 'Peking' meant 'northern capital' and 'Peiping' only meant 'northern plain'." The Nationalists had changed its name when they "christened their new capital 'Nanking' or 'southern capital'. Thus for the Communists to acquiesce in the use of the Nationalist term 'Peiping' would deny their own legitimacy. (Dulles) expressed surprise that nobody had ever explained this to him and said he would immediately explain it to Eisenhower."[111]

Geneva was acceptable to the Chinese as the site for the negotiations for a number of reasons. The talks were a logical extension of the consular level meetings that were begun in Geneva as a result of Zhou's highly successful performance at the Geneva Conference. As an international center, Geneva facilitated publicity and through the consulate relatively secure and efficient communication channels existed.[112] Since the talks were not expected to take long and the people qualified to staff the talks were available in the PRC's diplomatic posts in Europe, it was faster and more efficient to hold the talks in Geneva. And not to be underrated was the fact that Zhou was familiar with Geneva. By mutual agreement at the staff level, the talks were conducted in a small meeting room in the League of Nations building (Palais des Nations). To Ambassador Wang the "meeting room was furnished simply and solemnly with a large oval conference table in the center" that provided an atmosphere of solemn dignity and importance as befitted a meeting between the representatives of two major powers.[113] From Ambassador Johnson's perspective it was a "modest room" away from the center of activity.

The Chinese wanted the press present or fully briefed at each session, the United States wanted private talks. They agreed that after a short photography session at the beginning "to mark in history" the talks, the first meeting would be held in private. Nevertheless, the PRC delegation used the press very effectively. At a meeting with the press just prior to the beginning of the talks on 1 August, Ambassador Wang announced that the PRC had released "eleven American spies" (the airmen tried in November) on 31 July. "This decision by Premier Zhou really created a favorable start for the talks and enabled us (the PRC) to take the initiative in the talks."[114]

The meetings early developed a small ritual of their own, albeit not so solemn as to be humorless. Both negotiators actively cultivated a more relaxed and pleasant atmosphere than had characterized previous Sino-American talks. From the very first meeting they shook hands and exchanged pleasantries to neutralize between themselves the tensions that underlay the talks.[115] In 1958, during one of Wang's trips back to the PRC, Mao endorsed this pattern that Zhou and Wang had been using for three years when he told Wang that during the "talks it is necessary to think more, to be modest and prudent, and to pay attention not to use these stimulating expressions once used during the Panmunjom talks and not to hurt the national feelings of the Americans."[116] Because of the extremes of these two styles, this change provided the Chinese negotiator with another arrow for his quiver. The return to an adversarial style, even for a brief exchange, would cause considerable trauma for American policymakers.

Many years later during Zhou's talks with Kissinger, there was an occasion when Zhou used a confrontational approach, which he said was at Mao's behest. This incident plus Mao's aforementioned rather late endorsement of Zhou's more prudent and considerate approach suggests that Mao may have been largely responsible for the adversarial approach that dominated at Panmunjom and during other vituperative exchanges.[117]

As at Panmunjom the rule was separate and equal. The two delegations entered from opposite sides of the room from doors behind their seats. They alternated giving the opening statement with Ambassador Wang making the first speech at the first meeting at Ambassador Johnson's suggestion. Similarly they alternated in closing the meeting, after a one-time contest over who had the greater bladder capacity. Even the room rent of $1.15 was split equally.[118]

The first meeting lasted about 45 minutes and dealt with such procedural affairs as the degree to which the meetings should be private or open to the press and the agenda. Wang probed with questions the meaning of Johnson's three part proposal that the talks be conducted in private in order to facilitate a frank and informal exchange, that any press release be jointly agreed upon, and that each side notify the other in advance if either felt compelled to issue a separate press release. Then, agreeing in principle, Wang proposed that the subject be discussed again at the next meeting. This pattern became standard for both sides throughout the talks. One side would present a proposal or counterproposal that would then be followed by a discussion to explore its purpose and meaning as well as areas of possible interest and flexibility on both sides. The recipient would then normally reserve the right to comment more fully at a subsequent meeting.[119]

The Chinese agreed at the second meeting to the US proposal for privacy only to have a news story appear in the *New York Times* of 4 August concerning the position of the US at the next meeting.[120] The reporter obviously had inside information. When filtered through the aura of distrust that surrounded Sino-American relations and the Chinese obsession with equality, the leak reinforced concerns in Beijing that they were being used. This incident undoubtedly influenced decisions concerning several later

Courtesy Associated Press Photo

Wang Bingnan, center, sits at the conference table with his advisers at the opening of US-PRC talks in Warsaw, 15 September 1958.

indiscretions that originated with the *New China Agency*.[121]

There was no initial debate over the agenda. Ambassador Wang simply proposed an agenda of two items: (a) the repatriation of civilians desiring to return to their own country, and (b) other practical matters now at issue between the United States and China. Since his proposal was in accord with the 25 July announcements by Dulles and Zhou, Johnson immediately accepted it.

Evaluating Possible Outcomes

Ambassador Wang Bingnan and his delegation were assembled from different PRC posts in Europe for a task that each believed could be accomplished quickly.[122] Zhou himself had laid the groundwork and set the agenda with Dulles through the British. With little wasted effort Ambassador Wang moved to get the negotiations started. He was convinced that if the Americans were serious about being willing to negotiate, he could reach an agreement in short order. He only had to reach an agreement on the repatriation of civilians, probe the United States over the issue of Taiwan in preparation for a Foreign Minister's meeting between Zhou and Dulles, and to establish some cultural relations, such as visits by Americans (possibly journalists or relatives of Americans in China) to the PRC.[123] Each of these were items that the Americans had indicated, in one form or another, that they would be willing to deal with. Another item that Wang raised was the "economic blockade" of China. Zhou knew that the United States was under considerable pressure from its allies in COCOM, particularly Britain, France, and Japan, to at least lower the restrictions on trade with China to the criteria used for the Soviet Union.[124] This was an important issue for China but not one on which Zhou was able to develop much leverage separate from other issues. This was an important weapon used by the United States against the PRC, a weapon of considerable negotiating leverage for the United States even as late as the 1980s. Although the allies disagreed over what the policy should be, their disagreement did not lead to any significant breach of their common trade policy.

The repatriation of civilians as the first item was the same issue that the consuls of the PRC and the US in Geneva had discussed, although with little acknowledged benefit by either side. It was a difficult subject for the Chinese because these civilians were the single source of leverage with the United States besides Taiwan. It was necessary to present a peaceful image in order to keep international pressure on the United States to deal with the PRC. Fortunately, the Nationalists enhanced this image by continuing their raids, reconnaissance flights and belligerent statements against the PRC during this period. But it also meant that Beijing could not overreact to the Nationalists, either politically or militarily. However for this posture to have any significance, cultivation of the press was a top priority and done with considerable skill, although not without occasional error.

The Chinese early established that they were going to treat the question of Chinese students in the United States as a parallel and equal problem to that of American civilians in China. Because the United States had earlier sought to have its interests in China represented by the British, it was appropriate that the PRC ask the Indians to represent the PRC's interests in the United States. The United States wanted the British to help in China but the idea of India having free rein to represent the PRC in the United States was unacceptable. The Nationalist government represented Chinese interests and any act by India on the behalf of the PRC would have put unacceptable pressure on Chinese in the United States. Representation as sought would thus have been one more step toward de facto recognition.

During the Korean War the United States had prevented Chinese, who had certain scientific skills that would have benefited the PRC's war efforts, from leaving the

United States. However, as the United States moved toward holding these talks, the last of these restrictions were removed. Nevertheless, the PRC negotiators dealt with the question of Chinese students in the United States as if it was parallel to that of US civilians imprisoned in China.[125]

Over the month of August these issues were argued until by late August the two delegations were concerned with specific words in the English language version of the announcement. In the original US proposal there was a phrase "promptly to exercise their right to return." The most common Chinese word for "promptly" also means "immediately," a concept which was not acceptable to the Chinese. "Promptly" also has the meaning of a command in some contexts, which, though not intended by the US side, made the word unacceptable to the Chinese in English. The Chinese proposed "as soon as possible" as a substitute, but the US side considered this phrasing too open ended. The Chinese version used the word *jinsu*(尽速), a combination of *jin*, meaning "to the greatest extent possible" and *su*, meaning "fast." Referring back to the Chinese version, the US side suggested the English equivalent "very quickly," but the Chinese, who (according to Johnson's interpreter Robert Ekvall) "need to have the last word . . . one of the compulsions of their negotiating posture" and feeling "compelled to suggest something that bears their own trademark" suggested "expeditiously." The Americans gladly accepted since this word to them obliged the Chinese far beyond what they had sought in "promptly."[126] However, the Chinese were translating from and would eventually comply with the Chinese language version in which *jinsu* (better translated "as fast as possible") was the operative word. Since *jinsu* is more conditional, execution of the agreement in the minds of the Chinese was appropriately dependent on other events, such as the workings of the Chinese judicial system. Of course, behind this semantic jousting was an argument in which the United States wanted the PRC to permit all US civilians in the PRC to return to the United States immediately. The PRC on the other hand had to project an image of being a sovereign equal to the United States. No longer was China to be ordered about by the major Western powers. Due process of law was an important sovereign right that was respected among western nations and should be respected where it involved the PRC. Since such nationalistic sentiments have little value if there is no leverage, keeping those Americans in prison whose crimes appeared to justify such punishment, was also important. As one Chinese interviewed remarked, "we were afraid that if we released all the Americans, the United States would break off the negotiations."

With the approach of an agreement on the repatriation of civilians, the Chinese moved to line up pressure on the United States, including the release of nine civilians the first week in September. By the time the September 10 announcement of an agreement was made, a widespread impression was growing in the international community that the United States was lowering its resistance to the recognition of the PRC and its entrance into the United States. Wang Bingnan had delivered round one for Premier Zhou.

Once the announcement was made Ambassador Wang was ready to proceed with other matters at issue. The United States was not. The more agreeable the Chinese had been during the talks, the more Dulles and his advisors had become nervous about where the talks were headed. Prior to the talks, when radical change appeared impossible, Dulles had been willing in private to speculate about China's future in the international community. But as the talks began to reflect a radical change in the PRC's approach toward the United States, unmatched by comparable political change in the United States, Dulles became increasingly less willing to show any flexibility in his opposition to the entry of the PRC into the United Nations, much less recognition by the United States. The political costs in the United States were just too high. Yet that was exactly where the Chinese were clearly pushing the talks.

Now that, from the Chinese perspective, the first topic was settled, the next step was to agree on the issues to be discussed within the ambiguous framework of the second topic. Beijing wanted to discuss the economic blockade of China and a Foreign Minister's meeting between Zhou and Dulles. The first was an expression of Mao's concern for China to stand independent. To free China from having to "lean to one side" meant opening the way to balancing relations with the Soviets through economic ties with the West, especially the United States. At the same time Britain, France and Japan were exerting pressures on Washington to lower the Chinese (Chincom) levels to the Soviet levels of COCOM. These nations wanted and needed to expand trade relations with the PRC. The second item was the first step to discussions of the Taiwan situation. Zhou apparently felt he could persuade Dulles of the viability of the Chinese solution if he could discuss it with him face to face.

These proposals were not surprises to Washington. They had been raised prior to and during the talks as subjects of interest to the Chinese through such third party contacts as Khrisna Menon's conversations with Ambassador Johnson in the first week of the talks. Even so, Dulles couldn't discuss these subjects. Hate and distrust of the Chinese Communists dominated the domestic political environment of the US. Beijing underestimated the strength of these emotions and the ability or desire of US political leaders to take initiatives contrary to these emotions.

For several meetings following the September 10 agreement, Dulles had Johnson pressure the Chinese to conform, as Washington perceived it, to the agreement to return all the Americans quickly. However, it soon became clear that the Chinese were not going to release them all at once and that there were no pressures that could be exerted to force a release. Unwilling to break off the talks, but not willing to engage the PRC's agenda, the United States proposed that the Chinese provide an accounting for the Americans still missing in Korea. Attempts at the Military Affairs Commission (MAC) at Panmunjom had been unfruitful. Wang retorted that this was an issue for the MAC in Korea and wanted to know if the United States wanted to provide an accounting for the Chinese that were never returned home. Frustrated with the delaying tactics of the United States, the Chinese turned to the press and to third parties, like India and Burma. As friends and interested observers, they were advised of the deteriorating nature of the talks. The pressures began to mount.

Still unwilling to discuss the topics proposed by the PRC, the United States in mid-October suggested that the United States and the PRC unilaterally and simultaneously renounce the use of force to obtain their objectives, particularly in the Taiwan area. Although he was critical of this proposal, Ambassador Wang did not reject the topic out of hand. Rather Beijing saw it as an opportunity and on October 27 advanced a draft agreement that would further their objectives of recognition and membership in the United Nations. The draft quoted the UN charter concerning force, referring to a joint declaration, and proposed a PRC-US "conference of Foreign Ministers" to negotiate the relaxation and elimination of tensions in the Taiwan area. The United States responded with a draft of 10 November that eliminated or neutralized each of the PRC's proposals and associated the renunciation of force specifically to the Taiwan area, "except for individual and collective self-defense."[127] Beijing couldn't accept this blatant intrusion into a domestic issue.

Even before the talks began, Zhou had laid out in a speech to the National People's Congress on 30 July, 1955 the principles that must govern in any agreement with the

United States concerning Taiwan. Referring to the situation in the Taiwan area, he said that "This is an international issue between China and the United States. The exercise by the Chinese people of their sovereign rights in liberating Taiwan is a matter of China's internal affairs. These two questions cannot be mixed up."[128]

The two drafts reflected the differences between Beijing and Washington. But there was common ground and Zhou was determined to obtain an agreement. "Seeking common ground while reserving differences," Zhou had Wang try again on the first of December. The proposal, according to Ambassador Johnson, came very close to meeting the requirements of the United States for an agreement, including an agreement sought by the United States to an indefinite extension of the talks. (At least until all the Americans imprisoned were repatriated.) Nor were there any oral ultimatums delivered.[129] Except for some minor word changes, Johnson's only concern was whether Taiwan ought to be specifically mentioned. He felt that if the draft was accepted for its political rather than its legal value, there was no need to include Taiwan. He reasoned that the international community would not accept a fine print distinction as justification for an attack on Taiwan.

Politically there just wasn't any way that Dulles could make a deal with the Communist Chinese that enhanced their legitimacy at the expense of the Nationalists. Dulles essentially rejected the Chinese proposal by requiring Johnson to propose amendments to add Taiwan and the concept of individual and collective self-defense. Wang argued that Taiwan is central to Sino-American differences and thus was included within his draft, but to no avail.

Zhou was determined to obtain an agreement so he took his case to the public in mid-January. The exchange in the press was vigorous, bringing to light much of what had transpired in previous talks. One beneficial side effect to Beijing was the generation of considerable anxiety and distrust on Taiwan. Clearly out of frustration there also was a brief return at the talks to some of the harsh rhetoric of Panmunjom. In April the United States tried another draft and in May the PRC responded with a draft that included extracts from the Five Principles of Peaceful Coexistence and raised the subject of a meeting of the foreign ministers. But by then the positions of both countries were too rigid to yield.

With government-to-government relations deadlocked, Zhou moved in mid-1956 to people-to-people relations and offered in August to invite American newsmen to China. Assuming another Trojan Horse, Dulles backed away. Pressure from the press and the public over the next 6 months gradually forced a change, but by then Zhou wanted reciprocity—an equal number of PRC reporters to visit the United States. The talks continued to discuss the problem of Americans imprisoned in China (there were only six remaining by the end of 1957) and visits of family members to those imprisoned. The talks also were a means to educate each other and minimize misunderstanding, such as when the United States deployed the Matador missile to Taiwan in mid-1957. Gradually the talks slipped into a pattern of once a month meetings of short duration.

Zhou was increasingly preoccupied with domestic problems. Dissatisfaction with the economy and the party's leadership impacted on the support that the Premier could muster for his approach to foreign policy. Therefore it appears that it was important to Zhou to simply maintain the Ambassadorial Talks at a minimum level of activity as an outward symbol of continuity and as a means to reopen the negotiations when conditions were more favorable domestically, both in China and the United States. Conversly, the talks had long since become of marginal interest to Dulles, whose energies were sapped by his efforts at European diplomacy and his bout with cancer.[130] Considering their diminished utility and the contention they generated, when Johnson came due for reassignment, Dulles initially considered ending the talks but instead decided to downgrade the diplomatic rank of his representative. On 12 December, 1957, Ambassador Johnson informed Ambassador Wang that he was being reassigned to Thailand and that he would be replaced by Edwin Martin. The Chinese commented on Martin's excellent qualification but, because he was not an ambassador, found him unacceptable. Since Dulles would not assign an ambassador the talks were suspended pending the assignment by the US of an ambassador to meet with Wang Bingnan.

Hard Bargaining and Closure

The Chinese bargained hard for the positions they wanted, using every pressure they could generate. Their primary objective was to be accepted as an equal major power. Because of their sensitivity to violations of their sovereignty, they often carried their insistence beyond that which westerners found reasonable; nevertheless, if they perceived sufficient common ground for an agreement, they would move fairly quickly to produce a compromise that preserved their principles while meeting the essential demands of the United States. These positions were easily identified by Johnson by the intensity of the negotiations and by how close the Chinese would come to breaking off the negotiations and yet not take that final step. There were two such periods in the Ambassadorial Talks, once before the repatriation agreement and once during the negotiations over the draft renunciation of force agreement.

Postconference Phase

The Ambassadorial Talks did not end with Ambassador Johnson's departure. After a hiatus of nine months and the emergence of the second Taiwan crisis, Secretary Dulles assigned Jacob Beam to reopen the talks with the Chinese, only this time in Warsaw, Poland where both Beam and

Wang were accredited. During the 1958 Taiwan crisis this channel provided both sides with a safety valve, if needed. Huang Hua was assigned from Beijing to Wang's staff to provide him with the latest thinking in Beijing and the assistance of an expert linguist and analyst. However, throughout the late 1950s, the early 1960s, the isolationism of the Cultural Revolution, and until the United States initiated contact during the Nixon Administration, the main purpose of these contacts in Europe was to provide "for the two big nations, which were mutually confronted, a channel to contact each other. . . . we can say that the ambassadorial talks were in a sense the relations between the two countries under the specific conditions of the time. In certain respects, the contacts between China and the United States were more frequent than contacts between countries with diplomatic relations."[131]

In Retrospect—A Chinese View

In the course of the interviews with Chinese who had knowledge of the Ambassadorial Talks, it became clear that these people felt that the 30–year break in relations between the PRC and the United States could have been avoided at Geneva, if the domestic politics of the United States had been different. Relations had not been possible in 1949. Mao had decided that China needed time to purge its system of foreign influence. However, 1955 was a different matter. The PRC wanted to establish a relationship with the United States, albeit not at any price. The effort was sincere and they felt that it went more than half way toward meeting the requirements of the United States. Unfortunately the United States rebuffed the effort and the window of opportunity during a period in Chinese domestic politics when normalization was possible, was lost. another opportunity was not to appear until 1971, only to once again close due to domestic politics in the United States as well as in the PRC (notably the succession question following the death of Mao).

Success is obviously relative, particularly when the Chinese evaluate the results of their efforts in negotiations with the United States. In terms of stated objectives, "aside from the issue of repatriation, no agreements were reached between the two sides on substantive issues involving Sino-US relations." But in broader terms, the talks provided an opportunity for "China and the United States [to] express their views and positions" about major international events. "As a result, the two countries knew each other very well even though they had no diplomatic relations."[132]

While individual Chinese interviewees acknowledged that mistakes were made by the Chinese during the talks, no one was willing to discuss specific mistakes. Rather their emphasis was on Chinese initiatives to compromise; China's greater effort to make the talks succeed. However, they also emphasized that China never compromised its basic principles during the talks. Wang Bingnan says that during this period "Premier Zhou Enlai displayed his talent in China's diplomacy, which was full of creativity, vitality, and distinguishing features. Sticking to principles and never wavering in the slightest degree, he adopted flexible strategies with courtesy, good reason, and restraint. He established a new style for China's diplomacy, which combined the firmness of principle with the flexibility of strategy."[133]

Thus the significance of the talks was that without Zhou's new style as fully developed during this period and without the "ambassadorial talks, it would have been impossible for the United States to establish diplomatic relations with China (in 1979) on the basis of recognizing Taiwan as its sacred territory." As Ambassador Johnson and Wang Bingnan have both observed, Zhou's steps to Sino-American relations were followed. Zhou in effect had the rough equivalent of a "foreign ministers" meeting when he met in Beijing with Kissinger, the President's national security advisor who was at least as powerful with respect to foreign policy as the US Secretary of State. The PRC and the United States established people-to-people relations in order to facilitate the normalization process, beginning with Ping Pong diplomacy. and the PRC and the United States discussed the Taiwan issue and even made some progress in finding ways to deal with some aspects of the problem. One can reasonably argue that many if not all of these events would have transpired even without the efforts of the Ambassadorial Talks, but from the Chinese perspective these Talks and the events leading to the Talks established the boundaries within which the ultimate solutions were found. Like building a stone house, a solid foundation for the relationship had to be laid, if the relationship was to endure. Although the foundation was laid much more slowly than desired or, in such cases as 1958, than some leadership elements found tolerable, there is a general sense among China's national leaders of the continuous nature of the process and of the linkage that exists between events in the relationship that must be kept in mind (and maybe coordinated) in order to reach China's longer range objectives.

6.
NEGOTIATION AS AN ART

THE CHINESE DIPLOMATIC NEGOTIATING STYLE, as seen in Sino-American relations since 1949, is as complex and diverse as the centuries of history and traditions that underlie it. It is neither so routinized as to be always predictable, nor so flexible as to be nondeterministic and lacking continuity. It is neither so unique as to completely obviate Western negotiating experiences and concepts, nor so characterless as to be undifferentiated. Knowledge of China's negotiators does not simplify an evaluation of the Chinese style, for they are neither so culturally or ideologically homogeneous that the individual's creativity and initiative can be ignored, nor are they so individualistic as to be independent actors in the negotiations.

The strategies and combinations of tactics used by the Chinese have varied with the bargaining issue, changes in the domestic and international environments, the degree of conflict between China and the United States, differences among the policies of the PRC's various administrations, differences between negotiators, and adaptations to accommodate lessons learned. Yet enough continuity exists to conclude that there is a Chinese style of negotiations, one that describes the Chinese approach since 1949 to negotiations with the United States.

Style

The diplomatic negotiating style of the PRC is based on strategies and emphasizes tactics that many Westerners find frustrating and difficult to understand. This style has been effective in helping Beijing achieve many of its objectives, particularly over the long term, but there are also weaknesses that have been exploited by US negotiators and weaknesses that have prevented the Chinese from taking advantage of some opportunities. As the PRC's leaders have gained experience in the international community, they have attempted to improve on their negotiating style by making adjustments in the selection and training of their diplomatic personnel and by taking advantage of technology. The greatest changes will most likely follow from the decentralization that is occurring under the Four Modernizations program. Some US diplomats have already sensed that the reduced amount of direct involvement by the central leadership in the coordination of objectives between ministries and their implementation at the negotiating table has lessened the apparent coherence of China's approach to the United States.

The Chinese manage Sino-American relations as a continuous bargaining process. They are fully aware that their ability to achieve their objectives and fulfill their principles is significantly dependent on the choices and decisions of the United States. Consequently, the Chinese expend considerable energy influencing these choices through persuasion, conciliation, and compromise—at a tactical level.

Persuasion and conciliation are major functions of people-to-people relations. These programs are well-funded and, in the long term, effectively support the continuous bargaining nature of Sino-American relations. They can also support formal negotiations, although not necessarily with great success. Compromises are tactical in nature and usually involve compromises over Chinese techniques that the United States has found troublesome.

Strategic objectives or principles are seldom compromised; indeed, Chinese participants argue that no compromises are made. Furthermore, where compromises are made concerning subordinate principles, they are usually conditioned in some way so as to leave the door open for that subject to be readdressed in the future.

For the Chinese, formal negotiations mark the end of a period of successful mediation by third parties, including increasingly informal staff contacts as a substitute for outside third parties, during which the framework of an agreement is established. Then, the principals meet to complete the details. This process led Dr. Kissinger to term their style "preemptive concession." If the Chinese misjudge the success of the mediation efforts and are disappointed with the formal negotatiations, they will attempt to use the negotiations, as at Panmunjom and Geneva, to influence US perceptions of Chinese "objective reality," thereby recovering the initiative and achieving their objectives. Their negotiating stand will harden, their concession rate will be slow, and concessions—mainly over techniques—will be made at the last minute to keep the negotiations open until circumstances become more favorable to an agreement or the exercise is no longer fruitful.

Chinese negotiators tend to exploit the psychological dimension of interpersonal relations. Such highly personalized diplomacy is intended to create obligations and attitudes receptive to psychological demands. The full implications of such techniques as old friends, shame and sympathy, criticism, and nonverbal communications are often not recognized by Americans. Generally, these techniques are very effective, stimulating the friendly or hostile responses that help the Chinese negotiator maintain the initiative. Occasionally, such techniques will have only a marginal impact on an American because he lacks a comparable cultural framework within which to interpret the maneuvers.

Courtesy Xinhua News Agency, Beijing

Winston Lord, Henry Kissinger, Richard Nixon, David Bruce, (unidentified), Ji Chaozhu, Zhou Enlai, and Qiao Guanhua meet to complete details of agreement in a process Kissinger called "pre-emptive concession." Beijing, 27 February 1972.

Negotiators

The Chinese style is not codified and is not, in general, proliferated via a formal education process. Rather, it is learned mainly through an apprenticeship of many long years. Chinese negotiators do not all acquire the exact same skills. Personal experiences and idiosyncrasies and the style of foreign opponents often contribute to a distinct character in an apprentice's negotiating style, but all learn to be disciplined advocates in whom considerable confidence is placed. They develop great skill in gaining the psychological initiative. They are masters of the record both by study as well as practical experience and they are all team players.

The qualifications of their senior delegate and his staff indicate a great deal about Chinese expectations for particular negotiations. Some delegates have been little more than messengers who presented their government's position and relayed the response of the US representative. Any PRC's representative who assumed the role at the other extreme, that of a mediator arguing the merits of both sides, did so between himself and the central leadership in such a manner that it was hidden from the Americans and, thus, not exploited. Most of the PRC's representatives have been negotiators or disciplined advocates of their government's position with enough support from their superiors and intimacy with the policy process to be as accommodating or insistent as the occasion required.

The closer the duties of a Chinese representative in the cases studied approached those of a negotiator versus a messenger, the more likely he was to be from Zhou Enlai's inner circle of lieutenants, to have a western-style education, a facility with a foreign language, and sufficient cross-cultural experience to feel reasonably comfortable in dealing with the West. Zhou gave each of his representatives a degree of autonomy commensurate to the situation, his ability, experience and closeness to Zhou. These men learned directly from Zhou and to the extent they reflect his style they are the models by which Zhou's style is transmitted to China's young negotiators of today.

The PRC's negotiators are experienced leaders as well as followers, men accustomed to making decisions—within China's consensus process—as well as taking orders. They understand the value of differing opinions, even advocacy, within the system, as well as the importance of loyalty and iron discipline when implementing a policy—even one with which they may not agree. Each one is a disciplined advocate.

They enjoy the confidence of their superiors, exercising considerable latitude in judgments involving tactics. Of particular importance is their ability to take the initiative psychologically, to create the appropriate atmosphere or mood at any given point in the negotiations.

Each man has mastered the record of Sino-American negotiations, first as a result of his personal experiences with large segments of that history, and second through study and the assistance of his staff, whose accumulated experience usually covers the spectrum of Sino-American relations. He feels uncomfortable when he lacks access to the official record and expects the same of Americans. The Chinese negotiator views the lack of attention to the historical record on the part of his American counterpart as trickery, especially when Americans "carelessly" change previously carefully worded phrases.

Each has been a team player who sought the opinions and observations of the members of his delegation, yet retained the initiative and authority of leadership. This process, reinforced by discipline, is another essential element of the repertoire used by these negotiators to create an environment favorable to their psychological initiatives.

Each negotiator is aware of his educational responsibility as a role model for his staff. Negotiation skills are learned by on- the-job training under the tutelage of a master negotiator. Often beginning as translators, listening from the sidelines and working with the written text, the junior diplomats gradually acquire the language proficiency and political skills to become interpreters and then assistants to the negotiator. Formal negotiations provide the rough equivalent of a "one-room schoolhouse" in which those at each level of skill are simultaneously student and model.

Chinese negotiators will continue to be educated by this role model method. However, Sino-American relations have expanded so rapidly that the Chinese with formal negotiating skills cannot meet the demand. Negotiators with the appropriate skills find themselves called upon for duties that younger men should have learned, but didn't, during the Cultural Revolution. Some Chinese consider the pressures for quantity plus quality antithetical to the tutorial process employed more or less since 1949, further increasing pressure for change in the recruitment and training process of diplomats. Earlier and better foreign language training alongside a more Western style social science education emphasizing analysis as opposed to patterned reasoning is a formula that will probably diffuse the impact of Zhou's model in the 1990s as a younger generation assumes the positions of responsibility in the Ministry of Foreign Affairs.

Success or Failure

The Chinese interviewed were ambivalent when asked about their own success as negotiators. They were unanimous that the PRC's national objectives and negotiating principles were correct and sure that each of the periods of Sino-American negotiations examined had contributed to the PRC's objectives and sustained its principles; each expressed unabashed adulation for Zhou Enlai as the PRC's model negotiator. However, they acknowledged indirectly that the PRC's negotiators did not always do as well as expected. There was a surprising degree of frankness about their perceptions of what improvements are needed, particularly in three categories: communications and decisionmaking, public relations, and the qualifications of a negotiator and his staff.

Physical communications were a problem in both case studies and the relative disadvantage has continued to the present. US delegations have always appeared to the Chinese to be able to communicate with Washington faster and in greater volume. The US superiority in computers and communication satellites has continued this sense of relative deprivation.

Those interviewed were even more concerned with the less easily remedied slowness of the Chinese bureaucracy to respond to developments during the negotiations. Decisions in Beijing were frustratingly tardy for the negotiator in the field, often requiring him to temporize with old arguments. There was a tendency among Chinese bureaucrats to either pass or elevate a decision—a problem exacerbated in later years by the Cultural Revolution—greatly lengthening the response time as decisions were moved several echelons closer to the center than necessary. Initial reports of Deng's recent efforts to decentralize responsibility and to stimulate initiative have given the Chinese negotiator the reverse problem of negotiating an agreement that does not have a central leadership consensus: an agreement that may conflict with one reached in another sector of government.

Public relations was mentioned as an area in which the US has been more successful. The Chinese have lacked the knowledge, experience, and sufficiently skilled staff to compete in the international community with American public relations techniques and gadgetry. The Chinese do know the importance of the media in shaping opinions, as evidenced by their domestic public relations programs and efforts to control these programs by contending political factions. However, they also feel that they lack sufficient knowledge of the foreign media to compete internationally.

The qualifications of younger members of the diplomatic corps is the third major Chinese concern. In the early days of the PRC's foreign service corps, those who received mentor training under Zhou Enlai were the most effective, judging by those who were selected to represent the PRC to the West as negotiators. Most of them had foreign or foreign–sponsored educations and foreign language skills. But as the foreign service expanded rapidly in the mid to late 50s and again in the late 70s and 80s, it had to depend more and more on ill-prepared young people that the Foreign Ministry provided with little more than language training. Divisions occurred concerning the effectiveness of the Foreign Ministry's language oriented training program. While all believe foreign language is important, some experienced diplomats feel that the Ministry's trainees lack sufficient training in such areas as political science, economics, international law, and the culture of other countries. In short, the new generations of foreign service professionals have tended to be excellent linguists but not as effective as their Western counterparts with other equally important tools of the foreign service or as those Chinese diplomats who were trained "on-the-job" by the likes of Zhou Enlai.

Characteristics

Prescriptions suggest recommended counterstrategies and tactics for predicted strategies and combinations of tactics to be used by the Chinese. The results of this study do not suggest that the Chinese are that predictable. They have shown considerable flexibility and creativity over the years both as tacit, strategic bargainers and at the tactical negotiating table. However, US negotiators should consider the following five Chinese characteristics before entering into government-to-government negotiations with their PRC counterparts.

1. Chinese distrust of international law, dependence on moral principles, and a domestic legal system focused on criminal rather than civil law, have generally resulted in approaches asymmetrical to those of the United States with respect to problems that transcend national boundaries, problems ranging from nuclear nonproliferation and arms control to the protection of economic interests. These differences must be understood by US negotiators. The Chinese will spend years building trust in the international system and creating a domestic legal infrastructure that will sustain the PRC's international commitments. At the same time, the United States should continue to press the PRC to join international conventions and to make and enforce laws to protect foreign interests. On such key issues as the nuclear nonproliferation agreements, which the Chinese have not signed, the United States must press for more than oral assurances from the reluctant Chinese. Certainly, the US implicit tolerance of the PRC's position shows understanding but this policy may be counterproductive to further US-PRC agreements.

2. The Chinese are most flexible during the prenegotiation phase before public positions are taken to justify domestic and international policies, before bureaucratic lines are drawn, and before factions have committed themselves. In most cases, "quiet diplomacy" during this phase is be the most effective way to approach the Chinese.

3. A corollary to quiet diplomacy is third party communications. This essentially means warning a Chinese decisionmaker before presenting him with a problem directly. A common method is to raise the problem through a third party such as a mutual friend or acquaintance or even a subordinate. This technique is similar to informal staff

coordination used widely within the US bureaucracy, and with minor mental and procedural adjustments, these staff techniques can be used effectively by Americans with the Chinese, avoiding China's famous "barbarian handlers."

4. In general, such easily seen cultural differences between the United States and China as dress and eating habits can be easily accommodated by both sides, but psychological differences are less evident to each and can easily lead to serious misunderstandings. What may appear to be dishonest in one society may be merely good, practical politics in the other. Both sides would be well served to insure that at least one member of their negotiating team is knowledgable of both cultures as well as the topic of discussion and is assigned to watch for such cultural disconnections. Each negotiator should continuously review and test the assumptions he makes in his thought process with his counterpart. Frank discussions about the possibility of any disconnections can be useful.

5. The Chinese often assert that demands on the ground of principles must be met before negotiations can be held or relations improved. But, this did not prove to be an insuperable obstacle to negotiations with the Chinese in either case study, after the Chinese determined that conditions were right for a meeting. This should have been kept in mind when evaluating China's three preconditions for the improvement of relations with the Soviet Union. The Sino-Soviet border, Vietnam, and Afghanistan were currently important obstacles to improved Sino-Soviet relations, but when the Soviet Union made a gesture in anyone of these areas, there were at least corresponding changes in the policies of the PRC. The Chinese do not practice an "all-or-nothing" type of diplomacy but recognize the efficacy of a "step-by-step" approach.

Historical Insights

American scholars have often lamented the "lost opportunity in China" of 1949, arguing that the United States should have recognized the PRC and thereby avoided a quarter of a century of hostility. The Chinese, however, don't agree that bilateral relations in 1949 were possible. Interviewees from all quarters observed that Mao was determined to "sweep China clean of all foreign influence" before accepting any foreign guests. The central leaders decided to consolidate their power and establish the new order before establishing relations with any of the powers that had had strong political, economic, and cultural influence in China prior to 1949, especially the United States.

Although Mao and others were disposed to seek US assistance at the time of the "Dixie Mission," beginning with Ambassador Hurley's activities they began to see that such assistance was not possible. Since US domestic politics would have prevented any substantial foreign aid to the PRC and the USSR was willing to assist, the policy of "leaning to one side" easily gained dominance within the central leadership. Nevertheless, Mao's prime concern was to rid Chinese society of foreign socio-economic influence. Even the restrictions placed on the Soviets in their interaction with the Chinese in the 1950s appear, in retrospect, to support this thesis.

The second historical insight that surfaced in the interviews is that the leaders of the PRC seriously sought to open relations with the West, particularly the US, during the period from 1954 to 1957. The Chinese made derogatory remarks about Soviet arrogance and its conditional assistance in the early 1950s, attitudes guaranteed to grate on Chinese pride and desire for independence and self-reliance. Contemporary foreign policy makers felt a strong desire to move the PRC's foreign policy to a position between that of the USSR and the United States, not too dissimilar from the 70/30 balance sought in the early 1980s.

Following the PRC's "victory" in Korea, there was a steady, "step-by-step" approach in China's foreign policy to construct a bridge to the West. First, through the non-aligned movement and the restoration of relations with China's southern neighbors, particularly India, Zhou Enlai gradually broke China's isolation. At the Bandung Conference he cultivated a limited amount of support among America's Asian allies—notably Foreign Minister Romulos of the Philippines—and then at the Geneva Conference on Korea and Indonesia, the PRC quietly established contact with the United States while simultaneously normalizing relations with Britain. With the assistance of a number of third parties, the stage was set for a major step toward normalization at the Ambassadorial Talks in 1955, only to have Secretary Dulles shunt the efforts aside. By the time President Kennedy assumed office the window of opportunity in Chinese policy had long since been closed by domestic developments in China.

Strategy of Conflict

The connotative difference found between the meanings that Chinese and American diplomats attribute to the word "negotiate" point to fundamental differences in their respective concepts of negotiations. The Chinese emphasiize the inflexible nature of general principles, "strategy of conflict," agreements to limit conflict, and moral suasion to insure compliance. Their approach contrasts with the American emphasis on quid-pro-quo compromises supported by law and judicial processes as a basis for insuring compliance. These fundamentally different approaches reflect the asymmetry in Chinese and American cultures. What might be a rational decision in one society may not seem so in the other.

If "negotiation" is defined broadly as a process for combining divergent viewpoints to reach a common agreement, then the Chinese "strategy for conflict" conforms to the definition, but if "negotiation" is more narrowly construed to describe the resolution of a *specific conflict* across the formal negotiating table, then the definition is too restrictive. For the Chinese, formal negotiations take place to confirm agreements that have been worked out informally at any given point in the process and are a vehicle for influencing and changing reality for the next step in the strategic process. The formal process and, to a lesser extent the strategic process are not designed to divide between the US and China the total product of their relationship. It is neither wholly a win-win nor a win-lose situation. While the Chinese recognize the advantages of a win-win strategy, considering their stress on common interests, they also recognize a danger in too much emphasis on this approach. First, a win-win strategy deprives one of the initiative and can lead to the compromise of basic principles. Second, sovereign nations should not be overly demanding in telling others how to define their interests, particularly since there are many remaining conflicts of interest with the US which would involve win-lose scenarios if resolved bilaterally.

Because of the strategic perspective the Chinese bring to formal negotiations, those interested in the table process of bargaining will find it difficult to adjust the events to conform to a closed loop analysis. While the sequence of events tends to conform to that traditionally found in Western negotiations, the strategic perspective of the Chinese enables them to remain somewhat more detached from the process than westerners and to be able to redirect it more readily.

The Chinese can best be described as approaching negotiation as an art. Zhou was for the Chinese the Rembrandt of negotiators and today's diplomats appear to aspire to duplicate his techniques. Most of those interviewed believed that it would be difficult for anyone to be as talented as Zhou was, but he nevertheless provided the ideal standard against which China's negotiators are measured today.

NOTES

Introduction

1. Michael Pillsbury, "US-Chinese Military Ties?" *Foreign Policy* (Fall 1975), 50-60; A. Doak Barnett, "Military-Security Relations between China and the United States." *Foreign Affairs* 55 (April 1977): 584-597.

2. J. C. Harsanyi, "Approaches to the Bargaining Problem Before and After the Theory of Games," *Econometrica* 24 (1956): 149.

3. Gordon W. Rule, *The Art of Negotiation* (Washington: 1962), 52.

4. Otomar J. Bartos, *Process and Outcome of Negotiations* (New York: Columbia University Press, 1974), 303-305.

5. R. Dennett and Joseph Johnson (eds.), *Negotiating with the Russians* (New York: Columbia University Press, 1974), 303- 305; Nathan Leites, *A Study of Bolshevism* (Glencoe, Ill.: Free Press, 1953); Arthur Lall, *Modern International Negotiations* (New York: Columbia University Press, 1966).

6. Fred C. Iklé, *How Nations Negotiate* (New York: Harper and Row, 1964).

7. Michael Blaker, *Japanese International Negotiating Style* (New York: Columbia University Press, 1977).

8. William H. Vatcher, Jr., *Panmunjom: The Story of the Korean Military Armistice Negotiations* (New York: Frederick A. Praeger, 1958); Admiral C. Turner Joy, *How Communists Negotiate* (New York: The MacMillan Company, 1955); Allan E. Goodman, *Negotiating While Fighting: The Diary of Admiral C. Turner Joy at the Korean Armistice Conference* (Stanford: Hoover Institution Press, 1978).

9. Arthur H. Dean, "What It's Like to Negotiate with the Chinese." *New York Times Magazine*, 30 October 1966, 44-45.

10. Kenneth T. Young, *Negotiating with the Chinese Communists: The United States Experience, 1953-1967* (New York: McGraw-Hill, 1968).

11. Arthur Lall, *How Communist China Negotiates* (New York: Columbia University Press, 1968).

12. Wang Bingnan, *Nine Years of Sino-US Talks in Retrospect*, serialized in *Guangzhou Robao* , September 1984-February 1985, and in *Shijie Zhishi* (Beijing) 4-8, 1985, trans. in Foreign Broadcast Information Service, *Daily Report: Peoples Republic of China*).

13. Lucian Pye, *Chinese Commercial Negotiating Style* (Cambridge, Mass: Oelgeschlager, Gunn & Hain, Publishers, 1982).

14. I. William Zartman, ed., *The 50% Solution* (Garden City: Anchor Press/Doubleday, 1976), 33.

15. Conversations with PRC scholars in China and the United States indicate that very few Chinese scholars and researchers have been authorized access to the Foreign Ministry's archival records pertaining to Sino-American relations. Limited scholarly access appears to have been directed in support of studies concerned with contemporary foreign policy issues. On the other hand, there are some indications that the availability of selected policy related documents will increase. In the last few years, the Editorial Committee of Party Literature under the Central Committee of the CPC has made a number of documents available to the public for the first time and plans future releases. The releases to date are designed to support the distinction being made between the collection of all the statements of Mao Zedong—including his errors—and Mao Zedong thought as a scientific theory representing the collective wisdom of the CPC. The latter is stated to be the embodiment of the experiences of the Chinese people, including the contributions of Zhou Enlai, Liu Shaoqi, Zhu De, Chen Yun, and other revolutionaries of the older generation. This argument was presented by Wang Qi, the leader of the Party History Research Center, CPC in an article "Inheriting the Developing Mao Zedong Thought," *Beijing Review* 26, no. 52 (26 December 1983): 22. Releases include the following:

Selected Works of Zhou Enlai (1926-1949), vol. 1, Chinese ed. December 1980, English ed. 1981.

Selected Works of Liu Shaoqi (1926-1949), vol. 1, Chinese ed. (December 1981), English ed. (1984).

Selected Works of Zhu De (1931-1962), Chinese ed. August 1983.

The Selected Letters of Mao Zedong, December 1983.

The Selected Letters of Mao Zedong with Reproductions of the Original Calligraphy, English ed. December 1983.

Selected Works of Chen Yun (1926-1949), vol. 1, Chinese ed. March 1984.

16. In 1983-1984 Chinese diplomats and scholars occasionally mentioned this change of policy when discussing recently released memoirs of former United States Government officials.

17. For an example, see Wu Xiuquan, *The Experience of Eight Years in the Foreign Ministry, January 1950-October 1958* (Beijing: International Knowledge Publishers, 1983).

18. For an example, see Luo Ruiqing, Lu Zhengcao and Wang Bingnan, *Zhou Enlai and the Sian Incident* (Beijing: Foreign Language Press, 1983).

CHAPTER 1

1. Mao Tse-Tung, "Report to the Second Plenary Session of the Seventh Central Committee of the Communist Party of China," *Selected Works of Mao Tse-tung*, vol. iv, English ed. (Beijing: Foreign Language Press, 1967), 361.

2. Mao's comments on the importance of firm principles and flexible tactics to successful negotiations closely parallels Lenin's emphasis on principles and on temporizing when making compromises. V. I. Lenin, "Compromises," *Selected Works* VI, 16 September 1917, 208, in Stefan T. Possny, ed., *The Lenin Reader* (Chicago: Henry Regnery Co.), 454.

3. Roger Fisher and William Ury, *Getting to Yes* (New York: Penguin Books, 1983), xii.

4. *The Random House College Dictionary*, rev. ed. (1982).

5. *The New Merriam-Webster Pocket Dictionary*, Pocket Book ed. (1964).

6. Robert B. Ekvall, *Faithful Echo* (New Haven, Conn.: College and University Press, 1960), 79.

7. Fred C. Iklé, *How Nations Negotiate* (New York: Harper & Row, 1976), 143-149.

8. Jack C. Plano and Roy Olton, *The International Relations Dictionary* (New York: Holt, Rinehart and Winston, 1969), p. 218.

9. All definitions of Chinese characters and combinations of characters, unless otherwise indicated, are from the *Times Chinese- English Dictionary*, 1980 ed., that was compiled and edited by the Beijing Foreign Languages Institute, PRC.

10. *Ci Yuan* (Shanghai: Commercial Press, 1937) as cited by Ron Dolan, "Etymology of Selected Forms," 6 February 1984, memorandum to author, Library of Congress, Washington, DC.

11. Ibid.

12. For a useful discussion of whether or not modern Chinese is undergoing any profound linguistic change, see Paul Kratschvil, "Modern Chinese and Linguistic Change," *The China Quarterly* 92 (1982): 687-695.

CHAPTER 2

1. "Statement by the Spokesman of the Chinese Government—A Comment on the Soviet Government's Statement of August 21-September 1, 1963," *Peking Review* 36 (6 September 1963): 16 in William E. Griffith, *The Sino-Soviet Rift* (Cambridge, Mass.: The M.I.T. Press, 1964), 386.

2. See Documents 1-16 in Griffith, 241-490.

3. Samelson finds that in "the view of most western observers, the Soviets, and Chinese have . . . adopted fairly comparable obstructionist

negotiating techniques for dealing with the West . . . . a specific disregard . . . of many of the fundamental methods of traditional western diplomacy." He concludes that the model projected is the negative one quoted. Louis J. Samelson, *Soviet and Chinese Negotiating Behavior: The Western View* (Beverly Hills: Sage Publications, 1976), 52.

4. For example see Richard Pipes as quoted in Samelson, 6 and Paul E. Shroeder, "The Ohio-Hubei Agreement: Clues to Chinese Negotiating Practices," *The China Quarterly* 91 (September 1982): 486-491.

5. In the best and most recent example, Fisher and Ury state they "have evolved a practical method for negotiating agreements amicably without giving in." Fisher and Ury, *Getting to Yes* (New York: Penguin Books, 1983), vi.

6. This point was made by several Chinese officials and scholars. Several also noted that Zhou Enlai had made this point to several visiting American scholars of the "what if school" who had argued that if the United States had taken certain actions, the era of hostility could have been avoided.

7. Wang Bingnan, "Recalling 9 Years of Sino-US Talks," part 2, *Guangzhou Ribao*, 3 October 1984, 3, trans. in Foreign Broadcast Information Service, *Daily Report: People's Republic of China*, 19 October 1984, B-5.

8. Interviews with Chinese officials.

9. Ibid.

10. See statement of Chen Muhua, Minister of Foreign Economic Relations and Trade in *Beijing Review* 21 (21 May 1984): 111- 112, and June 5 press conference of Premier Zhao Ziyang in Brussels, *Beijing Review* 25 (18 June 1984), 7.

11. Kai-yu Hsu, *Chou En-lai: China's Gray Eminence* (Garden City, NY: Doubleday, 1968), 27-44.

12. Thomas C. Schelling, *The Strategy of Conflict* (Cambridge: Harvard University Press, 1960), 1-20.

13. Ren Tao (A member of the Economic Research Center under the State Council) and Zheng Tingsheng, "Chinese-Type Modernization: Why a Change in Emphasis?" *Beijing Review* 1 (3 January 1983): 16.

14. "Premier Zhao on Sino-US Relations and World Situation," *Beijing Review* 4 (23 January 1984): 19.

15. Ibid., 20

16. "Constitution of the Communist Party of China," *Beijing Review* 38 (26 September 1982): 8.

17. Mu Youlin, "China's Independent Diplomacy," *Beijing Review* 4 (24 January 1983): 4. See also Huan Xiang, "Uphold the Foreign Policy of Maintaining Independence and Keeping the Initiative in Our Own Hands." *Renmen Ribao*, (31 October 1982), 6 in *FBIS-PRC*, 1 November 1982, A1.

18. Hu Yaobang, General Secretary of CPC spoke of "The great friendship between the two Parties, the two countries and the two peoples of China and Korea . . . " while visiting Pyongyang in May 1984. "Hu Supports DPRK Talks Proposal," *Beijing Review* 20 (14 May 1984), 6. When visiting the United States, Premier Zhoa Ziyang spoke of the existing friendship between the Chinese and American peoples and the desire for the two countries to be friends. "Premier Zhao on Sino-US Relations and World Situations," *Beijing Review* 4 (23 January 1984): 20.

19. Pao Chao Hsieh, *The Government of China (1644-1911)* (New York: Octagon Books, 1966), 235-254.

20. "Report on Problems Concerning Peace Talks," *Selected Works of Zhou Enlai*, vol. 1 (Beijing: Foreign Language Press, 1981), 360-364.

21. "On the People's Democratic Dictatorship," *Selected Works of Mao Tse-Tung*, vol. IV (Peking: Foreign Language Press, 1967), 416.

22. Jerome Alan Cohen and Hungdah Chiu, *People's China and International Law*, vol. 1 (Princeton: Princeton University Press, 1974), 119.

23. Selected passages from Zhou Enlai's speech found in Yuan-li Wu, *China, A Handbook.* (New York: Praeger, 1973), 829-830, and Cohen and Chiu, 120-123.

24. In addition Cohen and Chiu suggest that the Chinese now apply these principles to their relations with all nations; China no longer applies the higher standards of "socialist internationalism" to other socialist nations because of the Soviet Union's "perfidy." In Zhao Ziyang's report to the Second Session of the Sixth National People's Congress, he stated that the Five Principles "are applicable in guiding relations not only between countries with different social systems but also between countries with similar social systems, including socialist systems."

25. Cohen and Chiu, 119.

26. Ibid., 7. See also Hsieh, *The Government of China*, 235-254.

27. Ibid., 10.

28. Chou Keng-Sheng, "The Principle of Peaceful coexistence from the Viewpoint of International Law," in Cohen and Chiu, 126-132.

29. Interview with Ambassador U. Alexis Johnson, March 1983, Washington, DC.

30. US Department of State, US-China Joint Communique, Current Policy No. 413, Bureau of Public Affairs, Washington, DC (August 1982). With respect to the Five Principles of Peaceful Coexistence, the three communiques state the following:

a. Joint Communique, February 28, 1972:

"There are essential differences between China and the United States in their social systems and foreign policies. However, the two sides agreed that countries, regardless of their social systems, should conduct their relations on the principles of respect for the sovereignty and territorial integrity of all states, non-aggression against other states, non-interference in the internal affairs of other states, equality and mutual benefit, and peaceful coexistence. International disputes should be settled on this basis, without reporting to the use or threat of force. The United States and the People's Republic of China are prepared to apply these principles to their mutual relations." Henry Kissinger, *The White House Years* (Boston: Little, Brown and Company, 1979), 1492.

b. Joint Communique, December 1978:

"The United States of America and the People's Republic of China reaffirm the principles agreed on by the two sides in the Shanghai Communique. . . . " US Department of State, "US Policy Toward China July 15, 1971-January 15, 1979," Selected Documents No. 9, Bureau of Public Affairs, Washington, DC (January 1979), 45.

c. Joint Communique, August 17, 1983 ("Shanghai II"):

"3. Respect for each other's sovereignty and territorial integrity and non-interference in each other's international affairs constitute the fundamental principles guiding United States-China relations. These principles were confirmed in the Shanghai Communique of February 28, 1972 and reaffirmed in the Joint Communique . . . (December 15, 1978). Both sides emphatically state that these principles continue to govern all aspects of their relations. . . .
.

5. The United States Government attaches great importance to its relations with China, and reiterates that it has no intention of infringing on Chinese sovereignty and territorial integrity, or interfering in China's internal affairs, or pursuing a policy of "two Chinas" or "one China, one Taiwan. . . .

8. . . . The two sides are determined, on the principle of equality and mutual benefit, to strengthen their ties. . . .

9. . . . , the two governments reaffirm the principles agreed on by the two sides in the Shanghai communique and the Joint Communique (December 15, 1978). . . . "

31. Zhao Ziyang, "Report on the Work of the Government," (Delivered at the Second Session of the Sixth National People's Congress on May 15, 1984), *Beijing Review* 24 (1 June 11 1984): document insert, XIV.

32. Walter G. Hermes, *Truce Tents and Fighting Front* (Washington, DC: Office of the Chief of Military History, US Army, 1966), 15.

33. Kenneth T. Young, *Negotiating with the Chinese Communist: The United States Experience, 1953-1967* (New York: McGraw-Hill Book Company, 1968), 371.

34. Kissinger, 752. It was a classical third-party approach in which the Chinese worked the issue through intermediaries until they perceived a possible agreement. They then moved rapidly to an agreement.

35. Samelson, 6, and Shroeder, 486-491.

36. Lin Yutang, somewhat more cynically, characterizes the Chinese character in terms of mellowness and pacifism. The Chinese live by a certain tolerant but hard-boiled pragmatism. They live neither for a utopia on earth nor in a life after but for order in life on earth in which they can work peacefully, endure nobly, and live happily despite its abundance of pain and sorrow—the original humanists. *My Country and My People* (New York: John Day Company, 1939), 42-66.

37. An interesting assessment by the K'ang-hsi Emperor partly explains why the Chinese avoided the court system. " . . . the good citizens, who have difficulties among themselves, will settle them like brothers, by referring them to the arbitration of some old man or the mayor of the commune. As for those who are troublesome, obstinate and quarrelsome, let them be ruined in the law-courts—that is the justice that is due to them." T. R. Jernigan, *China in Law and Commerce* (New York: 1905), quoted in Sybelle van der Sprenkel, *Legal Institutions in Manchu China, a Sociological Analysis* (London: Atlone Press, 1962), 114.

38. This description of China's traditional approach to conflict resolution is summarized from Sybelle van der Sprenkel, *Legal Institutions in Manchu China*, 99-100, 114-121. Her observations are supported in other fields of study by Cohen and Chiu, 119; Charles A. Moore, ed., *The Chinese Mind, Essentials of Chinese Philosophy and Culture* (Honolulu: University Press of Hawaii, 1967), 219; anthropologist Maurice Freedman, *Chinese Lineage and Society: Fukien and K'wang tung* (London: Atlone Press, 1966); and humanist Lin Yutang, 42-66.

39. There is considerable similarity between the clan wars of South China and how they were settled and the Korean War and the Armistice Talks. This comparison was brought to my attention by Mr. Charles Freeman, US Department of State, an astute observer of Chinese diplomatic negotiating practices.

40. Moore, 219.

41. "On Practice," *Selected Works of Mao*, vol. 1, 298.

42. Ibid., 295-309.

43. Jerome A. Cohen and Hungdah Chiu, *People's China and International Law*, vol. 1, (Princeton: Princeton University Press, 1974), 15-17.

44. "Disputes Solved by Arbitration," *Beijing Review* : 13 (26 March 1984), 9.

45. The term literally refers to the three religions of Confucianism, Daoism, and Buddhism and to the nine schools of thought of Confucian, Daoists, the "Yin-Yang", the Legalists, the Logicians, the Mohists, the Political Strategists, the Eclectics, and the Agriculturists. The term is commonly used to refer to all religions, sects, and academic schools of thought. *Beijing Review* 13 (26 March 1984): 24.

46. Mao makes this point in "Fourteen Great Achievements: 6. Overthrowing the Political Power of the Country Magistrate and his Bailiffs," *Selected Works of Mao*, vol. 1, 42-44.

47. Ibid, 342. For purposes of his argument, Mao used the following terms interchangeably' "unity, solidarity, combination, harmony, balance, stalemate, deadlock, rest, constancy, equilibrium, solidity, attraction, etc."

48. "On Contradictions," *Selected Works of Mao*, vol. 1, 315-319.

49. Interviews in Beijing, PRC, 1982.

50. Interviews in Beijing, PRC, 1982.

51. See an excellent discussion of the value of weiqi as an analogy for Chinese strategic thought in Scott A. Boorman, *The Protracted Game, a Wei-ch'i Interpretation of Maoist Revolutionary Strategy* (London: Oxford University Press, 1969), 11-21.

52. Walter G. Hermes, *Truce Tent and Fighting Front* (Washington: Office of the Chief of Military History, US Army, 1966), 20-23.

53. Interviews with Chinese officials, 1984.

54. Kai-yu Hsu, *Zhou EnLai: China's Gray Eminence* (Garden City, NY: Doubleday, 1968), 163.

55. One US diplomat stated during an interview in Beijing that initially after normalization, the US delegation did not keep very detailed records of the negotiations conducted in Beijing. However, they soon learned to do so as a defensive mechanism. The Chinese were constantly quoting from their records and the US diplomats had no capability of refuting their statements, much less of using such a tactic.

56. "More Agreements Reached with US," *Beijing Review* 2117 (21 May 1984), 11-12.

57. Chester L. Karrass, *The Negotiating Game* (New York: Thomas Y. Crowell, 1970), pp. 170-198.

58. "Past Year's Negotiating and the Prospects," *Selected Works of Zhou Enlai*, vol. 1 (Beijing: Foreign Language Press, 1981), 291.

59. For an effective generalization of the negotiating style of America's business see: John L. Graham and Roy A. Herberges, Jr., "Negotiators abroad-Don't shoot from the hip," *Harvard Business Review*, July-August 1983, 160-168.

60. Richard L. Walker, *The Multi-State System of Ancient China* (Westport, Conn.: Greenwood Press, 1953).

61. One of the better known stories from Chinese history, the story of Li Xiangru is the basis for a popular Peking Opera, *The Reconciliation of the General and the Prime Minister*, that is still played today. For a summary see Wei Tang, "The Return of the Jade," *China Reconstructs* 31 (October 1982): 69 and 72.

62. Chai Zemin, "Common Wish for Better Sino-US Relations," *Beijing Review* 17 (23 April 1984): 18.

63. Ogura Kazuo, "How the 'Inscrutables' Negotiate with the 'Inscrutables': Chinese Negotiating Tactics vis-a-vis the Japanese," *China Quarterly* 79 (September 1979): 529-552.

64. "Premier Zhao on Sino-US Relations and World Situation," *Beijing Review* 4 (23 January 1984): 18. This concept might also be seen as a Chinese version of a familiar Western phrase "no permanent friends, only permanent interests."

65. For an examination of many of these techniques as they are used by the Chinese in commercial negotiations with the United States, see Lucian Pye, *Chinese Commercial negotiating Style* (Cambridge: Oelgeschlager, Gunn & Hain, Publishers, 1982).

66. Interviews with Chinese officials, 1984.

67. Alfred D. Wilhelm, Jr., "National SecurityThe Chinese Perspective," in U. Alexis Johnson, George R. Packard, Alfred D. Wilhelm, Jr., *China Policy for the Next Decade: Report of the Atlantic Council Committee on China Policy* (Washington, DC: Oelgesehlager, Gunn and Hain, Publishers, 1984), 193-194.

CHAPTER 3

1. C. Turner Joy, *How Communists Negotiate* (NY: MacMillian, 1955), 10.

2. Admiral C. Turner Joy was Senior Delegate of the United Nations Command delegation to the Korean Armistice Conference from 10 July 1951 through 22 May 1952.

3. Fred C. Iklé, *How Nations Negotiate* (NY: Harper and Row, 1964), 123.

4. Ibid., 143-148.

5. Ibid., 143-163, 238-255. Also see Fred C. Iklé, "Negotiating Effectively," in *Modern Diplomacy: The Art and the Artisans* (Washington: American Enterprise Institute for Public Policy Research, 1979), 371-372.

6. Allan E. Goodman, ed., *Negotiating While Fighting: The Diary of Admiral C. Turner Joy at the Korean Armistice Conference* (Stanford: Hoover Institution Press, 1978), 19.

7. Ibid., 436-437.

8. Kenneth T. Yound, *Negotiating with the Chinese Communists: The United States Experience, 1953-1967* (NY: McGraw-Hill, 1968), 342.

9. Henry Kissinger, *White House Years* (Boston: Little, Brown and Company, 1979), 686.

10. Interview with Ambassador U. Alexis Johnson, Washington, DC, June 1984.

11. Kissinger, 752.

12. See Senator John Glenn, "China-Taiwan Policy," *Congressional Record, July 22, 1982*, S. 8873-8875; and *China Policy for the Next Decade, Report of the Atlantic Council's Committee on China Policy*, by U. Alexis Johnson, Chairman, Washington, DC: The Atlantic Council of the United States, 1983, 23. The committee noted, with respect to US decisions on arms sales, that "Others within and outside the US Government questioned whether such sales were in the long term US national interest The various offers seemed based on ad hoc, unrelated decisions, often prompted by "trip-book diplomacy," i.e., the need for each American visitor to Beijing to bring some new concession or expansion of the relationship in order to maintain "momentum" in consolidating the relationship."

13. These biographical summaries are drawn principally from the following sources:

a. Interviews held in Beijing, Hong Kong, Washington, and New York during 1982-1984 with some of the negotiators, former members of their negotiations staffs and other Chinese who have known these individuals personally.

b. Chai Chengwen, Wang Bingnan, Huang Hua, Zhou Enlai from Wolfgang Bartke, *Who's Who in the People's Republic of China* (Armonk, NY: M. E. Sharp, 1981).

c. Deng Hua, Bian Zhangwu, Ding Guoyu, Xie Fang, Chai Chengwen, Wang Guoquan from *Chung-kung Jen-min Lu (Chinese Communist Personalities)*, Taipei, Taiwan: Institute of International Relations, 1983).

d. Ed Hammond, *Coming of Grace, An Illustrated Biography of Zhou Enlai* (Berkeley: Lancaster-Miller, 1980).

e. Hsieh Fang, Pien Chang-wu, Teng Hua, Ting Kuo- yu, Tsai Chengwen from Walter G. Hermes, *Truce Tent and Fighting Front* (Washington, DC: Office of the Chief of Military History, US Army, 1966.

f. Kai-yu Hsu, *Zhou Enlai, China's Gray Eminence* (NY: Doubleday Anchor, 1969).

g. Teng Hua, Wang Ping-nan, Wang Kuo-ch'uan, Ch'iao Kuan-hua, Huang Hua, Zhou Enlai from Donald W. Klein and Anne B. Clark, *Biographic Dictionary of Chinese Communism, 1921-1965* (Cambridge, Mass: Harvard University Press, 1971).

14. Admiral C. Turner Joy, *How Communists Negotiate* (NY: MacMillan, 1955), 12-13.

15. Interview with a White House staff member shortly after Huang Hua's visit.

16. Wu Xiuquan, *Eight Years in the Foreign Ministry* (8th installment) from Hong Kong *Wen Wei Po*, 1 September 1983, Foreign Broadcast Information Service (FBIS), *Daily Report-China*, 1 September 1983, W5-W7.

17. Ibid., W7.

18. Luo Ruiqing, Lu Zhengcao, Wang Bingnan, *Zhou Enlai and the Xi'an Incident* (Beijing: Foreign Language Press, 1983).

19. Young, 15-17.

20. Kissinger, 188.

21. Ibid., 1054.

22. Chen Yun, "Strictly Observe Party Discipline," *Beijing Review* : 14 (2 April 1984): 17.

23. Ibid., 17-18.

24. Chen Yun, 19.

25. Zbigniew Brzezinski, *Power and Principle* (NY: Farrar, Straus, Girous, 1983), 226, 230.

26. Interview with US Government official shortly after negotiations.

27. Wu Xiuquan, W6.

28. Interview with Ambassador U. Alexis Johnson, Washington, DC., March 1982.

29. Luo, Lu, Wang, *Zhou Enlai and the Xi'an Incident*, 57-82.

30. Kissinger, 741-755.

31. Wang Bingnan, *Nine Years of Sino-US Talks in Retrospect* (part 3), in *Guangzhou Ribao*, 4 October 1984, trans. in Foreign Broadcast Information Service, Daily Report: People's Republic of China (FBIS-PRC), 19 October 1984, B6-B7.

32. During my interviews, several Chinese scholars and diplomats commented that many Americans have a distorted view of Chinese patience. One scholar felt that the American view was, to some degree, patronizing. He argued at length that the Chinese were individually probably as impatient as Americans, particularly to the extent that impatience reflects drive and ambition, but that deeply ingrained social conventions have in the past generally curbed most of the more direct and emotional manifestations of impatience. He illustrated his point by pointing to the impatience and rudeness associated with the competitiveness in recent years of Beijing's cab drivers. Their conduct reflects the radicalizations of China's youth who were taught during the Cultural Revolution to eschew old social conventions in order to express their true feelings more freely. He argued that the Chinese are not passively patient, but rather have collectively learned from bitter experience the value of fortitude and perseverance to eventual success.

33. Kissinger, 1056.

34. Ambassador Johnson issued the invitation after he obtained permission from Washington to take the initiative. Interview with Ambassador Johnson in March 1982.

35. FBIS-PRC, B6.

36. Donald Klein makes the point that the Ministry of Foreign Affairs has, over the years, provided the majority of its ambassadors from within its ranks or from related government agencies involved in foreign affairs. Of course during the early years this was not possible. There was a "borrowing" and "lending" of personnel among ministries according to the need of the moment. Donald Klein, "The Chinese Foreign Ministry," (Ph.D. diss., Columbia University, 1974), 95-117.

37. Maurice Collis provides in *Foreign Mud* (London: Farber and Farber, 1946), 125-132, an engaging description of some of the social-psychology behind the use by Chinese officials of Chinese merchants to buffer exchanges between the British "barbarians" and themselves in the early 19th century. These merchants were translators and held responsible for whatever went wrong in the realtionship. Kissenger reports in *The White House Years*, 741, that Nancy Tang (T'ang Wen-sheng), Brooklyn-born translator for Zhou Enlai during one of Kissinger's visits to China, considered herself to be more than just an interpreter. The extent of this feeling was illustrated by the extent to which she argued with Zhou in front of Kissinger over a point being discussed.

38. Donald J. Munro, *The Concept of Man in Early China* (Stanford: Stanford University Press, 1969), 167.

39. Arthur H. Dean, "What It's Like to Negotiate with the Chinese," *NY Times Magazine*, 30 October 1966, 52.

40. Panmunjom served as a training ground for Foreign Ministry linguists long after the armistice and political talks concluded. A number of diplomats, with whom I had conversations (1982-1984), perfected their English by translating a countless number of "boring speeches" at Panmunjom.

CHAPTER 4

1. Allan E. Goodman, ed., *Negotiating While Fighting: The Diary of Admiral C. Turner Joy at the Korean Armistice Conference* (Stanford: Hoover Institution Press, 1978), 436.

2. Arthur H. Dean, "What It's Like to Negotiate with the Chinese," *New York Times Magazine* (30 October 1966), 44.

3. U. Alexis Johnson, *The Right Hand of Power* (Englewood Cliff, NJ: Prentice-Hall, 1984), 127-128.

4. Henry Kissinger, *American Foreign Policy* (New York: W. W. Norton and Company, 1974), 11-12.

5. James F. Schnabel, *Policy and Direction: The First Year* (Washington, DC: Office of the Chief of Military History, US Army, 1972), 104-105.

6. Ibid., 194.

7. The success of the Chinese following their entry into the war generated a variety of reactions in the United States. For some it meant that US forces must inevitably retreat from the Korean peninsula in order to insure their survival to protect Japan. Some wanted to seek an armistice, while others wanted to carry the war to China. Still others argued for continuing to fight to retain a toehold on the peninsula. A working consensus only emerged after Ridgway did the unexpected and fought back to the 38th Parallel in March 1951. As the UN forces retreated south of the 38th Parallel, a message from the JCS, personal for MacArthur (JCS 80680, 9 January 1951), directed MacArthur to defend in successive positions, inflicting maximum damage to hostile forces in Korea, subject to the safety of his troops and his basic mission of protecting Japan. When he judged that evacuation was necessary to avoid severe losses of men and materials, he was to withdraw to Japan. Fredrick Aandahl, John P. Glennon, Harriet D. Schwar and Paul Claussen, eds., *Foreign Relations of the United States, 1951*, vol. VII, part 1 (Washington, DC: Government Printing Office, 1983), 42-43. On 10 January General MacArthur responded that his command was of "insufficient strength to hold a position in Korea and simultaneously protect Japan." He argued that under the limitations of his command, "its military position is untenable, but it can hold . . . up to its complete destruction." Aandahl et al., 55-56.

Two efforts made through the United Nations by the British, Indians, and others to encourage the Chinese to accept a cease-fire are discussed by Dean Acheson in *Present at the Creation* (New York: The New American Library, 1970), 661. Amplification of Acheson's account can be found among the documents in Aandahl et al., 1-93.

A National Intelligence Special Estimate was completed on January 11, 1951, "To estimate and enumerate the advantages and disadvantages of holding a UN beachhead in South Korea." The estimate as written generally advocated maintaining a beachhead, though such would be impossible in the event of a full-scale Soviet intervention. Aadahl et al., 61-63.

In a memorandum of 12 January to the Secretary of State, Assistant Secretary Dean Rush argued that the US should not abandon resistance in Korea if there is any practical way to continue it. Resistance could be continued from the many islands, including Cheju-do, and peninsulas along the south coast. From there the ROK government, armed forces and civilian refugees could be organized to develop unconventional operation within Korea. Off-shore air operations would continue. The results of these efforts might be applicable to opposing Asian communism in general. Aandahl et al., 66-67.

8. In February 1951, the commander of the Chinese forces in Korea, Marshall Peng Dehuai, reported to Mao in Beijing that the war "could not be won quickly." During the first three months of 1951, the Chinese gradually built a "defense-in-depth tunnel system" from which to conduct "positional warfare of a protracted nature." By the Spring of 1951, the Chinese had concluded that the war was at a military stalemate. Peng Dehuai, *Memoirs of a Chinese Marshall*, trans. Zheng Longpu, ed. Sara Grimes (Beijing: Foreign Language Press, 1984), 479-483.

On 5 April 1951, Dean Rusk, Assistant Secretary of State for Far Eastern Affairs told members of Congress that a strategic stalemate had developed in Korea in which neither side was able to drive the others out of Korea but that tactically there were important, impending operations. Executive session hearing before the Subcommittee on the Far East and the Pacific Ocean Area of the House Committee on Foreign Affairs, 5 April 1951 found in US, Congress, House, Committee on Foreign Affairs, *US Policy in the Far East, Part I* . Selected Executive Sessions Hearings, 1951- 1956, Historical Series Volume XVII (Washington, DC: Government Printing Office, 1980), 127. By July 1951, "A full year of bitter fighting had served only to bring the opposing forces into balance." Schnabel, 405. According to John M. Allison, Assistant Secretary of State for Far Eastern Affairs, by May 1952 both sides had built up to a depth of 30 miles on each side, making it a costly operation for each side to make an appreciable advance—a tactical stalemate. Executive session hearing before the House Committee on Foreign Affairs, *US Policy in the Far East*, 178.

9. Allen S. Whiting, *China Crosses the Yalu* (Stanford: Stanford University Press, 1960), 159. In 1951 the PRC conducted three mass movements. Two dealt with the domestic problems of land reform and the elimination of residual resistance from the civil war. The third was concerned with "smashing US imperialism's mad scheme to overrun and occupy the Democratic People's Republic of Korea and then to invade China's mainland." Mao Tsetung, "Great Victories in Three Mass Movements," *Selected Works of Mao Tsetung*, vol. V (Peking: Foreign Language Press, 1977), 59-61. "US occupation of Korea, separated from China by only a river, would threaten Northeast China. Its control of Taiwan posed a threat to Shanghai and East China." Peng Dehuai, 473.

10. Whiting, 151-160; Peng Dehuai, 473-474.

11. Sun Tzu, *The Art of War*, trans. Samuel B. Griffith (New York: Oxford University Press, 1963), 72.

12. Peng Dehuai briefly described the meetings on October 4 and 5, 1950 of the Party's Central Committee at which the reasons for not

sending troops to Korea were discussed. He then summarized the reasoning that lead him to support the logic that China should "dispatch troops to resist the US." Peng Dehuai, 472-474.

Two years later Mao summarized how the concerns of 1950 were handled in an appeal for the unity necessary to stay the course in Korea and to resolve the problems, particularly economic, that lay ahead. Mao Tsetung, "Let us Unite and Clearly Distinguish Between Ourselves and the Enemy, August 4, 1952," *Selected Works,* vol. V, 78-79.

13. For an example, see the section titled "Enemy Intentions," of "Draft Memorandum for the President [February 23, 1951]," Aandahl et al., 191, or Schanbel, *Policy and Direction*, 381.

14. Peng Dehuai states that the 37th Parallel was the limit of the ability of the Chinese Volunteers to defeat the Americans on the battlefield. Peng Dehuai, 480. My interviews supported Whiting's analysis of the Chinese, "Motivation Behind Intervention," in Whiting, 151-162.

15. Acheson, 686-687. See his analysis of "the Decision to Negotiate Through Ridgway."

16. Johnson, 122-123.

17. Donald J. Munro, *The Concept of Man in Early China* (Stanford: Stanford University Press 1969), 171-172.

18. Mao Tse-tung, "Problems of Strategy in China's Revolutionary War," December 1936 in *Selected Works*, Vol I (Peking: Foreign Language Press, 1967), 180.

19. Griffith, 73.

20. Interviews conducted in 1983-84 in Seoul and Hong Kong with Koreans and Nationalist Chinese who had fought against and negotiated with the Communist Chinese.

21. In *Red China's Fighting Hordes* (Harrisburg, Pa: The Military Service Publishing Company, 1951), 40-41, Robert B. Rigg notes that Peng Dehuai, the PLA commander in Korea, "holds the opinion that soldier morale and espirit de corps count more in the success of a campaign than the plan itself." Peng also believed that "What we lack in weapons will be balanced by our men's knowledge of what they are fighting for." Both concepts require time to instill in troops and neither are compatible with a wanton disregard for life. At the same time Peng believed that "with her great manpower, China can outlast any enemy in a long war of attrition." Marshall Liu Bozheng recorded his view in verse. "When you keep men and lose land, the land can be retaken. If you keep land and lose soldiers, you lose both." Rigg, 31.

Nevertheless, PLA commanders found it necessary to use the 'human wave' tactic of mass in Korea as they had in the liberation war. In July 1947 for example, Rigg saw at Tsining, Shantung "a dike across the Grand Canal made of human bodies produced by a 'human wave' attack." Rigg, 199. Such tactics were not invented by the communist, rather they have existed throughout China's revolutionary history (Boxer, Taiping, Nien, etc. Rebellions), whenever men, lacking material resources, have had to substitute the dedication of the many to achieve their end, having exhausted all other means.

22. Mao, vol. V, 79.

23. "They (the Chinese People's Revolutionary Military Commission and the People's Government) are willing to consider the establishment of diplomatic relations with foreign countries; such relations must be based on equality, mutual benefit, mutual respect for sovereignty and territorial integrity and, first of all, on no help being given to the Kuomintang reactionaries. They will tolerate no act of intimidation by any foreign government. A foreign government which wishes to consider establishing diplomatic relations with us must sever relations with the remnant Kuomintang forces and withdraw its armed forces from China." Mao Tse-tung, "On the Outrages by British Warships," 30 April 1949 *Selected Works*, vol. IV, 402. A footnote states that the statement was drafted by Mao and set forth as the foreign policy of the new China which was soon to be established.

24. Donald W. Klein, "The Chinese Foreign Ministry" (Ph,D. diss., Columbia University, 1974), 56.

25. Acheson, 621-622.

26. Ibid., 585. Whiting, 110.

27. Whiting, 117-118. Peng Dehuai, 474-477.

28. Schnabel, 236, 253-256.

29. Peng Dehuai, 472-474; Mao, vol. v, 78-79.

30. Wu Xiuquan, *Eight Years in the Foreign Ministry* (8th installment), from Hong Kong *Wen Wei Po*, 1 September 1983, Foreign Broadcast Information Service (FBIS), *Daily Report-China*, 1 September 1983, W7.

31. Acheson, 661-662. Wu's rejection of the efforts of the allies resulted in their closing ranks behind the proposal of the United States to condemn Chinese aggression, albeit reluctantly. See the series of exchanges between the Secretary of State and US ambassadors to Britain, Canada, France, India, and the United Nations leading up to the 1 February 1951 adoption in UN of Resolution 498 on the finding of Communist China guilty of aggression in Korea. Aandahl et al., 100-151.

32. Aandahl et al., 91-92.

33. Acheson, 682. Also see US, Congress, Senate, Committees on Armed Services and Foreign Relations, *Hearings to Conduct an Inquiry into the Military Situation in the Far East and the Facts Surrounding the Relief of General of the Army Douglas MacArthur from His Assignments in that Area*, 82d Cong., 1st sess., 1951, 3479-3480. Also see discussion of how in latter years Acheson reasoned that the Russians and Chinese, for

other historical reasons, might have felt tricked by the refusal of the US to accept the 38th Parallel as the armistice line. Acheson, 689-690.

34. Those members of the Chinese delegation from the Foreign Ministry whose jobs included frequent contact with the United States were given temporary military ranks equivalent to those of their US counterparts. As an example, one of the key liaison officers was Colonel Pu Shan. Walter G. Hermes, *Truce Tent and Fighting Front* (Washington, DC: Office of the Chief of Military History, US Army, 1966), 159-160. A Harvard Ph.D in economics, Dr. Pu had accompanied Wu Xiuchuan to the United Nations in 1950. Wu, W5. After the war, Dr. Pu returned to the Foreign Ministry. Like many other Western educated intellectuals in the Party, he suffered severely from the revolving door effect of the anti-rightest campaigns of 1957-58 and the Cultural Revolution. In the early 1980s he transferred to the Chinese Academy of Social Sciences where he headed the Institute of International Economics. Similarly, many of the Chinese translators rose to prominence in the Foreign Ministry, such as Bi Jilung, a Chinese member of the UN permanent staff in the early 1980s and Ji Chao Zhu, Minister-Counselor of the PRC Embassy in the US, 1982-85. A large number of China's current American experts have served at Panmunjom either during the negotiations or at the postarmistice talks.

35. Dean, 52. Dean underplayed the importance of Dr. Pu Shouchang in the negotiations by describing him as Huang's official interpreter. Dr. Pu performed as Huang's deputy, but, because of his impeccable American (Harvard) English, he often had to assist during difficult sessions or to correct interpreter errors during the proceedings. Dr. Pu returned to China to become Zhou Enlai's executive assistant and later when Huang Hua became Foreign Minister, Dr. Pu became Vice Foreign Minister until his retirement in 1984. Then he joined the Chinese Academy of Social Sciences as an advisor. Dr. Pu is also the brother of Dr. Pu Shan.

36. Acheson, 684. Aandahl, "Telegram, The Ambassador in the Soviet Union (Kirk) to the Secretary of State," *Foreign Relations*, 1951, 548-549.

37. Aandahl, "Editorial Note," *Foreign Relations*, 1951, 546-566. Uncertainty is indicated by the flurry of cables that took place between Washington and US Embassy, Moscow, and others.

38. Aandahl, "Telegram," 560-562.

39. Aandahl, "Memorandum of Conversation, by the Director of the Office of Northeast Asian Affairs (U.A. Johnson), June 28, 1951," *Foreign Relations*, 1951, 566-571.

40. Aandahl, "Telegram," *Foreign Relations*, p. 577-578; Schnabel, 403.

41. Schnabel, 404. Ridgway accepted Kaesong, suggested the 10th or earlier, and suggested a meeting of liaison officers on July 5 or a soon

thereafter as possible. The communists accepted and set the date as the 8th.

42. Hermes, 20-22.

43. Before a meeting in 1835 between British Lord Napier and three Chinese mandarins representing the Viceroy of Canton, local merchant/interpreters, acting as third-party intermediaries, took ceremonial "chairs to the (British) reception room, and there arranged three of them facing south, the quarter of happy augury toward which authority always faces in China, with two rows of four chairs at right angles to them and facing east and west." The three Mandarins would sit facing south and the Hong merchants facing east and west. The British would stand. Although the protocol has changed, similar seating arrangements are still used in China today. Maurice Collis, "The Victory of the Chairs," *Foreign Mud* (London: Faber and Faber, Ltd., 1946), 144-154.

44. Hermes, 21. "For the mandarins when confronted with the (reversal of the placement of the) chairs to have shown the smallest sign of surprise or vexation would have been a breach of manners, a blow of dignity and so, a loss of face". Collins, 151.

45. *History of the Korean War-Korean Armistice Negotiations (July 1951-May 1952), Part One* (Tokyo: Military History Section, Headquarters, Far East Command, United Nations Command), 13.

46. Ibid., 8, 12.

47. Arthur Dean described the environment of Panmunjom as "A worse place for peaceful negotiations could not have been found. There was no way in which the normal tensions of difficult diplomatic negotiations could be relieved, and no way in which private negotiations or suggestions could be carried out." Dean, 47.

48. On 15 July 1951 Joy recorded in his journal, "Our opponents seemed willing and anxious to get down to business as if they wanted to show results or determine our position as quickly as possible." On 16 July he wrote, "By their comments Commies appeared interested in arriving at agenda. Several concessions on their part indicated their interest." Goodman, 19-20.

49. After the war Joy wrote that "Among men who adhere to logic, an agenda is understood to be only a list of topics to be discussed, concerning which agreed conclusions are later required." In contrast, "the Communist concept of an agenda was a set of conclusions which would restore the situation in Korea to that obtaining before they launched their aggression." As an example an American agenda might be: "1. Place the game is to be played. 2. Time the game is to start. 3. Selection of umpires." The Communist proposed agenda might be: "1. Agreement that game is to be played in Shanghai. 2. Agreement that game be played at night. 3. Agreement that umpires be Chinese officials." Admiral C.

Turner Joy, *How Communists Negotiate* (New York: MacMillan, 1955), 18-19.

50. In 1966 Le Duan, First Secretary, Lao Dong Party in Hanoi, stated in a letter to General Nguyen Chi Thanh, NLF Commander-in-Chief in the south that "the general strategy has to pass through several transitional phases . . . Heavy emphasis is to be placed on the political struggle which includes the diplomatic struggle ... the strategy on war and negotiations must . . . serve the political and military aims of our strategy on PITTING THE WEAK AGAINST THE STRONG (emphasis added)." In the next paragraph he relates these ideas to the Chinese experience. "The problem of war and negotiation is not quite new in the history of our country. Nguyen Trai had once used such a strategy to defeat the feudalist elements of Ming's dynasty. Our comrades in China had also adopted the 'fight-and-negotiate' policy in their struggle against the US and Chiang Kai-shek. The same strategy was used in the Korean War." He then observes that the US holds "that negotiation is to be conducted from a strong (military) position." For Le Duan "the political struggle is of major importance . . . we must constantly take the initiative, our strategy on negotiation must serve in a practical manner our concrete political aims.

In April 1966 General Nguyen Van Vinh said "In a war between a powerful country which waged aggression and a weak country, as long as we have not yet acquired adequate strength, a situation where fighting and negotiations are conducted simultaneously does not exist. Fighting continues until the emergence of a situation where both sides are fighting indecisively. Then a situation where fighting and negotiations are conducted simultaneously may emerge." Later he says that "The Americans find it necessary to negotiate, but negotiate from a strong position, partly because they have deceitful motives, and partly because the situation has compelled them to negotiate. Yet, they want us to make concessions to them." John T. Thomas, Jr., "Negotiating With the North Vietnamese, a Military Perspective" (MMAS thesis, US Army Command and General Staff College, Ft. Leavenworth, Kansas, 1975), 10-14.

51. Both the Departments of State and Defense "agreed that UN forces should not stop hostilities in the absence of a formal, supervised arrangement with the other side. This meant that fighting should continue during the period of negotiations." "UN forces had to maintain military pressure if we were going to achieve an armistice within a reasonable period." "It was a delicate situation, because the military was naturally reluctant to ask men to do battle if a cease-fire was likely the next day." Johnson, 122; also see Aandahl, "Conversation," attachment, part III. UN Military Operations before and during Cease-fire Discussions," *Foreign Relations, 1951*, 571, and "Memorandum by the Officer

in Charge of Korean Affairs, June 28, 1951," *Foreign Relations, 1951,* 571-572.

52. Mr. Acheson released a statement following receipt of Premier Zhou's message in which he said that "The reply of the Chinese Communist . . . is still further evidence of their contemptuous disregard of a world-wide demand for peace . . . outright rejection . . . shown a total lack of interest in a peaceful settlement. . . . " Aandahl, UN document A/C.1/653, *Foreign Relations, 1951*, 92-93.

53. Acheson, 681-692, 830-838.

54. For the text of Admiral Joy's opening statement concerning the United Nations Command Delegation's initial position on the demilitarized zone see Aandahl, message "Armistice Conference at Kaesong, 27 July 1951," *Foreign Relations, 1951*, 739-745, and Hermes, 36.

55. *History of the Korean War*, chap. II, 8-13; For an example of typical arguments advanced by both sides see account of 10 August 1951 meeting in Aandahl, "Telegram," 801-811.

56. Aandahl, "Telegram," 1065-1188.

57. Hermes, 116-121; Aandahl, "Telegram," 1087-1089, 1092-1093; *History of the Korean War*, chap. II, 13.

58. During the establishment of security procedures for the negotiations, the United States insisted that during the talks the trucks of the Communists, which would travel to Kaesong to support the talks, must be marked on top with white crosses. In addition, the Communists must inform the United States of the time and route of their convoys in order that US pilots would not attack these vehicles. Because there was no reciprocal requirement for the United States, the Chinese saw this as an unequal demand, an 'imperialist' type requirement which the powerful impose on the weak."

59. US Department of the Army, *Pamphlet 27-1: Treaties Governing Land Warfare* (Washington, DC: GPO, 7 December 1956), 109.

60. Ambassador U. Alexis Johnson, 129-144, provides an interesting description of the evolution of the positions and rationale that emerged in the US government during the development of the US position involving the one-for-one voluntary repatriation of POWs. This policy was ultimately decided by President Truman on moral grounds and recognized as a reversal that would create enormous difficulties at Panmunjom. According to Johnson, US policymakers were less concerned about Chinese reactions to the US proposal than they were about those in Moscow. "The prospect of communist POWs going where they liked after a war opened up too wide a rent in the Iron Curtain for them to accept. The Kremlin, as well as members of our (US) government, saw that it might be more difficult in the event of 'hot' war elsewhere, in Europe of instance, for the Soviets to guard against large-scale defections

of soldiers and civilians from Eastern European satellites if we were known to offer an inviolable sanctuary to POWs." Johnson, 134.

61. Article IV, Armistice Agreement in Hermes, 531.

62. See a memorandum of a conversation between President Rhee and Secretary Dulles, 5 August 1953 in Edward C. Keefer, ed., *Foreign Relations of the United States, 1952-1954*, vol. XV, Korea, part 2 (Washington, DC: GPO, 1984), 1468-1471.

63. Ibid., 1492-1510.

64. Peng Dehuai, 483-484.

65. Ibid., 484.

66. Ibid., 474-483.

CHAPTER 5

1. Wang Bingnan, "Recalling Nine Years of Sino-US Talks," part 23, *Guangzhou Ribao*, 20 January 1985, trans. in Foreign Broadcast Information Service, *Daily Report: People's Republic of China* (*FBIS-PRC*), 1 February 1985, B-5.

2. *FBIS-PRC*, 25 January 1985, B-2. He Long once told Wang Bingnan that "when the central authorities were selecting the negotiator, there were several candidates .... Due to my experience in foreign affairs for 10 years or so in the party and to having had long-term contacts with, and being familiar with the Americans, I was selected as chief negotiator on the Chinese side." *FBIS-PRC*, 18 January 1985, B-2.

3. Dick Wilson, *Zhou Enlai, A Biography* (New York, Viking Penguin Press, 1984), 190.

4. *FBIS-PRC*, 18 January 1985, B-2.

5. The guiding group was composed of:

- Group Leader—Zhang Hanfu, Vice Minister of Foreign Affairs. He was a key aide of Zhou along with Wang Bingnan in Hankow (1937), Chongqing (1938-1945), and during the Marshall Mission. He was in the United States for about 6 months for the creation of the United Nations at San Francisco in April 1945. During these six months, a number of talented Chinese scholars were recruited, including Dr. Pu Shan and Dr. Pu Shouchang, by the delegation of Dong Biwu, Zhang Hanfu and Chen Jiakang.
- Deputy Group Leader—Qiao Guanhua, Assistant Minister of Foreign Affairs, brother-in-law of Zhang Hanfu. He was a member of the Party's South China bureau, foreign affairs team that was established in Chongqing in 1939 under the leadership of Wang Bingnan. Later he spent much of the war in Hong Kong as a key Party representative, returning to China to work with the Marshall Mission. He died in late 1983.

- Secretary-General—Dong Yueqian, Director of Staff Office (Succeeded Wang Bingnan), Deputy Director to Wang Bingnan 1949-1952. He also worked with Zhou during the Marshall Mission.
- Member—Gong Peng (female), Director of Information Department. Like Huang Hua, she was a student at Yenching University at the time of Leighton Stuart. In 1939, as a member of Wang Bingnan's foreign affairs team, she was in charge of contacts with reporters from foreign countries. She later worked with the Marshall Mission and was in charge of the press for Zhou Enlai at the Geneva Conference. She died in 1970.
- Member—Pu Shan, Ph.D. in economics from Harvard, taught in US for several years prior to returning to China. In 1950 he accompanied Wu Xiuquan to the United Nations. During the Armistice Talks at Panmunjom, he was a senior liaison officer with the rank of Colonel. In 1954, as a section chief in the Ministry of Foreign Affairs, he attended the Geneva Conference. He supported Wang Bingnan during the four Johnson-Wang private meetings and conducted the two additional liaison meetings with Alfred LeS. Jenkins, Department of State. By 1983, he had moved from the Ministry of Foreign Affairs to be the Director, World Economics and Politics Institute, Chinese Academy of Social Sciences, Beijing.
- Member—Wang Baoliu. Partial sources:

–1945 UN team: *FBIS-PRC*, 18 January 1985, B-5.

–Guiding group: *FBIS-PRC*, 18 January 1985, B-2.

–South China team: *FBIS-PRC*, 18 January 1985, B-3.

–Marshall Mission and foreign ministry duties: Donald W. Klein, "The Chinese Foreign Ministry," (Ph.D. diss., Columbia University, 1974), 8-38.

6. *FBIS-PRC*, 19 October 1984, B-5.
7. Ibid., *FBIS-PRC*, 1 February 1985, B-2.
8. Huang Hua, "Looking Back on Bandung," *Beijing Review* 15 (April 15, 1985): 16.
9. *FBIS-PRC*, 25 January 1985, p. B-5.
10. U. Alexis Johnson, *Right Hand of Power* (New Jersey: Prentice-Hall, 1984), 239.
11. Andrew H. Berding, *Dulles on Diplomacy* (Princeton, New Jersey, D. Van Nostrand, 1965), 56-57.
12. Johnson, 94.
13. Interview with Ambassador U. Alexis Johnson, March 1983, Washington, DC.
14. *FBIS-PRC*, 19 October 1984, B-5.
15. Ibid.
16. Cable from US Embassy in London reports on cable from British office in Beijing concerning a conversation between Indian Ambassador

Raghavan and Zhou Enlai. US Department of State, *Foreign Relations of the United States, 1952-1954*, vol. XV, Korea, Part 2, (Washington: GPO, 1984), 1509-1510, hereafter cited as *FRUS-Korea.*

17. Ibid.

18. Ibid., "Editorial Note, 1503. On 28 August 1953 the General Assembly passed Resolution 711 (VII) calling for UN participation at the Korean political conference, which was called for in the Korean Armistice, to be limited to those nations "'contributing armed forces under the Unified Command." The resolution also called for participation by the Soviet Union, if the North Korean and Chinese side desired, and then called for communication of the resolution to both "Peking and Pyongyang."

19. Ibid., 1509.

20. Ibid., 1523. See "Memorandum of Conversation" pertaining to luncheon conversation among Arthur H. Dean, Krishna Menon, and Rajeshwar Dayal, Permanent Representative of India to the UN. For October 10 message see *Department of State Bulletin*, October 26, 1953, 551, cited in *FRUS-Korea* 1530.

21. Ibid., 1531.

22. Ibid., 1651-1652, 1655-1657. See Arthur Dean's 8 December 1953 cable to Washington in which he mentions the demand for a conference prior to the release of POWs. Ibid., pp. 1651-1652. On 12 December he describes his last meeting with Huang Hua. This cable was retransmitted to Paris for Dulles, who was attending the NATO Ministerial meeting. Ibid., pp. 1655-1657.

23. Ibid., 1675-1676. Kenneth Young, Deputy Representative for the Korean Political Conference discussed in a cable on December 29 to the Secretary of State some of the issues surrounding the charges of 'perfidy' and 'agent'. Dean found it difficult to believe the Chinese were as upset about his charge as he was with their use of the term "perfidy." In a 29 December cable to Young he inquires, "we don't wish to eat crow and we certainly would not wish to be placed in position of making that offer and then having Communists reject it publicly without formally retracting 'perfidy' charge. Do you think it possible that they do not quite understand full connotation of 'perfidy' in English (remember Huang's chief assistant is Dr . . Pu Shouchang, Harvard PhD, whom Under Secretary Walter Bedell Smith later complimented at Geneva for his flawless and beautifully pronounced English) and that they might be willing to withdraw or expunge ... without our having to make any retraction or expunging ... their statement that General Harrison did not act in good faith?" Dulles provided additional information in his instructions to Young on January 12, 1954. Ibid., 1717-1718.

24. Ibid., 1672-1673. Also, Young's cable of 26 January 1954 from Young to the Department of States. See Arthur Dean's observations of a

conversation between Huang Hua and India's General Thimayya, chairman of the NNRC, which he gave during a briefing conducted on December 21, 1953 in Washington for the UN representatives of the nations that provided forces to the UN Command in Korea.

25. Ibid, 1736. See cable of 26 January 1954 from Young to Department of State.

26. Ibid., 1678. See Arthur Dean memorandum of 30 December 1954 for Secretary of State.

27. Dwight D. Eisenhower, *The White House Years, Mandate for Change, 1953-1956* (Garden City, NY: Doubleday & Company, Inc., 1963), 214-215, 342-343; and Townsend Hoopes, *The Devil and John Foster* (Boston: Little, Brown and Company, 1973), 204-206; See message from Chief of Mission to Far East, General Van Fleet to Secretary of Defense Wilson concerning views in Korea and Formosa that British and French exercise veto over US Far East policy. *FRUS-Korea,* 1820-1821.

28. "NSC Staff Study on US Policy Toward Communist China," *Foreign Relations of the United States, 1952-1954,* vol. XIV, China and Japan, Part 1 (Washington: GPO, 1985), 305-306, hereafter cited as *FRUS-China.*

29. See Article IV, "Recommendations to the Governments Concerned on Both Sides," Korean Armistice Agreement, July 27, 1953 in Robert L. Branyan and Lawrence H. Larsen, *The Eisenhower Administration, 1953-1961: A Documentary History* (New York: Random House, Inc.), 170-171.

30. See "Terms of Reference," in William H. Vatcher, *Panmunjom* (New York: Frederick A. Praeger, Inc., 1958), 308.

31. The PRC and North Korea entered into three agreements, during Kim Il Sung's visit to PRC in November 1953, in which the PRC promised assistance for the restoration of North Korea's war damaged economy, communications and transportation, the promotion of technical cooperation, etc. The PRC agreed to annul debts up to 280 million yuan and primised a gift of 800 million yuan from 1954 to 1957 in the form of commodities. Douglas M. Johnston and Hungdah Chiu, *Agreements of the People's Republic of China, 1949-1967, A Calendar* (Cambridge, Mass.: Harvard University Press, 1968), 22-23.

32. By July 1954, eight out of nineteen Chinese armies had been withdrawn from North Korea. North Korean forces had been increased from six to seven corps and the effectiveness of each had also been increased. While the decrease in Chinese forces ensured that the forces of the United Nations were stronger than the Communists, there had also been an increase in UN strength such that they were relatively stonger than they had been at the time of the Armistice. *FRUS-Korea,* 1838.

33. Ibid., 1668. See memorandum of Dean's 21 December 1953 briefing.

34. Ibid., 1731. See 23 January 1954 cable from Young to Department of State.

35. Ibid., 1713. See 9 January 1954 cable from Young to Department of State.

36. Ibid.

37. Hoopes, 205-207; Anthony Eden, *The Memoirs of Anthony Eden, Full Circle* (Boston: Houghton Mifflin Company, 1060), 94-100.

38. Hoopes, 206; Eden, 97-99.

39. As part of the Quadripartite Communique of 18 February 1954, the four foreign ministers of Britain, France, the United States and the USSR agreed to a conference "in Geneva on April 26 for the purpose of reaching a peaceful settlement of the Korean question; (and) It is understood that neither the invitation to, nor the holding of, the above-mentioned conference shall be deemed to imply diplomatic recognition in any case where it has not already been accorded." *Department of State Bulletin*, 1 March 1954, 317-318.

In a 21 April 1954 note to the United States, the USSR put the PRC on equal footing with the four convening powers. In a 23 April reply, the United States rejected the contention that the "Chinese People's Republic should enjoy any special position with respect to conference at Geneva." *Foreign Relations of the United States, 1952-1954, Vol. XVI, The Geneva Conference* (Washington: GPO, 1981), 126-127, 130-131, hereafter cited as *FRUS-Geneva Conference.*

40. *FBIS-PRC*, October 19, 1984, B-5.

41. *FRUS-China*, 354. See Dulles cable of 30 January 1954 to President Eisenhower reference his dinner conversation with Soviet Foreign Minister Molotov on January 29.

42. *FBIS-PRC*, October 19, 1984, B-6.

43. Ibid.

44. Ibid.

45. Several participants in the conference have recorded their observations. One of the more critical of US policy is Chester Ronning, *A Memoir of China in Revolution* (New York: Pantheon Books, 1974), 213-241. Others include Eden, 120-163; Johnson, 201-236; *FBIS-PRC*, parts 2-12; Humphrey Trevelyan, *Living with* the Communists (Boston: Gambit, 1971), 77-85; and for specific technical but insightful vignettes see Ekvall, *Faithful Echo*, (New Haven" College and University Press, 1960), chapters XII-XVI. For selected US Government records see *FRUS-Geneva Conference.*

46. Wang Bingnan reports that Under Secretary Walter Bedell Smith approached Zhou Enlai and said "As the (Geneva) conference draws to

an end, I am very pleased and honored to be able to make your acquaintance. You have played a major role at this conference. Whether it is Korea or Vietnam, we hope that peace will be restored." *FBIS-PRC,* part 8; Also see Ronning, 213-239.

47. *FBIS-PRC*, part 3.

48. Ibid., part 4.

49. Ibid., part 8.

50. See note 40.

51. *FBIS-PRC*, part 4. Ambassador U. Alexis Johnson recalls that the Vietnamese delegation did not arrive in Geneva until near the end of the Korean Conference. From comments by U. A. Johnson on draft of this chapter, 22 July 1985, Washington, DC.

52. Robert Ekvall, an interpreter with the US delegation, recounts that during the final session, Belgian Prime Minister Paul Henri Spaak spoke in defense of the UN statement. His remarks were translated from French to English to Chinese, during which a phrase was added by a translator that irritated Zhou Enlai, who offended Spaak in turn. In the confusion and heated exchange that followed, both men apparently tried to reverse the misunderstanding. In the subsequent high speed translations, Zhou's interpreter left out a key qualifying phrase in one of Zhou's pleas. Spaak thought he heard a concession by Zhou and in response made a statement that the other UN members from the West interpreted as the dissolution of the agreement and unity they had achieved prior to the final meeting. For nearly an hour confusion and ill will reigned. Ekvall, 107-114. Other accounts are less clear as to the source of confusion. See Ronning, 232-235 and US Delegation cable of 16 June 1954 reporting on the 15th Plenary Session on Korea of 15 June *FRUS-Geneva Conference*, 376-385.

53. Although the British had left a chargé d'affaires in Peking in 1949, the Chinese had not accepted his credentials nor granted him high-level access. Normalization in 1954 involved the exchange of representatives at the level of chargé d'affaires and appropriate access. The first PRC representative to Britain was Huan Xiang, who had been the Director of the Western Europe and Africa Department of the Ministry of Foreign Affairs since October 1949 and was a member of the PRC delegation to the Geneva Conference. He remained in Britain from September 1954 until March 1962, including duty as an advisor to the Chinese delegation at the Laos Conference in Geneva in 1961 and 1962. Purged during the Cultural Revolution, he resumed work in the Ministry in 1976 as Ambassador to Belgium, the European Community, and Luxemborg. In 1978 he returned to China to become vice-president of the Academy of Social Sciences and a leading intellectual in the field of foreign policy. He resigned from the Academy in 1983 to become the General Director of the State Council's Center for International Issues, which he founded.

54. See cable of 30 July 1954 from Dulles to US Embassy in France in *FRUS-China*, 513-514.

55. Klein, "The Chinese Foreign Ministry," 57-59.

56. *FBIS-PRC*, October 25, 1984, B-3. Zhou proposed that "The states participating in the Geneva conference agree that they will continue their efforts toward achieving an agreement on the peaceful settlement of the Korean question on the basis of establishing a united, independent and democratic Korea. As regards the question of the time and place for resuming appropriate negotiations, it shall be decided separately by the states concerned through negotiation." *FRUS-Geneva* 381. Under Secretary Smith rejected Zhou's proposal "to effect that this conference could not accept responsibility for settlement of the Korea question indefinitely since it is not a permanent body. He was not prepared [to] accept Zhou's proposal and 16-nation [UN participants in Korea War] declaration made clear conditions to be made by Commies for any resumption negotiations." *FRUS-Geneva*, 383.

57. *FRUS-China*, 437 and 438-441. See Under Secretary Smith's cables of 28 and 30 May to Department of State.

58. Ibid., 436-437. See Dulles cable of 28 May to Geneva.

59. Ibid., 443. See Dulles cable of 3 June to Geneva.

60. Ibid., 436, 440-441. See Dulles cable of 28 May to Geneva and 31 May Memorandum of Deputy Assistant Secretary State for Far Eastern Affairs, Drumright, to Dulles.

61. *FBIS-PRC*, part 10.

62. Smith cable of 30 May, FRUS-China, 438-440.

63. Ibid., 443. See Dulles cable of 3 June to Geneva.

64. *FBIS-PRC*, part 10.

65. This account of the four plenary and two staff meetings is drawn from the following accounts: Trevelyan, 83-85; *FBIS-PRC*, parts 9-12; Johnson, 233-236; interviews with some the American and Chinese participants; and the pertinent cables to and from Geneva between 23 May 23 and 29 July found in *FRUS-China*, 430-513.

66. The first meeting was held on Saturday, 5 June, and was attended for the British by H. Trevelyan, Britain's representative in Beijing and J. F. Ford, both of the British delegation. The US delegation sent U. A. Johnson accompanied by Edwin W. Martin and Col. Robert Ekvall (interpreter). The PRC delegation was represented by Wang Bingnan accompanied by Ge Bonian (Director of the Department of American and Australian Affairs, MOFA), Huan Xiang (Director of the Department of West European and African Affairs, MOFA) and an interpreter. Somewhat to the annoyance of the United States, where the delay was perceived as calculated, Wang opened the meeting by noting that this would have to be a preliminary meeting as Mr. Ge had a prior appointment in Berlin he must attend. Wang recommended that they meet again

on Thursday, 10 June, the day after Mr. Ge returned. Under Secretary Smith's cable to State, *FRUS-China*, 462-463.

67. Ibid., 463-464. See cable of 7 June 1954 from Under Secretary Smith to State and State's response.

68. Ibid., 468-471. Under Secretary Smith's cable of 15 June 1954.

69. Ibid., 503-505. Cable from U. A. Johnson on 22 June 1954.

70. *FBIS-PRC*, parts 10 and 11.

71. Johnson, 235.

72. *FRUS-China*, 378-386. Karl Lott Rankin, *China Assignment*, (Seattle: University of Washington Press, 1964), 105, 122-123, 174. Cited in Ralph N. Clough, *Island China* (Cambridge, Mass.: Harvard University Press, 1978), 10.

73. *FRUS-China*, 205, 209, 219. See cables to State Department from US Embassy in Taiwan.

74. Ibid., 187, 193, 194. See State cables of 13 and 23 April 1953.

75. Ibid., 300-301, 307-310, 318. "NSC Staff Study on US Policy Toward Communist China" and "United States Objectives and Courses of Action With Respect to Formosa and the Chinese National Government."

76. Under Mao Zedong, the five principal members of the Political Bureau (Politburo) of the Communist Party's Central Committee were Liu Shaoqi, Zhou Enlai, Zhu De, Chen Yun, and Kao Kang. Chen was a Vice Premier of the Government Administration Council and Chairmand of the Finance and Economic Committee and Kao Kang was Chairman of the State Planning Committee, a Vice Chairman of the Central People's Government Council and had a strong regional bias toward the northeast, where he was Chairman of the Northeast Administrative Committee and Commander and Political Commissar of the Northeast Military Region. "National Intelligence Estimate—13-54," *FRUS-China*, 447-448.

77. Huang Hua, "Looking Back on Bandung," *Beijing Review* 15 (April 15, 1985): 14-15.

78. The first was the isse of US prisoners, both civilian and military, held by the Chinese. The future of Korea was another issue until the Geneva Conference essentially neutralized that problem.

79. For his assessment of the PRC's use of Taiwan as a lever in the 1950s, see Johnson, 236. For his assessement of Taiwan as a "control rod" see, George R. Packard Rapporteur, "The Policy Paper: China Policy for the Next Decade," in U. Alexis Johnson, George R. Packard, Alfred D. Wilhelm, Jr., *China for the next decade: Report of the Atlantic Council's Committee on China Policy* . (Washinton, DC: Oegeschlager, Gunn and Hain, Publishers, 1984), 35. The phrase "control rod" is taken from a supporting study within the Atlantic Council study that analyzed the use of negotiations by the PRC as an instrument of national security

policy. See Alfred D. Wilhelm, Jr., "National Security- The Chinese Perspective" in Johnson et al., 193-201.

80. "Memorandum of Discussion at the 199th Meeting of the National Security Council, May 27, 1954," *FRUS-China*, 434.

81. Ibid., 426. Cable of 20 May 20 from Ambassador Rankin in Taipei.

82. Ibid., 473, 541-542. Memorandum of conversation of 22 May 22 between President Eisenhower, Secretary Dulles, Admiral Radord (Chairman, JCS), and memorandum of conversation of May 27.

83. Ibid., 473. Telephone conversation between the President and Secretary Dulles. "Our plane flies high, spots these boats, tells Chiang where they are, and he picks them up . . . it's a little illegal, but no one so far has picked it up." "Tuapse Case" summary.

84. Ibid., 480-481. See Ambassador Rankin cable of 22 June 1954.

85. Ibid., 505. Cathey-Pacific airlines is a British commercial firm in Hong Kong. The aircraft was in route from Bangkok and was about 30 miles south of Hainan Island when downed. Memorandum of telephone conversation between Secretary Dulles and the President.

86. Ibid., 510-511. Telephone conversation between State Department's Director, Office of Chinese Affairs and First Secretary, British Embassy.

87. Ibid., 548. Memorandum by Assistant Secretary Robertson of 25 August 1954.

88. Clough, 11.

89. Eisenhower, 463.

90. Ibid., 465.

91. The I Chiang Shan (*Yijiangshan*) attack was a double victory for the PLA. The first was the capture of the island. The second came as a result of the resentment in a lot of quarters of the PLA of the attitude of the Soviet military advisors in China. The Russians were insensitive to the successes of the Chinese in combat over the preceding 10 years and instead spoke of their successes against the Germans and how the Chinese should copy their model. Thus the second victory was that the PLA's own plans and tactics had been successful without the cost of lives that the Soviet plan would have cost.

92. Ibid., 467-470; Hoopes, 272-275.

93. It was widely assumed at the time that a conflict between the United States and the PRC over Taiwan would lead to a general war in Asia. The President had approved in October 1953 the planning assumption that nuclear weapons would be used in such limited war situations. Nuclear retaliation as a doctrine was beginning to have an impact on the range of military options available to the United States. Eisenhower, 477; Hoopes, 196.

94. It dropped from 25 to 5 percent of the total PRC propaganda. Eisenhower, 480.

95. Ibid., 483.

96. "Letter from Comrade Zhou Enlai to Comrade Deng Yingchao on eve of the Bandung Conference," *Renmin Ribao*, 24 April 1985, 1, in *Foreign Broadcast Information Service, China Report* (JPRS-CPS- 85-052), 24 May 1985, 24.

97. Hoopes, 282.

98. Ibid.

99. Huang Hua, "Looking Back on Bandung," *Beijing Review* 15 (15 April 1985): 18.

100. Hoopes, 283; Eisenhower, 482. For the press conference of 26 April, see the *Department of State Bulletin*, 9 May 1955, 754-759.

101. Dwight D. Eisenhower, *Public Papers of the Presidents of the United States, 1955* (Washington, DC: Office of the *Federal Register*, National Archives and Records Service, 1953-), 425-440.

102. Supplement in the *People's China*, 16 June 1955.

103. *Department of State Bullentin*, 13 June 1955, 953.

104. U Nu, *U Nu: Saturday's Son* (New Haven and London: Yale University Press, 1975), 205-1.

105. See cables of 3, 6, and 11 December from Ambassador Lodge at the United Nations to Department of State, *FRUS-China*, 987-988, 993-994, and 1016-1017. Kenneth T. Young, *Negotiating with the Chinese Communists: the United States Experience, 1953-1967* (New York: McGraw-Hill Book Company, 1968), 40-41; Interviews in April 1984 with Ambassador U. Alexis Johnson in Washington and with Chinese observers.

106. Hoopes, 353-354; Johnson 22 and 241.

107. Young, 51.

108. *FBIS-PRC*, 25 January 1985, B-4.

109. Ibid.

110. Young, 48-49.

111. Johnson, 238-239.

112. During the Geneva Conference of 1954, some of the communications between Beijing and the Chinese delegation in Geneva may have been by mail, given the difficulty the delegation had in getting a timely response from Beijing. However, by the time the Ambassadorial Talks got under way, their communications were by telegram. On occasion the delegation found itself receiving a cable just before a meeting with little or no time to prepare for the talks. These difficulties highlight the importance that Wang Bingnan placed on the direct telephone line that was installed, with the help of the Soviet Union, between Warsaw and Beijing when the talks were moved to Warsaw in 1958. During that

period Zhou always personally called Wang in order to give instructions and to emphasize certain issues. *FBIS-PRC*, 28 March 1985, B-9.

113. *FBIS-PRC*, 25 January 1985, B-5.

114. Ibid.

115. The Chinese perceived that Dulles had instituted a no-handshake policy during the Geneva Conference of 1954. This perception was reinforced by Dulles' refusal to let his delegation sit next to any Communist delegation, despite the international convention of seating delegations alphabetically, and Dulles' internationally reported refusal to shake hands with Zhou during a recess at the first session on Korea. *FBIS-PRC*, part 8, and Johnson, 204. Wang recounts an incident, similar to the Zhou-Dulles incident, that occurred in Denmark in about the same timeframe as the Geneva Conference. An American military attaché offered to shake hands with the PRC military attaché, but the Chinese officer refused, causing both to be embarrassed. Wang was in charge of the case and instructed by Zhou to insure that Chinese diplomats were not so rigid in the future. The Chinese were not to take the initiative to shake hands, but if the Americans volunteered, the Chinese were not to refuse. *FBIS-PRC*, part 9.

116. *FBIS-PRC*, 28 March 1985, B-7.

117. Henry Kissinger, *White House Years* (Boston: Little, Brown and Company, 1979), 781-782.

118. Johnson, 242.

119. This account of the talks is drawn from Young, *FBIS-PRC*, Johnson, and interviews with Ambassador U. Alexis Johnson and Chinese participants and knowledgable observers during 1982, 1983, and 1984.

120. Elie Able, "US Ban Expected on Peiping's Plan of Student Check," *New York Times*, 4 August 1955, 1, and the associated special to the *New York Times* titled "Washington's position," 2.

121. Interviews with Ambassador U. Alexis Johnson in April 1983 in Washington, DC.

122. To illustrate the naivete of their belief that the talks would not take more than a few meetings, Wang points out that when he departed Warsaw at the end of July, he only took a few summer clothes. Others interviewed reported similar experiences. It was also pointed out that it was not until several months after the start of the talks that the Foreign Ministry decided to assign a staff member to Geneva full-time to handle the administration associated with the Talks. *FBIS-PRC*, 25 January 1985, B-4. Some of the principal members of Wang's delegation were:

- Li-Huichuan, a member of the Chinese Embassy in Moscow, a Russian linguist and specialist who was also able to speak English. He retired in 1983 while Director of the Foreign Ministry's Institute of International Relations. Li's wife, Zhou Yan, is also a foreign affairs expert and fluent in English. Among her assignments related to Li's work at Geneva was her work as an interpreter during the Marshall Mission peace talks in Beijing (1946-1947) and as an interpreter with Dr. Pu Shan during General Wu Xiuquan's 1950 trip to the United Nations in New York.

- Li Peng, rose to the rank of Ambassador.
- Qui Yingjue, interpreter, acquired his English in his youth in Malaysia. He served at Panmunjom and then under Wang Bingnan in the Foreign Ministry. In 1983 he was the permanent staff member on the UN Security Council Staff from the PRC.
- Huang Hua joined Ambassador Wang at Warsaw in September 1958; see chapter 4.
- Lai Yali joined Wang in January 1956 as the replacement of Li Huichuan, both at the talks and as the Counsellor in the PRC Embassy in Moscow.
- Wang Baoliu replaced Lin Ping in January 1956.
- Guo Jiading joined Wang in Warsaw as an additional interpreter.

123. Wang Bingnan has described the objectives of the PRC at the Ambassadorial Talks as "We held that the talks had to emphasize discussing some substantial problems such as the Taiwan issue, arrangements for direct talks between Secretary of State Dulles and Premier Zhou Enlai, and the establishment of cultural ties between the two countries." The United States "insisted on repatriating Americans detained in China and demanded that China not resort to force over Taiwan. In order to make a start at the talks, we finally agreed to discuss the question of repatriating American nationals first . . . . " *FBIS-PRC*, January 25, 1985, B-5.

124. COCOM is the Coordinating Committee established in 1949, composed of most NATO countries plus Japan, that regulates the flow of advanced Western technology to all Communist countries, including China.

125. Americans in China: The US and the PRC first dealt directly concerning the repatriation of each other's nationals during the 1954 Geneva Conference. In the second meeting (10 June 1954), Wang Bingnan stated the Chinese position. The Chinese people are friendly to the American people and all are free to leave China, unless they have (a) engaged in espionage or sabotage, (b) taken part in Chiang Kai-shek's civil war, or (c) violated Chinese territorial air or waters. In these cases China has the right and duty to presecute according to the laws of a sovereign state. To prove they are free to leave, he noted that 1485 Americans had left China since 1949: "582 in 1950, 727 in 1951, 143 in 1953, and 33 in 1953 [1954]." *FRUS-China*, 464-466. The United States focused on the approximately 155 Americans who were in prison or denied exit permits between 1949 and 1955. Johnson, 232. As of May

1954, the Chinese thought there were 80 Americans in China of which 30 were in prison. *FRUS-China*, 434-435. The United States was not certain either when it submitted a list of 83 in June, including 14 military who were subsequently determined to have died in action. *FRUS-China*, 471.

Toward the end of the conference, the Chinese approved six American exit requests, possibly to entice the United States to continue the Geneva contact. Subsequently the talks were continued at the Consul-General level in Geneva. *FRUS-China*, 501. By the time these talks were elevated to the ambassadorial level in August 1955, the exchange of information enabled the United States to focus on 41 civilians and 35 military detained in China. Johnson, 233. On August 4, 11 US airmen were freed (*New York Times*, 4 August 1955, 1) at the start of the talks by China to gain the initiative. *FBIS-PRC*, 25 January 1985, B-4. On 6 September, as the negotiations on the repatriation of civilians was reaching a critical point, the PRC released 12 civilians and then on September 10 with the signing of the "Agreed Announcement," the PRC released 10 more. *Department of State Bulletin*, 12 September 456-457. On 13 October, the *People's Daily* reported that there were 66 Americans in China, 19 who had violated Chinese law and were in prison and 47 who were free to leave whenever they wanted. Young, 79. (Of the 47, 17 were POWs from Korea who elected not to return to the United States and 30 were civilians who elected to live and work in China after 1949). Five more civilians were released in October/November in an effort to influence the Big Four Foreign Minister Conference in Geneva. Johnson, 256. In March 1956 the Chinese accounted for the 99 Americans in China at the end of July 1955; of 59 ordinary residents, 13 had asked to leave and 46 remained free to leave whenever they wished; of 40 criminals, 27 had finished their term and left and 13 remained in prison. Over the next 12 years the number in prison was gradually reduced until the last one was released with President Nixon's visit in 1972.

Chinese in the United States: In 1954 there were approximately 117,000 Chinese aliens resident in the US. Of these, about 34 were in state prisons for murder and narcotic crimes, up to 175 had been issued orders (based on 1918 legislation revived during the Korean War) at one time or another barring them from leaving the United States because of their US educations in such technical fields as weapons design, nuclear energy, and rocketry, and the remainder were free to leave at any time. Johnson, 235-243.

In 1954 the PRC focused on the 5,400 students in the United States, probably because of the need in China for their talents; because they are likely to be the most vulnerable both to appeals to patriotism and to family ties; and they are the easiest to identify. *FRUS-China*, 441. Of those free to go, the United States paid the fares of 767 of 4000 students cut off from frinancial support by the 1949 victory and who chose between 1949 and 1955 to return to China. Johnson, 235. Of the 124 that were barred from departing in June 1954, initially 57 wanted to return to the PRC. The United States decided to release 15 of their names at a time, with the first list given to the PRC on 221 June 1954. *FRUS-China*, 475-477. By April at least 75 students had been permitted to leave. *New York Times*, 4 August 1955, 1. When the Ambassadorial Talks began in August, the PRC expanded its interest in Chinese aliens in the United States to all 117,000, probably because it provided a vehicle for seeking de facto recognition by the United States in lieu of the ROC, as well as influence within this community. In May 1956 Johnson offered to let an Indian representative interview each of the 34 prisoners for the PRC. Wang refused, and the United States had the International Red Cross conduct the interviews. One wanted to return to the PRC and two wanted to go to Taiwan. One of each subsequently changed their minds. Johnson, 257.

While the categories were parallel, the conditions that created the categories were significantly different, as well as were the goals of each country in seeking repatriation. As a result, Wang Bingnan and, needless to say, Zhou Enlai had to demonstrate considerable skill to treat the repatriation of Chinese nationals as a parallel and equal problem to that of US nationals.

126. Ekvall, 89-93. Ekvall cites an example of the difficulties of wording an agreed text so that the key words and phrases, both the English and Chinese versions, have the same connotations. The example deals with the difference between mandate versus authorized.

127. Young, Appendix C, 425-427.

128. *People's China*, 16 August 1955, 3-8.

129. Young, 100-101.

130. As long as the talks continued, Secretary Dulles could reply to his critics that there was an ongoing dialogue with the Chinese and thereby deflect any pressures to be more forthcoming to the Chinese. The talks also kept pressures and tensions in the Taiwan Straits down. From comments by Ambassador U. Alexis Johnson on a draft of the chapter on 22 July 1985 in Washington, DC.

131. *FBIS-PRC*, 2 May 1985, B-9.

132. Ibid.

133. Ibid.

APPENDIX—THE PANMUNJOM AGENDA

The Agenda, 10 July 1950

Original UN Position

1. Adoption of Agenda.

2. Location of and authority for IRC representatives to visit POW camps.

3. Limitation of discussion to purely military matters related to Korea only.

4. Cessation of hostilities and of acts of armed force in Korea under conditions which will assure against resumption of hostilities and acts of armed forces in Korea.

5. Agreement on a demilitarized zone across Korea.

6. Composition, authority and functions of military armistic commission.

7. Agreement on principle of inspection within Korea by military observer teams, functioning under a military armistice commission.

8. Composition and functions of these teams.

9. Arrangements pertaining to prisoners of war.

Original Communist Position

1. Adoption of Agenda.

2. Establishment of the 38th Parallel as the military demarcation line between both sides and establishment of a demilitarized zone, as basic condition for the cessation of hostilities in Korea.

3. Withdrawal of all armed forces of foreign countries from Korea.

4. Concrete arrangements for the realization of cease fire and armistice in Korea.

5. Arrangements relating to prisoners of war following the Armistice.

The Agenda as Finally Agreed Upon, 26 July 1950

1. Adoption of Agenda.

2. Fixing a military demarcation line, between both sides so as to establish a demilitarized zone as a basic consideration for a cessation of hostilities in Korea.

3. Concrete arrangements for the realization of cease fire and armistice in Korea, including the composition, authority and functions of a supervising organization for carrying out the terms of a cease fire and armistice.

4. Arrangements relating to prisoners of war.

5. Recommendations to the governments of the countries concerned on both sides.

SELECTED BIBLIOGRAPHY

I. Societal Factors Influencing the Chinese Negotiator

Bai, Shouyi. *An Outline History of China.* Beijing: Foreign Languages 1982.

Bonavia, David. *The Chinese.* New York: Lippincott & Crowell, Publishers, 1980.

Boorman, Scott A. *The Protracted Game, A Weo-Ch'i Interpretation of Maoist Revolutionary Strategy.* London: Oxford University Press, 1969.

Chen, Theodore Hsi-en. *Chinese Education Since 1949: Academic and Revolutionary Modesl.* New York: Pergamon Press, 1981.

Chu, Godwin C., and Francis L. K. Hsu, eds. *Moving a Mountain: Cultural Change in China.* Honolulu: University Press of Hawaii, 1979.

Chu, Valentin. *Ta Ta, Tan, Tan (Fight, Fight, Talk, Talk).* New York: W. W. Norton & Company, 1963.

Cohen, Jerome A., ed. *China's Practive of International Law: Some Case Studies.* Cambridge, Mass.: Harvard University Press, 1972.

———.and Hungdah Chiu. *People's China and International Law.*
Vol 1 & 2. Princeton: Princeton University Press, 1974.

Collis, Maurice. *Foreign Mud.* London: Farber and Farber, 1946.

Crozier, Ralph C. *China's Cultural Legacy and communism.* New York: Praeger Publishers, 1970.

De Bary, Theodore, ed. *Sources of Chinese Tradition.* New York: Columbia University Press, 1960.

Fei, Hsiao-Tung. *Peasant Life in China.* London: Routledge & Kegan Paul, 1939.

Freeman, Maurice. *Chinese Lineage and Society: Fukien and K'wangtung.* London: Atlone Press, 1966.

———. *Liniage Organization in Southeast China.* London: Atlone Press, 1958.

Hammond, Ed. *Coming of Grace, An IllustratedBiography of Zhou Enlai.* Berkeley: Lancaster-Miller, 1980.

Harrison, James P. *The Long March to Power.* New York: Praeger Publishers, 1972.

Hsiao, Kung-chuan. *A History of Chinese Political Thought.* Vol. 1. Translated by F. W. Mote. Princeton: Princeton University Press, 1979.

Hsieh, Pao Chao. *The Government of China (1644-1911).* New York: Octagon Books, 1966.

Hsu, Francis L. K. "Chinese Kinship and Chinese Behavior." In *China in Crisis.* Vol. 1, Book 2. Edited by Ping-ti Ho and Tang Tsou. Chicago: University of Chicago Press, 1968.

Hsu, Kai-yu. *Chou En-lai: China's Gray Eminence.* Garden City, NY: Doubleday, 1968.

Hu, Hsien-Chin. "The Chinese Concept of 'Face'." *American Anthropologist* 46 (1946): 45-65.

Hur, Douglas. *The Arrow War, An Anglo-Chinese Confusion (1856-1860).* New York: Macmillan Company, 1967.

Kratschvil, Paul. "Modern Chinese and Linguistic Change." *China Quarterly* 92 (1982): 687-695.

Kwong, Julia. *Chinese Education in Transition.* Montreal: McGill-Queen's University Press, 1979.

Li, Tien-min. *Chou En-lai.* Taipei: Institute of International Relations, 1970.

Lin, Mousheng. *Men and Ideas.* Introduction by Pearl S. Buck. New York: The John Day Company, 1942.

Lin, Yutang. *My Country and My People.* New York: John Day Co., 1939.

Luo, Ruiqing, Zhengcao Lu, and Bingnan Wang. *Zhou Enlai and the Xian Incident.* Beijing: Foreign Language Press, 1983.

Moore, Charles A., ed. *The Chinese Mind, Essentials of Philosophy and Culture.* Honolulu: University Press of Hawaii, 1967.

Mote, Frederick W. *Intellectual Foundations of China.* New York: Alfred A. Knopf, 1971.

Munro, Donald J. *The Concept of Man in Early China.* Stanford: Stanford University Press, 1969.

Ogden, Suzzane P. "Chinese Conceptions of the Nations, State and Sovereignty." Ph.D. dissertation, Brown University, 1975.

Pye, Lucian. *The Dynamics of Chinese Politics.* Cambridge, Mass.: Oelgeschlager, Gunn & Hain, Publishers, 1981.

Ridley, Charles P., Paul H. B. Godwin, Dennis J. Doolin. *The Making of a Model Citizen in Communist China.* Stanford: The Hoover Institution Press, 1971.

Rozman, Gilbert. *The Modernization of China.* New York: The Free Press, 1981.

Scalapino, Robert A. *Elites in the People's Republic of China.* Seattle: University of Washington Press, 1972.

Schurmann, Franz. *Ideology and Organization in Communist China.* 2d ed. Berkeley: University of California Press, 1970.

Solomon, Richard H. *Mao's Revolution and the Chinese Political Culture.* Berkeley: University of California Press, Sprenkel, Sybelle van der. *Legal Institutions in Manchu China, A Sociological Analysis.* London: Atlone Press, 1962.

Sun Tzu, The Art of War. Translated by Griffith, Samuel B. New York: Oxford University Press, 1963.

Walker, Richard L. *The Multi-State System of Ancient China.* Westport, Conn.: Greenwood Press, 1953.

Weber, Max. *The Religion of China.* Translated by Hans H. Gerth. New York: The Free Press, 1951.

Winfield, Gerald F. *China: The Land and the People.* New York: William Sloane Associates, 1948.

II. US-China Negotiations: 1949-1953

Berger, Carl. *The Korean Knot: A Military-Political History*. Philadelphia: University of Pennsylvania Press, 1957.

Dean, Arthur H. "What It's Like to Negotiate with the Chinese." *New York Times Magazine*, October 30, 1966, pp. 44-45.

Dille, John. *Substitute for Victory*. New York: Doubleday and Company, 1954.

George, Alexander L. *The Chinese Communist Army in Action*. New York: Columbia University Press, 1967.

Gilbert, Jerry D. "John Foster Dulles' Perceptions of the People's Republic of China: A Study of Belief Systems and Perceptions in the Analysis of Foreign Policy Decisionmaking." Ph.D. dissertation, Texas Tech., 1973.

Goodman, Allan E., ed. *Negotiating While Fighting: The Diary of Admiral C. Turner Joy at the Korean Armistice Conference*. Stanford: Hoover Institute Press, 1978.

Goodrich, Leland M. *Korea: A Study of US Policy in the United Nations*. New York: Council on Foreign Relations, 1956.

Hedley, John H. "The Truman Administration and the Loss of China." Ph.D. dissertation, University of Missouri, 1964.

Hermes, Walter G. *Truce Tent and Fighting Front*. Washington: Office of the Chief of Military History, US Army, 1966.

Joy, Admiral C. Turner. *How Communists Negotiate*. New York: The MacMillan Company, 1955.

Kinkead, Eugene. *In Every War but One*. New York: W. W. Norton and Co., 1959.

Kinney, Andrew J. "Secrets from the Truce Tent." *This Week, New York Herald-Tribune*, August 31, 1952.

Kuan, John C. "The Kuomintang-Communist Party Negotiations, 1944-1946." Ph.D. dissertation, Fletcher School of Law and Diplomacy, Tufts, 1975.

May, Ernest. *The Truman Administration and China, 1945-1949*. Philadelphia: Lippincott, 1975.

Military History Section, Headquarters, Far East Command. *History of the Korean War-Korean Armistice Negotiations(July 1951-May 1952)*. Part I. Tokyo: 1952. Located in the Office of the Chief of Military History, US Army, Washington, DC.

Murray, James C. "The Korea Truce Talks: First Phase." *US Naval Institute Proceedings* 79 (September 1953): 908-909.

Ojha, Ellen Frost. "State Power and Buraucracy in Communist China, 1949-1957." Ph.D. dissertation, Harvard University, 1962.

O.S.S./State Department Intelligence and Research Reports: Asia 1950-1961. Washington: University Publications of America, 1979.

Peng, Dehuai. *Memoirs of a Chinese Marshall.* Translated by Zheng Longpu. English Text edited by Sara Gromes. Beijing:Foreign Language Press, 1984.

Poats, R. M. *Decision in Korea.* New York: McBride Co., 1954.

Possony, Stephen, ed. *The Lenin Reader.* Chicago: Henry Regnery Company, 1966.

Purifog, Lewis M. *Harry Truman's China Policy: McCarthyism and the Diplomacy of Hysteria, 1947-1951.* New York: New Viewpoints, 1976.

Rigg, Robert B. *Red China's Fighting Hordes.* Harrisburg, Pa.: The Military Service Publishing Company, 1951.

The Selected Letters of Mao Zedong. Chinese ed. Beijing: Foreign Language Press, 1983.

A Selection of Letter by Mao Zedong with Reproductions of the Original Calligraphy. Beijing: Foreign Language Press,1983.

Selected Works of Chen Yun. Vol. 1 (1926-1949). Chinese ed. Beijing: Foreign Language Pres, 1984.

Selected Works of Liu Shaoqi. Vol 1. (1926-1949). Beijing: Foreign Language Press, 1984.

Selected Works of Mao Tse-Tung. Vol. 1 (1924-1937). Beijing: Foreign Language Press, 1965.

______. Vol 2 (1937-1941).

______. Vol 3 (1941-1945).

______. Vol 4 (1945-1949). Beijing: Foreign Language Press, 1961.

______. Vol 5 (1949-1957). Beijing: Foreign Language Press, 1977.

Selected Works of Zhou Enlai. Vol 1. (1926-1949). Beijing: Foreign Language Press, 1981.

Selected Works of Zhu De. (1926-1962). Chinese ed. Beijing: Foreign Language Press, 1983.

Service, John S. *The Amerasia Papers: Some Problems in the History of US-China Relations.* Berkeley: University of California Press, 1971.

Smith, Cordell A. "A Marshall Mission: Its Impact Upon American Foreign Policy Toward China, 1945-1949." Ph.D. dissertation, University of Oklahoma, 1963.

Schnabel, James F. *Policy and Direction: The First Year.* Washington: Office of the Chief of Military History, US Army, 1972.

Stone, W. T. "Negotiating with the Reds." *Editorial Research Reports* 2 (1953): 649-665.

Truman, Harry S. *Memoirs: Years of Trial and Hope, Vol II.* New York: Doubleday, 1956.

Tsou, Tang. *The Embroilment over Quemoy: Mao, Chiang, and Dulles.* Salt Lake City: University of Utah Press, 1959.

———. *America's Failure in China, 1941-1950.* Chicago: University of Chicago Press, 1963.

Tsuan, Tai-hsun. "An Explanation of the Change in United States' Policy Toward China in 1950." Ph.D. dissertation, University of Pennsylvania, 1969.

Tucker, Nancy B. *Patterns in the Dust: Chinese-American Relations and the Recognition Controversy, 1949-1950.* New York: Columbia University Press, 1983.

Tuchman, Barbara W. *Stilwell and the American Experience in China, 1911-1945.* New York: Bantam Books, 1972.

Vatcher, William H. Jr. *Panmunjom: the Story of the Korean Military Armistice Negotiations.* New York: Frederick A. Praeger, 1958.

US Congress. House. Committee on Foreign Affairs. *US Policy in the Far East, Part I.* Selected Executive Session Hearings, 1951-1956. Historical Series Vol. 17. Washington: GPO, 1980.

———. Senate. Committee on Armed Services and Committee on Foreign Relations. *Military Situation in the Far East, Hearings.* 82d Cong., 1st Sess. Washington: GPO, 1949.

———. *Hearings to Conduct an Inquiry into the Military Situation in the Far East and the Facts Surrounding the Relief of General of the Army Douglas MacArthur from His Assignments in the Area.* 82d Cong, 1st sess., 1949. Washington: GPO,

______. Committee on Foreign Relations. *The United States and Communist China in 1949 and 1950: The Question of Rapproachment and Recognition.* Washington: GPO, January 1973.

______. *The United States and the Korean Problem documents, 1943-1953.* AMS Press, 1953. Reprinted., 1976.

______. *Economic Assistance to China and Korea: 1949-1950.* Washington: GPO, 1974.

______. Committee on the Judiciary. Subcommittee to Investigate the Administration of the Internal Security Act and Other Internal Security Laws. *Institute of Pacific Relations, Hearings.* 82d Cong., 1st-2d sess., 1951-52. Washington: GPO.

______. *The Amerasia Papers.* Washington: GPO, January 1970.

______. Subcommittee of the Committee on Foreign Relations. *State Department Employee Loyalty Investigation Hearings.* 81st Cong., 2d sess., 1950. Washington: GPO.

US Department of Army. *Pamphlet 27-1: Treaties Governing Land Warfare.* Washington: GPO, 1956.

US Department of State. *Foreign Relations of the United States, 1959.* Vol. 6, East Asia and the Pacific. Washington: GPO, 1976.

______. Aandahl, F., John P. Glennon, Harriet D. Schwar, P. Claussen, eds. *Foreign Relations of the UnitedStates, 1951.* Vol 7, Korea and China. Parts 1&2. Washington: GPO, 1983.

______. *In Quest of Peace and Security: Selected Documents on American Foreign Policy, 1941-1951.* Washington: GPO,

______. *The China White Paper, August 1949.* Washington: GPO.

______. *United States Relations with China.* Washington: GPO.

Wei, Tang. "The Return of the Jade." *China Reconstructs* 31 (October 1982): 69 & 72.

Whiting, Allen S. *China Crosses the Yalu.* New York: MacMillan Company, 1960.

Wu, Xiuquan. *The Experience of Eight Years in the Foreign Ministry.* Beijing: International Knowledge Publishers, 1983.

III. US-China Negotiations: 1954-1967

Able, Elie. "US Ban Expected on Peiping's Plan of Student Check." *New York Times*, 4 August 1955, 1, and associated article "Washington's Position," 2.

Acheson, Dean. *Power and Diplomacy.* Cambridge: Harvard University Press, 1958.

———. *Present at the Creation.* New York: W. W. Norton & Co., 1969.

Alsop, Stewart. "The Story Behind Quemoy: How We Drifted Close to War." *Saturday Evening Post*, December 13, 1958, pp. 26-27.

An, Tai Sung. "Communist China and 'Peaceful Coexistence.'" Ph.D. diss., University of Pennsylvania, 1963.

Bachrack, Stanley D. *The Committee of One Million: 'China Lobby' Politics, 1953-1971.* New York: Columbia University Press, 1976.

Beal, John R. *John Foster Dulles, 1888-1959.* New York: Harper, 1959.

Berding, Andrew. *Dulles on Diplomacy.* Princeton: Van Nostrand, 1965.

Boorman, Howard L., A. Eckstein, P. E. Mosley, and B. Schwartz. *Moscow-Peking Axis: Strengths and Strains.* New York: Harper, 1957.

Branyan, Robert L. and Lawrence H. Larsen. *The Eisenhower Administration, 1953-1961: A Documentary Histroy.* New York: Random House.

Chang, Parris Hsu-cheng. "Patterns and Processes of Policymaking in Communist China, 1955-1962: Three Case Studies." Ph.D. diss., Columbia University, 1969.

Chen, Nai-Ruenn and Walter Galenson. *The Chinese Economy under Communism.* Chicago: Aldine, 1969.

Chen, Stephen Chin-shan. "American Recognition and Nonrecognition Policies in China: A Legal, Historical and Political Analysis." Ph.D. diss., Southern Illinois University, 1964.

Clark, Sharon W. "History of the Political Organization of Chinese People's Liberation Army: Organizational Conflict and Charismatic Change." Ph.D. dissertation, University of North Carolina, 1972.

Clough, Ralph N. *Island China.* Cambridge, Mass.: Harvard University Press, 1978.

Cohen, W. J. *America's Response to China: An Interpretive History of Sino-American Relations.* New York: Wiley, 1971.

Communist China, 1955-1959: Policy Documents with Analysis. Forward by robert R. Bowie and John K. Fairbank. Cambridge, Mass.: Harvard University Press, 1962.

Datt, V. P. *China's Foreign Policy, 1958-1962.* Bombay: Asia Publishing House, 1964.

Drummond, Roscoe. *The Duel at the Brink.* Garden City, NY: Doubleday, 1960.

Dulles, Eleanor Lansing. *John Foster Dulles: The Last Year.* New York: Harcourt, Brace and World, 1963.

Eden, Anthony. *The Memoirs of Anthony Eden: Full Circle.* Boston: Houghton Mifflin, 1960.

Eisenhower, Dwight D. *The White House Years: Mandate for Change, 1953-1956.* New York: Doubleday, 1962.

———. *The White House Years: Waging Peace, 1956-1961.* New York: Doubleday, 1965.

Ekvall, Robert B. *The Faithful Echo.* New York: Twayne Publishers, 1960.

Fairbank, John K. *The United States and China.* 4th ed. Cambridge, Mass.: Harvard University Press, 1982.

Gittings, John. *The World and China, 1922-1972.* New York: Harper and Row, 1975.

Gould-Adams, Richard. *The Time of Power: A Reappraisal of John Foster Dulles.* London: Weindenfeld and Nicolson, 1962.

Griffith, William E. *The Sino-Soviet Rift.* Cambridge, Mass.: The MIT Press, 1964.

Gurtov, Melvin. *Negotiations and Vietnam: A Case Study of the 1954 Geneva Conference.* Santa Monica, Calif.: Rand Corporation, 1968.

———. "The Foreign Ministry and Foreign Affairs during the Cultural Revolution." *China Quarterly* 40 (Oct.-Dec. 1969): 65-102.

Hefron, Peter O. "Ideology and Chinese Foreign Policy during the Eighth Central Committee, 1956-1969." Ph.D. dissertation, Fletcher School of Law and Diplomacy, Tufts, 1976.

Hilsman, Roger. *To Move a Nation.* Garden City, NY: Doubleday, 1967.

Hinton, Harold C. *China's Turbulent Quest, An Analysis of China's Foreign Relations Since 1949.* Rev. ed. Bloomington: Indiana University Press, 1972.

Hoopes, Townsend. *The Devil and John Foster Dulles.* Boston: Little, Brown, & Company, 1973.

Huang, Hua. "Looking Back on Bandung." *Beijing Review* 15 (April 15, 1985): 16.

Important Documents Concerning the Question of Taiwan. Peking: Foreign Language Press, October 1955.

Johnson, U. Alexis. *Right Hand of Power.* Englewood Cliffs, NJ: Prentice-Hall, 1984.

Kalcki, J. H. *The Pattern Of Sino-American Crises: Political-Military Interactions in the 1950s.* London: Cambridge University Press, 1975.

King, Ambrose Yeo-chi. "The Chinese Ombudsman Institution in a Historical and Comparative Perspective." Ph.D. dissertation, University of Pittsburg, 1970.

Lall, Arthur. *How Communist China Negotiates.* New York: Columbia University Press, 1968.

Lee, Chae-Jin. *Communist China's Policy Toward laos: A Case Study, 1954-1967.* Lawrence, Ks.: Center for East Asian Studies, University of Kansas, 1970.

Onate, Andres David. "Foreign and Domestic Conflict Behavior in Communist China, 1949-1970: A Quantitative Study." Ph.D. diss., University of Arizona, 1972.

Pollack, Jonathan D. "Perception and Action in Chinese Foreign Policy: The Quemoy Decision." Ph.D. dissertation, University of Michigan, 1976.

Dwight D. Eisenhower, 1955. *Public Papers of the Presidents of the United States.* Washington, DC: Office of the *Federal Register*, National Archives and Rewcords Service.

Rankin, Karl Lott. *China Assignment.* Seattle: University of Washington, 1964.

Ronning, Chester. *A Memoir of China in Revolution.* New York: Pantheon Books, 1974.

Salisbury, Harrison E. *War Between Russia and China.* New York: W. W. Norton & Company, 1969.

Schlesinger, Arthur M. *A Thousand Days.* New York: Crest Books, 1967.

Schram, Stuart. *Basic Tactics.* London: Pall Mall Press, 1967.

Schrecker, John E. *Imperialism and Chinese Nationalism.* Cambridge: Harvard University Press, 1971.

Scott, Gary L. "Chinese Treaties: The Post Revolutionary Restoration of International Law and Order." Ph.D. diss., University of Washington.

Sethi, J. D. "Negotiating with China." *China Report* 6 (Nov.-Dec. 1970): 5-20.

Smoker, P. "A Time-Series Analysis of Sino-Indian Relations." *Journal of Conflict Resolution* 13 (June 1969): 171-191.

Snow, Edgar. *The Other Side of the River.* New York: Random House, 1961.

Sorenson, Theodore C. *Decision-Making in the White House.* New York: Columbia University Press, 1963. Steele, A. T. *The American People and China.* New York: McGraw-Hill, 1966.

Steibel, Gerald L. *How Can We Negotiate with the Communists?* New York: National Strategy Information Center, 1972.

Sutter, Robert G. *China-Watch: Toward Sino-American Reconciliation.* Baltimore: John Hopkins University Press, 1978.

Teiwes, Frederick C. *Politics and Purges in China (1950-1965).* New York: M. E. Sharpe, 1979.

Thorton, Richard C. *China, the Struggle for Power, 1917-1972.* Bloomington: Indiana University Press, 1974.

Trieman, Jack. "State Practice and the Rule of Continuity of Treaties: The Russian and Chinese Experience." Ph.D. diss., University of Chicago, 1969.

Trevelyan, Humphrey. *Living with the Communists.* Boston: Gambit, 1971.

Tsou, Tang. *China's Policies in Asia and America's Alternatives.* Chicago: University of Chicago Press, 1968.

U Nu. *U Nu: Saturday's Son.* New Haven: Yale University Press, 1975.

US Congress. House. Committee on Foreign Affairs. Subcommittee on Far East and Pacific Affairs. *United States Policy Towards Asia.* Washington: GPO, 1966.

Committee on Un-American Activities. *Communist Commitment to Force and Violence.* Washington: GPO, 1968.

———. *Language as a Communist Weapon.* Washington: GPO, 1959.

———. Joint Economic Committee. *Economic Profile of Mainland China.* Washington: GPO, 1967.

US Congress. Senate. Committee on Foreign Relations. *US Policy with Respect to Mainland China.* Washington: GPO, 1966.

———. Committee on Government Operations. Subcommittee on National Security and International Operations. *International Negotiations.* Washington: GPO, 1970.

———. *Peking's Approach to Negotiations-Selected Writings.* Washington: GPO, 1969.

US Department of State. *Chinese Communist World Outlook.* Washington: GPO, 1962.

———. *Foreign Relations of the United States, 1952-1954.* Vol 14, China and Japan, Part 1&2. Washington: GPO, 1985.

———. John P. Glennon, Harriet D. Schwar, Louis J. Smith, eds. *Foreign Relations of the United States, 1955-1957.* Vol. III, China. Washington, DC: GPO, 1986.

———. Vol. 15., Korea, Part 1&2. Washington: GPO, 1984.

———. Vol. 16., Geneva Conference, Washington: GPO, 1981.

Wang, Bingnan. *Recalling Nine Years of Sino-US Talks.* Serialized in *Guangzhou Ribao* (29 Sep 1984-3 Feb 1985) and *Shijie Zhishi* (Beijing, 16 Feb 1985-16 Apr 1985), in Foreign Broadcast Information Service, *Daily Report: People's Republic of China,* 19 Oct 1984-2 May 1985. Springfield, VI: National Technological Information Service.

Weakland, John H. *Chinese Communist Patterns of Strategy and Negotiations.* Palo Alto, Calif: Mental Research Institute, May 1970.

Wilson, Dick. *Zhou Enlai, A Biography.* New York: Viking Penguin Press, 1984.

Worsnop, Richard L. "East-West Negotiations." *Editorial Research Reports* 2 (1962): 737-754.

———. "Negotiating with Communists." *Editorial Research Reports* 1 (1965): 283-300.

Wu, Yuan-li. *A Handbook.* New York: Praeger, 1973.

Young, Kenneth T. *Negotiating with the Chinese Communists: The United States Experience, 1953-1967.* New York: McGraw-Hill, 1968.

Zablocki, Clement J., ed *Sino-Soviet Rivalry: Implications for US Policy*. New York: Praeger, 1966.
Zagoria, Donald S. *The Sino-Soviet Conflict, 1956-1961*. Princeton: Princeton University Press, 1962.

IV. US-China Negotiations: 1968-1985

Barnds, William J., ed. *China and America: The Search for a New Relationship*. New York: New York University Press, 1977.

Barnett, A. Doak. *Uncertain Passage: China's Transition to the Post-Mao Era*. Washington: Brookings Institution, 1974.

———. "Military Secutiry Relations Between China and the United States." *Foreign Affairs* 55 (April 1977): 584-597.

———. *China Policy: Old Problems and New Challenges*. Washington: The Brookings Institution, 1977.

Borisov, O. B., and B. T. Kolaskov. *Soviet-Chinese Relations, 1945-1970*. Bloomington, Ind: Indiana University Press, 1975.

Brezezinski, Zbigniew. *Power and Principle*. New York: Farrar, Straus and Girous, 1983.

Chen, King C., ed. *China and the Three Worlds, 1972-1977*. New York: M. E, Sharpe, 1978.

Chiu, Hungdah, ed. *Normalizing Relations with the People's Republic of China: Problems, Analysis and Documents*. Baltimore: University of Maryland Law School, 1978.

———. *China and the Taiwan Issue*. New York: Praeger Publishers, 1979.

Dickinson, William B. Jr., ed. *China and US Foreign Policy*. Washington: Congressional Quarterly, 1973.

Dulles, Foster R. *American Policy Toward Communist China: The Historical Record, 1949-1969*. New York: Crowell, 1972.

Ellsberg, Daniel. *Papers on the War*. New York: Simon and Schuster, 1972.

Fairbank, John K. *Chinese-American Interactions: A Historical Summary*. New Brunswick, NJ: Rutgers University Press, 1975.

———, ed. *Our China Prospects: A Symposium*. Philadelphia: The American Philosophical Society, 1977.

Ford, Gerald R. *In Time to Heal: the Autobiography of Gerald Ford*. New York: Harper and Row - Reader's Digest, 1979.

Galloway, L. Thomas. *Recognizing Foreign Governments: The Practice of the United States*. Washington: American Enterprise Institute, 1978.

Harding, Harry, Jr. *China: The Uncertain Future.* Headline Series, no. 233. New York: Foreign Policy Association, December 1974.

Hellman, Donald C., ed. *China and Japan: A New Balance of Power.* Lexington, Mass: Lexington Books, 1976.

Hinton, Harold C. *Bear at the Gate: Chinese Policymaking Under Soviet Pressure.* Washington: AEI for Public Policy Research, 1971.

______. *Three and a Half Powers.* Bloomington, Ind: Indiana University Press, 1975.

Hsiao, Gene T., and Michael Witunski, eds. *Sino-American* Normalization and its Policy Implications. New York: Praeger Publishers, 1983.

Hsiung, James T., ed. *Contemporary Republic of China, The Taiwan Experience, 1950-1980.* New York: Praeger Publishers, 1981.

Johnson, U. Alexis, George M. Packard, and Alfred D. Wilhelm, Jr., eds. *China Policy for the Next Decade: Report of the Atlantic Council's Committee on China Policy.* Boston: Oelgeschlager, Gunn and Hain, 1984.

Kalb, Marvin and Bernard. *Kissinger.* Boston: Little and Brown, 1974.

Kay, Michael Y. M., ed. *The Lin Piao Affair.* New York: M. E. Sharpe, 1975.

Kissinger, Henry A. "The Vietnam Negotiations." *Foreign Affairs* 47 (1969): 211-234.

______. *The White House Years.* Boston: Little, Brown & Company, 1979.

Klein, Donald W. "The Chinese Foreign Ministry." Ph.D. diss., Columbia University, 1974.

Lai, Fung-wai. "Policy Oscillations in the People's Republic of China: A Quantitative Appraisal." Ph.D. diss., University of Hawaii, 1977.

Li, Victor H. *De-recognizing Taiwan: The Legal Problems.* Washington: Carnegie Endowment for International Peace, 1977.

Lieberthal, Kenneth. *A Research Guide to Central Party and Government Meetings in China, 1949-1975.* New York: M. E. Sharpe, 1975.

Lin, Kuo-chung. "Classical Chinese Concepts of International Politics and their Influence on Contemporary Chinese Foreign Policy." Ph.D. diss., Univeristy of Oklahoma, 1974.

Moorsteen, Richard and Abramowitz, Morton. *Remaking China Policy: US-China Relations and Governmental Decision-Making.* Cambridge, Mass: Harvard University Press, 1971.

Nixon, Richard. *The Memoirs of Richard Nixon.* New York: Grossett and Dunlap, 1978.

———. *United States Foreign Policy for the 1970s: Building for Peace.* New York: Harper and Row, 1971.

Oksenberg, Michael and Oxnam, Robert B. *China and America, Past and Future.* Headline Series, no. 235. New York: Foreign Policy Association, April 1977.

———, eds. *Dragon and Eagle, United States-China Relations: Past and Future.* New York: Basic Books, 1978.

Pillsbury, Michael. "US-China Military Ties?" *Foreign Policy* (Fall 1975): 50-60.

Pye, Lucien W. "The Puzzels of Chinese Pragmatism." *Foreign Policy* (1978): 119-136.

Randolph, R. Sean. "Carter as Negotiator: The Taiwan Issue." In *About Face: The China Decision and Its Consequences.* Edited by John Tierney, Jr., New Rochelle, NY: Arlington House Publishers, 1979.

Samelson, Louis J. *Soviet and Chinese Negotiating Behavior: The Western View.* Sage Professional Papers in International Studies, IV. Beverly Hills, Calif.: Sage Publications, 1976.

Selected Works of Deng Xiaoping (1975-1982). Beijing: Foreign Language Press, 1984.

Shroeder, Paul E. "The Ohio-Hubei Agreement: Clues to Chinese Negotiating Practices." *The China Quarterly* 91 (Sept 1982): 486-491.

Simon, Jeffrey. *Comparative Communist Foreign Policy, 1965-1976.* Santa Monica, Calif.: Rand Corporation, August 1977.

Sutter, Robert G. *Chinese Foreign Policy After the Cultural Revolution, 1966-1977.* Boulder, Co.: Westview Press, 1977.

———. *US-PRC Normalization: Arguments and Alternatives.* Washington: Congressional Reference Service, Library of Congress, 1977.

US Congress. House. Committee on Foreign Affairs. Subcommittee of Asian and Pacific Affairs. *Future Importance of*

Taiwan and the Republic of China to US Security and Economic Interests. Washington: GPO, 1975.

______. Committee on International Relations. Subcommittee on Asian and Pacific Affairs. *Normalization of Relationswith the PRC: Practical Implications, Hearings*. Washington: GPO, 1977.

______. Subcommittee on Future Foreign Policy Research and Development. *Shifting Balance of Power in Asia: Implications for Future US Policy*. Washington: GPO, 1976.

______. *United States-China: Future Foreign Policy Directions*. Washington: GPO, August 10, 1976.

______. *United States-Soviet Union-China: The Great Power Triangle*. Washington: GPO, 1976.

______. Special Subcommittee on Investigations. *United States-China Relations: The Process of Normalization ofRelations*. Washington: GPO, 1976.

______. Joint Economic Committee. *China: A reassessment of the Economy*. Washington: GPO, July 1975.

______. Senate. Committee on Foreign Relations. *Legislative History of the Committee on Foreign Relations, 93d Congress*. Washington: GPO, 1975.

______. Senator John Glenn. "China-Taiwan Policy." *Congressional Record*, July 22, 1982, S. 8873-8875.

______. *Sino-American Relations: A New Turn*. Washington: GPO, January 1979.

______. *Taiwan*. Washington: GPO, 1979. US Department of State. "US Policy Toward China, July 15, 1971- January 15, 1979." Selected Document No. 9, Bureau of Public Affairs. Washington: GPO, January 1979.

______. "US-China Joint Communique." Current Policy No. 413, Bureau of Public Affairs. Washington: GPO, August 1982.

Vance, Cyrus. *Hard Choices, Critical Years in American Foreign Policy*. New York: Simon & Schuster, 1983.

Wang, Sheng. *An Analysis of the Chinese Communist Tactics of Peace Talks*. Taipei: World Anti-Communist League, 1978.

Whiting, Allen S. *China and the United States: What's Next* ? Headline Series no. 230. New York: Foreign Policy Association, April 1976.

Whitson, William W., ed. *The Military and Political Power in China in the 1970s.* New York: Praeger, 1972.

Wu, Fu-mei. "The China Policy of Richard M. Nixon from Confrontation to Negotiation." Ph.D. diss., University of Utah, 1976.

Index

THE AUTHOR

Dr. Alfred D. Wilhelm, Jr., completed this study while a military professor of Asian Studies on the faculty of the National Defense University, National War College, from 1984-86. During this time he also negotiated the first bilateral agreement between the US National Defense University and the National Defense University of the People's Liberation Army of China. This agreement involved academic exchanges between the two universities and was formally signed in 1986 by the two university presidents, Lieutenant General Richard D. Lawrence and General Zhang Zhen. Dr. Wilhelm later served as the first exchange professor with the People's Liberation Army from the US military.

After graduating from West Point, Dr. Wilhelm served in Vietnam and then studied Chinese in Taiwan. Other military assignments included duty in air defense, airborne artillery, and special forces units, appointments to the staffs of the Department of the Army and Office of the Secretary of Defense and to the faculty of the US Army Command and General Staff College and the National War College. He completed his service as the US Army Attaché in Beijing. Currently Dr. Wilhelm is the Vice President of the Atlantic Council of the United States, where he is also Director of the Council's Atlantic and Pacific Interrelationships Program. He earned a Master's degree in Asian studies from the University of Michigan and a Ph.D. in political science from the University of Kansas. In addition, Dr. Wilhelm has held postgraduate fellowships at the Atlantic Council and the National Defense University.

☆ U.S. GOVERNMENT PRINTING OFFICE:1994-282-306/40008